# WITH HONOR AND PURPOSE

# WITH HONOR AND PURPOSE

An Ex-FBI
Investigator
Reports from
the
Front Lines of
Crime

Phil Kerby

St. Martin's Press ⋈ New York

WITH HONOR AND PURPOSE. Copyright © 1998 by Phil Kerby. Printed in the United States of America. No part of this book may be used or reproduced in any manner whatsoever without written permission except in the case of brief quotations embodied in critical articles or reviews. For information, address St. Martin's Press, 175 Fifth Avenue, New York, N.Y. 10010.

Design by Bryanna Millis

Library of Congress Cataloging-in-Publication Data

Kerby, Phil.
    With honor and purpose : an Ex-FBI investigator reports from the front lines of crime / by Phil Kerby — 1st ed.
        p.    cm.
    ISBN 0-312-18224-4
    1. Kerby, Phil.    2. United States. Federal Bureau of Investigation—Officials and employees—Biography.    3. Criminal investigation—United States.      I. Title.
    HV7911.K39A3    1998                                97-40381
    364.1'0973—dc21                                         CIP

First edition: April 1998
10 9 8 7 6 5 4 3 2 1

# Contents

# Author's Note

**W**hen a madman killed a Washington, D.C., police officer and also wounded an FBI agent with an automatic rifle, Special Agent Martha Dixon Martinez was in an adjoining work area. A partition shielded her from his view. A door beckoned her to the hallway where she could have sought help safely. But this SWAT team member entered the room knowing the potential consequences. Despite fighting the good fight, she died in a hail of bullets.

She'd been through it all before during the prison riot at Talladega, Alabama, and when a fugitive from justice blew his brains out in front of her in the Tennessee woods. Every day from one end of this country to the other, and in embassies all over the world, FBI agents face the same fate. Yet day after day they go out and do what they signed up to do—collect and preserve evidence and put the bad guys behind bars.

After the funeral for Martha Dixon Martinez, in which agents and FBI Director Louis Freeh had been so kind and helpful, the Dixon family wrote Director Freeh: "Your words were helpful in comforting us that Martha died a hero, with honor and for a purpose."

Like Martha, I make no claim to honor and purpose. An FBI agent's work speaks for itself. The tribute of the title—the book itself—is dedicated to Martha Dixon Martinez and all of the FBI heroes who have gone before her with Honor and Purpose.

# Acknowledgments

Every book includes a supporting cast of characters who made it possible. In this case, the list includes all the people who made my career in the FBI possible, for without that, there would have been no book. Among those I would like to thank are:

Charlie Donlan, Bill Ahrens, and all the instructors who taught us the ropes at Quantico.

Jim Glavin, Ed O'Connor, Ed McShane, Tom Kelly, and the rest of the old guard in Albany, who tolerated me while I learned. Especially Bob Kolevar, who worked in Director Hoover's office and provided invaluable insight.

Bud Goodwin, and Tom Mitchell, my supervisors in Columbus, and also John Morley, my supervisor in Saginaw. Who could have asked for better supervisors? All true gentlemen.

The old-timers in Columbus who were so kind to Debbie and me when we arrived—especially the Fusts, who even helped us make curtains for our house.

My fellow agents in Columbus who taught me about life in the Bureau, especially those who helped me to resurrect the memories necessary for the writing of this book. Special thanks to Mike Chretien, Dick Cleary, Bob Federspiel, Flint Gabelman, Anson Hopper, Emmett Scott, Gerald Jones, Al Heffernan, Tom Decker, Bob Gillespie, George Murray, Jim Rogers, and my pal, Paul Miller.

Special thanks also to John Warren and all the others at the Columbus Police Department robbery squad, and Steve Martin, chief deputy at the Franklin County Sheriff's Department, who through the years has been like a brother to me. Also William Milligan, Al Ritcher, and Tommy Thompson, the federal prosecutors who prosecuted all the bad guys in Columbus.

Dick Farley, for the Chicken Delight story. Sheila Reagan, who paved the way for many women to follow with dignity and humor.

Thanks to the students at Bryant Junior High who cared, such as Elmore Timms, Derek Aldridge, Nate Johnson, and the many dedicated teachers who stayed with a stressful and difficult profession for the sake of the children.

The Michigan agents who helped me reconstruct many of the dim memories of our investigations, Bob Rudge, Dave Welker, Paul Koch, Jerry Redd, Jerry Cox. Also thanks to all of the agents who worked with me and for me. I'll never forget the deep commitment of such stars as Al DiBrito, Ron Dick, Dave Kleinpaste, Mark Hamrock, Joe Johnson, Derek Siegle, Leon Fantroy, Ben Walker, and especially Frank the Crank Lauden, who made my thirty days in Decker fly by in good humor in spite of the massive tragedy. Even the least productive and most contentious agents who worked for me all made significant contributions to the safety of society, and I commend them all, each and every one.

To the Detroit management, who over the years were so supportive, especially Hal Helterhoff, who was the great mediator and who taught me so much about ways to utilize the individual talents of each agent; and Tony Riggio, who offered such wise counsel for so long.

To the secretaries and other support personnel, who labor in obscurity day after day—especially my secretaries who doubled as psychologists, including Nancy Schrems, Tammy Proux, Linda Hamrock, and Diane Krajkowski. Although I chose to honor Martha Dixon Martinez, Diane pointed out the letter from which the title was derived.

Michael Hluchaniuk, the primary U.S. attorney in Bay City, and his staff, who prosecuted all of the cases coming out of the Saginaw FBI office.

To all of the Michigan law enforcement professionals, both patrol and investigative, many thanks for all the help and for being out there every day for all of us. And especially Dave Hall for his insight into the Oklahoma City bombing, as well as for being a solid and caring investigator.

To the Michigan State Police, including the BAYANET team, which was always there to take on the next drug conspiracy—especially Ken Bennett, John Charney, and Bill Burns, who led the teams over the years.

To Gary Loster, the mayor of Saginaw, who has been like a brother to me over the years and who was the driving force behind the gang task force. And to Jim Osterman, Mike Van Horn, Brian Berg, Terry Williams, Mark Miller, Bill Lauman, Bob Lucas, Joaquin Guerrero, Mark Garabelli, Craig Oatten, and all the other team members who were so instrumental in the success of the task force and providing information for the book.

I will especially remember the victims, whose lives were dramatically changed by criminals. Tony and Geri Dambro, Si Jin and Ken Ahn, James Crawford and his family, and the many others whose lives formed the basis for this book. I also want to acknowledge the directors of the FBI, from J. Edgar Hoover to Louis Freeh. They have an impossible job and will always receive criticism before praise. So, for the record, let me praise each one heartily—especially Louis Freeh, who personally changed my life; and William Webster, who did a superb job and restored confidence in the FBI. His aloofness did not shield his accomplishments from me.

To the people of Saginaw, which Debbie and I call home. Without your support, the FBI could not function and there would be no gang task force. Saginaw has been a great place to live and raise our children.

A special thank you is due George Martinez for allowing me to honor his wife, who died in service to her country. I told him in an honest and straightforward way all of my mistakes and triumphs. He listened carefully and opened up his heart enough to share her.

Aside from the FBI, there's my real family, to which I owe a million thanks: particularly my mother, Virginia R. Harrison, my stepfather, Floyd Harrison, my father, Wayne C. Kerby, my dear wife,

Deborah A. Kerby, my beloved sons, Stephen and Scott, and my brother Bill.

I also want to thank Drs. Bart Grossman and James Monte of the U. of M. Hospital and Fathers James Gannon and Brendan Wrobelewski, who all combined to help me through cancer.

A number of people at newspapers helped us track down old clippings, which were crucial for the precise dates, times, and other minutiae that often elude human memory. They included John Wilson at the *Detroit News*, Joe Frolik at the *Plain Dealer* in Cleveland, Jim Hunter at the *Columbus Dispatch*, and Steve Verburg at the *Saginaw News*. Jim Marion, the retired security director of Nationwide Insurance, also dug up some old clippings and generously shared his memories.

PHIL KERBY
SAGINAW, MICHIGAN
MARCH 1, 1996

# PRELUDE TO A BOMBING

February 10, 1995

The tension in the colonel's voice startled me. When I asked if the National Guard was keeping Soviet tanks on a camp in the middle of Michigan hunting country, I was prepared for scorn, sarcasm, disbelief—but not anxiety. "Who told you about that?" he demanded.

"Somebody who's planning to blow them up," I replied.

There was a long silence on the other end of the phone. "Tell me about it," the colonel finally asked.

I thought about the snitch who walked into an FBI office that morning. Twitching and fidgeting like a bundle of nerves, he took several hours to tell his story in lurching fits and starts.

He identified himself, finally, as a "counterintelligence officer" for the Michigan Militia, a shadowy far-right-wing paramilitary group active in the state's northern counties. The Militia had learned there were four Russian tanks at Camp Grayling, the giant 700,000-acre base in northern Michigan where most of the Midwest's National Guard units trained. And, certain that the tanks were the advance guard of a foreign invasion—it was an article of faith to the Militia that the U.S. government was riddled with traitors who intended to turn the country over to a conspiracy guided by the United Nations and international bankers—the Militia had decided to raid Camp Grayling and blow them up with homemade C-4 explosive.

"And if anyone at the base tries to stop them, any military police or someone like that, they've been given orders to kill," the man said. That was why he had come in. Blowing up Russian tanks was one thing, but he wasn't at all certain about the patriotism of killing American soldiers.

Quickly I sketched out the snitch's story. "Now tell me about the tanks," I asked the colonel. "Because, frankly, we thought the guy was probably crazy."

"No, he's right," the colonel said. "I guess I really shouldn't be surprised that people know about it—we're not really keeping it secret anymore. Force of habit, I guess."

It was called Operation Chicken Little. For years the Pentagon had been shipping to Camp Grayling tanks captured or purchased from Soviet client states. There U.S. military pilots came from all over the Midwest to practice shooting at the tanks with radar gunsights that were programmed to lock onto a particular vehicle's profile. The training had proven its worth during the Gulf War, when American helicopters were able to make armored mincemeat out of Iraq's Russian-made tanks. The Iraqis must really have thought the sky was falling.

Throughout the Cold War, Operation Chicken Little had been shrouded in government secrecy, with the tanks delivered under wraps in the middle of the night. With the collapse of the Soviet Union, the program's cover had been dropped, and one of the Michigan Militia's nutball followers had seen some of the tanks on a flat car at a railroad siding in Bay City, 1 ½ hours south of the camp.

"There's something else you should know, too," the colonel added. "A couple of weeks ago, I got a letter from some guy who claimed to be the commander in chief of the Michigan Militia. He ordered me—*ordered me*—to vacate the camp and turn it over to the Michigan Militia. There wasn't any explicit 'or else' in the letter, but you could certainly read it between the lines."

I knew what he meant. For the past couple of years, I had been watching the growth of the Militia and other far-right groups with increasing unease. They had guns, explosives—we'd helped local cops bust up a bomb factory the year before—and an overabundance of hatred. As far as I was concerned, they were damned dangerous, although not everyone at the Bureau shared my opinion.

"When is this attack on the tanks supposed to happen?" the colonel asked.

"Anytime during a two-week window that begins February 12 at 7 P.M.," I said. "The man gave us the names of three Militia members who are supposedly part of the advance team for the raid. We're trying to find them. And I'll see about getting some help for you at Camp Grayling."

The camp, a creaky collection of World War II–era Quonset huts and wooden barracks was half-buried in drifted snow when we arrived the next day. The temperature was below zero and felt much colder, thanks to a thirty-mile-an-hour wind that clawed at my eyes like a wild animal as I scurried from the car into one of the office buildings.

It was the weather more than anything that had us worried. "How long are we going to have to protect these tanks before you can get them out of here?" asked Joe Martinolich, the special agent in charge of the FBI's Detroit office, to which my ten-agent office in Saginaw answered.

"We're working on it," the colonel said. "But we've got to arrange for a train to pick them up, and we've got to find a place to put them. It might be twenty-four hours, maybe a little bit more."

"How long can your people stay out in this weather?" Martinolich asked the head of the Bureau's Detroit-based SWAT team.

"Not that long," the SWAT commander replied. "We just don't have the equipment to deal with this kind of weather."

"We do," offered a man at the other end of the table. He was from the Hostage Rescue Team, the FBI's most elite unit, which was equipped for every conceivable terrain, climate, and crisis. It wouldn't have surprised me to learn the HRT had a standard operating plan for protecting Russian tanks from right-wing terrorists.

"Good," Martinolich said, "because I think we're going to need you. How soon can your men be here?"

The answer turned out to be less than twenty-four hours. The

HRT flew into the Saginaw airport, an hour and a half south of Camp Grayling, on its own jet. After nearly twenty-six years in the FBI, I had my first look at the team. It was worth the wait. Our local agents looked on in amazement as the plane was unloaded: Sniper rifles with night vision scopes, an array of electronic motion and heat sensors, satellite telephones that linked the team directly with FBI Director Louis Freeh back in Washington—even its own field hospital, with the military's top trauma surgeon in tow.

Within hours, the HRT agents were scattered around the Camp Grayling tank range, a meadow that the snow had turned into a vast, immaculately frosted caketop. Nonetheless, the HRT was invisible. The agents, wearing special heated uniforms that allowed them to stay out for hours at a time, burrowed into the snow and vanished. Although the team had come to Michigan directly from a deployment in a jungle climate, the 100-degree swing in temperature didn't seem to bother the agents a bit.

While the HRT dug in, the investigation continued. The computers were humming in Detroit, compiling background on the Militia, while surveillance teams were scattered around the Detroit area, looking for the raiders. But still there was no definite word. The fearful man who had warned the FBI of the attack had dropped out of sight. For the hundredth time, I wished we had some informers inside the Militia, someone to turn to for information.

It was the next morning before we got a break in the case. "It looks like your guys can come in from the cold," Martinolich told the HRT commander. "The Militia has called off the attack. They suspect a security leak."

*My God,* I thought as the HRT agents began emerging from the snow, *the Militia has better intelligence than we do.* As I trudged out to my car, I silently vowed that I wouldn't be caught like that again, shadowboxing a foe who was playing for keeps.

Right-wing nuts were nothing new to America, nor to me. Back in 1969, as a rookie agent in Albany, New York, I was assigned to do a background check on a candidate for a high government position. When I went to a mountaintop home to interview one of his references, the man turned out to be a member of the John Birch Society. I had to listen to a long lecture on the connection between Lenin and fluoride.

The Bircher struck me as comical more than anything else. But in the late 1980s, I had to travel up to the little northeastern Michigan town of Caseville to interview an elderly man whose son had just been arrested in the state of Washington after a shootout between the FBI and a right-wing racist group called The Order.

The founder was an irascible anti-Semite named Robert Matthews who believed that in the wake of World War II the United States had fallen under control of a secret Jewish cabal he called ZOG, the Zionist Occupation Government. The Order, he decreed, would wage guerrilla warfare against the cabal, financing itself through counterfeiting and bank robberies. He meant business. When FBI agents tracking The Order's crime spree tried to enter the basement of a house where Matthews was hiding, he unleashed a burst of bullets through the floorboards that nearly killed them all. A couple of days later, Matthews was killed in the same house during a gun battle with an enhanced Los Angeles SWAT team, while his followers were arrested.

The interview with the old man was heartbreaking. For months, he had been able to communicate with his son only through letters sent to aliases at mail drops. "You know," he told me sadly, "I fought in World War II. I was a marine, went ashore at Okinawa. And now my son thinks I was fighting on the wrong side."

My next brush with the ultraright came a few months later, when an agent took a call from a Saginaw woman who was alarmed by the militant rhetoric of one of her neighbors. The man was always talking about how the U.S. government ought to be overthrown, she said.

"The world is full of crackpots, ma'am, and they're entitled to their opinion, no matter how nutty," I said, trying to soothe her.

"I think this man may be more than a talker," the woman replied. "There's a rumor that he was involved in a bank robbery. And if I'm right, I'll bet he gave the money to Robert Miles. Do you remember him?"

I certainly did. A former insurance agent, Miles was a Ku Klux Klan official who led the fight against busing children in Pontiac, Michigan, during the early 1970s. He was eventually convicted of fire-bombing school buses and sentenced to six years in prison. After his release, he became a prolific author of hateful racist and anti-Semitic pamphlets. There was some evidence he was a secret member of The Order.

"You're not going to believe this, but my neighbor let Miles impregnate his wife," the woman said. "He told me he wanted her to carry the seeds of The Master."

That was sufficiently creepy to get my full attention. "I'm going to look into this," I told her. "I'll see if there's anything the FBI can do to find out the truth."

But I already knew what our office in Saginaw could do: nothing, at least on our own. Any time there's a political overlay to a potential investigation, it has to be cleared from Washington, which alone can decide if a case meets the attorney general's guidelines.

The guidelines originated with Edward Levi, Gerald Ford's attorney general. He was in office when the scandals about FBI intelligence-gathering and harassment of extremist organizations during the 1960s broke open. Levi put serious reins on our ability to collect information against anybody with a political agenda, no matter how potentially bloodthirsty they might appear.

In practical terms, there was no way to get Washington's approval for one of these cases without first getting Detroit's. I called one of the senior officials there and explained what the woman had told me. "Do you think we can open an antiterrorism investigation against this guy?" I asked.

"Is there any hard evidence he's committed a crime, or is about to commit one?" the official asked.

"None that I'm aware of," I admitted.

"Then you know we can't do it," he said. End of discussion.

I wasn't annoyed by the negative reply; I knew the case was pretty doubtful when I called. But the lady's story stuck in my mind, and I began noticing things. Once or twice a month we were getting phone calls from citizens around the state complaining that the Klan was meeting in their town, or some other racist organization was leaving lurid flyers in their mailboxes. Curious, I called a few sheriff's offices. I soon concluded that every cop in northern Michigan had a desk drawer full of this stuff, collected from angry folks in their town.

"But we can't do anything more about it than you can," one detective told me. "We got whacked with all the same lawsuits you did from the Red Squad stuff in the old days. We've got strict rules about keeping intelligence files on people or groups."

In 1994, one of the groups finally crossed the line. In Midland, a couple of right-wing fanatics drove a black couple out of a grocery store, yelling "Get out of here, you niggers!" and other epithets. Michigan's "hate crimes" law makes ethnic intimidation a felony, and the skinheads were arrested. The cops who worked the case became increasingly convinced that the fanatics were behind another infraction they were investigating, a series of letters sent to prominent Jews warning them to get out of town. When I heard the cops were going to get a search warrant for their home, I called to ask if we could send an agent over to observe. I had a feeling we might be able to stick them with a federal bomb-making charge. "Be my guest," replied the prosecutor.

Sure enough, the police found several pipe bombs—including one lettered with the message KILL NIGGERS—and supplies to make plenty more. There was also a boa constrictor.

The radicals hadn't even gone to trial when I got another call, this one from Saginaw. A woman who owned a photocopying shop noticed two men huddled secretively around one of her machines, darting furtive glances around the room as they made their copies. Edging closer, the woman peeked over their shoulders. They were copying an illustrated manual on how to make bombs. "They hustled right out of there when they saw me looking at them, but I got their license plate number," she said proudly. When we traced it, it turned out to belong to a member of the newly formed Michigan Militia.

The Militia was a worrisome new development, because it was so big—Militia leaders claimed to have signed up twelve thousand members in just a few months—and because it was so overtly paramilitary. The Militia members wore camouflage uniforms, carried weapons, and assigned themselves military ranks. Local cops who drove by their meetings told me that Militia members took care to back their cars in when parking so their license plates couldn't be seen, and uniformed men usually patrolled a perimeter around the meeting.

The militia movement sprang up in 1994 in angry protest against two disastrous federal law enforcement forays: A Bureau of Alcohol, Tobacco and Firearms raid on the compound of the Branch Davidian fundamentalist religious sect in Waco, Texas, which led to a seven-week standoff that climaxed in the fiery deaths of more than eighty Branch Davidians, including dozens of women and children; and a U.S. marshal's raid on the mountaintop home of a right-wing racist that ended with his wife and teenage son killed by gunfire and made Idaho's Ruby Ridge infamous.

The Militias claimed their legitimacy was established in the U.S. Constitution's Second Amendment, which says: "A well-regulated militia being necessary to the security of a free state, the right of people to keep and bear arms shall not be infringed." The Michigan Militia was by no means the only one—they cropped up in at least twenty states in 1994—but it was one of the biggest, perhaps because it had its own highly effective publicist: Mark Koernke, a University of Michigan janitor who claimed to be a former military intelligence officer on his nightly shortwave radio show, where he billed himself as "Mark from Michigan."

A lot of the Militia members were just guys who liked to get together, drink beer, and bitch about taxes and welfare. But many of them, in my judgment, were seriously crackers. They believed: Washington was going to hand the country over any day to the United Nations, which was planning to exterminate many Americans and imprison the rest; massive crematoriums had already been built in Kansas City, Indianapolis, and Oklahoma City to handle all the bodies; two thousand Russian tanks, which had entered the country at Gulfport, Mississippi, since 1993, were waiting on a base in Fort Polk, Louisiana, for the green light, after which they would be guided around the United States by the bar codes on the back of traffic signs.

Everybody has the right to an opinion, no matter how loony; I understood that. But the question in my mind was, if a paramilitary group seriously believes the country is on the verge of takeover by a foreign army, how long before it acts on that belief? There were already signs that the Militia was doing so. In September, police in Fowlerville, just outside the state capital of Lansing, had stopped a car on a routine traffic violation. Inside they found three men wearing fatigues, their faces smeared with camouflage paint. The car was full of guns. The men said they were performing surveillance on local law enforcement officers. They didn't show up for their arraignment a few days later, but fifty Militia members chanting slogans did.

I decided it was time for the FBI to act. I called Marty Lauer, the Detroit supervisor in charge of terrorism cases. I told him I wanted to open a terrorism investigation against the Militia members spotted photocopying the bomb manual.

"We have strict and specific guidelines on this kind of thing, Phil," he said. "This was the sort of stuff that got us in a lot of trouble in the 1960s, and we're not going to let it happen again. You can go ahead and draw up the paperwork for a request, but it doesn't sound like you've got much. Photocopying a document isn't a crime."

I knew he had a point: Reading about bombs is not the same thing as building them or setting them off. The FBI is not the thought police. But I also knew that every cop instinct in my body told me that we were behind the curve and this was not a time for excess caution. I decided to call John Bell, the No. 2 man in the Detroit office.

"I think we need a meeting—you, Lauer, and the six agents outside Detroit with supervisory responsibility," I told him. "All of us out here are getting daily calls from people worried about these groups. The Militia is growing like hell, and the Klan and the Nazis are popping up all over the place, too. We all have a general idea of what the AG guidelines say. But we need some instruction on the nuances. We need to know just how far we can go without violating the guidelines."

"That sounds very interesting and very useful," Bell said. But before he could end the conversation, I charged ahead.

"I also think it's time Martinolich and the U.S. attorney's office start denouncing these groups," I continued. "It's time to use the bully pulpit, to say that hatred and intimidation are wrong. Because if we don't, something terrible is going to happen. This is just how it got started in Germany—the Nazis pushed around the Jews, in small ways at first, and no one said anything. We can't let that happen here. We need to stand up to these people and say: 'This will not be tolerated.' Because if we don't, later on everyone will be saying, 'Where was the FBI? They were asleep at the switch.' "

"That's an intriguing idea, Phil," Bell said. "But you know it's not simple. A lot of people would have to agree to something like that. We'll discuss it, and I'll get back to you."

*Don't wait too long,* I wanted to add as I hung up the phone, but I didn't. I was both exasperated and apprehensive. The FBI, at times, is capable of quick and overwhelming responses. But it can also move as slowly as the worst pork-barrel agency in Washington. I remembered something Winston Churchill once said: "In the perfect bureaucracy, no one is in charge."

Meanwhile, I could almost hear northern Michigan going *tick . . . tick . . . tick . . .*

# 2

# JOINING UP

Whenever I read a biography, it always seems that the author finds plenty of clues that point, at a very early age, to the way a life's going to turn out. Winston Churchill played with toy soldiers when he was a boy. Wolfman Jack loved the crystal radio set he got as a kid. Mickey Mantle's dad had him swinging a bat the moment he could stand up straight.

But I've scoured my own childhood for leads and I can't find a single hint that I was headed for a career in the FBI. I never played cops and robbers as a kid, didn't watch *The Untouchables* on TV, and rarely read *Dick Tracy* in the Sunday comics. In high school, when we took our senior trip to Washington, D.C., I didn't even get out when we stopped for a tour of the Justice Department building. I was more interested in some serious necking—well, as serious as it got in 1963—with a girl who stayed on the bus.

I grew up just outside Flint, Michigan. Years later, the movie *Roger and Me* would turn Flint into an appalling symbol of urban decay in the Rustbelt, a place where all the jobs had gone south and the survivors were reduced to slaughtering cute little bunny rabbits to feed themselves. Telling people you were from Flint was like saying you hopped the last train out of Pompeii.

But it wasn't like that in the late 1950s and early 1960s, when I was growing up. Back then, the only things made in Japan were the crummy transistor radios that we listened to Four Seasons records on. A booming America was buying station wagons as fast as the General Motors assembly line in Flint could slap them together. Unemployment was something we heard about in social studies class when the teacher talked about the Great Depression. If you could dress yourself in the morning, GM had a job waiting for you.

My dad owned his own truck, an oil tanking rig, and he made his living delivering heating oil to homes around the Flint area. My mom worked as a secretary at an inner-city elementary school. We lived in a rural-flavored suburb a little bit east of town, in a tiny frame house. There were two bedrooms—my dad built the second one himself after my brother Bill and I came long—but just one midget bathroom. My dad used to say it wasn't really small, just efficient: You could sit on the toilet, wash your hands in the sink and your feet in the bathtub all at once. No time wasted in the Kerby household.

Looking back on it, I suppose you would call us lower-middle class. But at the time, I felt like a millionaire. Nobody ever went hungry or ragged. There were big fields right out the back door where Bill and I could play ball or, in the fall, hunt pheasant. Our neighbors owned horses, and sometimes I went riding after school.

All that exercise, coupled with a frame that grew out to a muscular six-foot-three, turned me into a jock. By the time I graduated from high school in 1963, I made all-league teams in both football and basketball. But my grades were good, too. My mom made sure of that.

Her own mother had died when Mom was twelve, leaving behind a dazed husband and a baby boy. My mom spent what should have been her childhood struggling to raise an infant and hold a family together in the middle of the Depression. It left her with a low tolerance for goof-offs and screw-ups. There was never any chance that Bill or I—or, for that matter, my dad—would veer off the straight and narrow path.

Working all those years in school, my mother developed a tremendous admiration for teachers. They were educated, they were doing something constructive, and the work was steady. "You'd make a fine teacher, Phil," my mom used to say—a lot—and without really thinking about it, I adopted her ambition as my own. When I finished high school, I went to Central Michigan University in Mount Pleasant, a couple of hours northwest of Flint, to get a teaching degree. In 1967, three months after graduation, I returned to Flint to teach social studies and English at Bryant Junior High School.

I wish I could say that I got the Bryant job because the principal was floored by my unique combination of intellect and empathy, that he recognized a born teacher when he saw one. The reality was that few graduates wanted to teach at Bryant, which was in a decent neighborhood that was getting seedy. My most outstanding attribute as a job applicant was that I *was* a job applicant. If the principal gave anything else even passing consideration, it was probably that because I was six-foot-three, only a few of the students would be capable of challenging me.

That's not what I thought at the time, of course. The 1960s didn't have the same impact in Flint and Mount Pleasant as they did in Stanford and Berkeley. But nobody could come out of college in those days without at least a mild case of save-the-world, we-are-all-brothers-itis. Man, I had seen *To Sir With Love*. I knew I could reach out to those kids. All you need is love.

My enthusiasm was such that I wasn't even fazed when the principal told me that, with the other rookie teachers, I'd have to attend sensitivity training sponsored by the Urban League. In every school I'd ever attended, the kids had to adjust to the teachers rather than the other way around. But I was willing to give it a try.

The training turned out to be an early experiment in playing on white guilt. The idea was that, as whites, we'd been handed the keys to the kingdom at birth, while the black kids we'd be teaching had never gotten a single break. I didn't exactly buy that—we Kerbys, alas, were almost never mistaken for Rockefellers—but I didn't completely reject it, either. Growing up, I had sometimes played at the elementary school where my mother worked. You didn't have to be Joan Baez to see that those kids lived in a different world than the one I knew.

Some of the other new teachers, however, took the training completely to heart. One guy was truly enraptured. You could almost see the blood dripping out of his heart. "These aren't bad children," he said during one of the discussion periods. "These are children wounded by racism. It's up to us to close those wounds."

"Okay, once or twice a week, we're going to play a little game called Stump the Star. We'll have a contest, something related to U.S. history, and anybody who can beat me gets a prize." My voice was hearty, but I was a little uneasy as I scanned the room. Most of the faces looked bored or indifferent, and on a couple I even thought I detected signs of incipient malice. My plan to show the kids that school could be *fun* as well as useful didn't seem to be catching on.

Trying to shrug it off, I handed out the first contest: A blank map of the U.S. "See how many states you can label in the next twenty minutes," I instructed them. "Like I said, anyone who beats me gets a prize." I had thought long and hard about what to use for the first one. I thought labeling the states would be difficult enough to challenge the students, but not so hard that they'd say the hell with it.

Half an hour later, as I graded the last paper, I didn't know whether to laugh or cry about all my careful preparation. The top scholar in my class had managed to correctly label exactly three states: Michigan, California, and Florida An appalling number of the kids didn't get a single correct answer. How in the *hell* had any of these children reached the eighth grade?

As the year wore on, I started wondering how some of them had *lived* to reach the eighth grade. There were several that I surely wanted to strangle. They talked constantly and my polite requests (which were getting less polite by the minute) to keep it down were greeted as though I were speaking Martian.

The worst was a kid named Fred Johnson. Though I loved him, he was one of the brighter students, and he absolutely couldn't keep his mouth shut. Anytime anyone said anything, Fred answered back in a singsong rhyme. If I said, turn to page five in the book, Fred would call out: "I'm turning to page five, Mr. Jive." If I asked another student to read aloud, he'd yell: "Time to get down, clown." Inevitably the entire class would start cackling. Usually, I had to fight down my own laughter—some of his rhymes were pretty clever. But it was impossible to even try to teach when he was in the room.

By the end of the third day, I'd had enough. When Fred started his rap, I interrupted: "Just a minute, while I step next door to get someone." A low *ooooooohh* rippled through the room. Everybody knew what "stepping next door" meant: A paddling. The Flint schools permitted us to use wooden paddles on the kids as long as another teacher was present. But when I returned with a math teacher in tow, Fred was still laughing and firing rhymes. He didn't seem worried at all, although I was a good foot taller and probably sixty pounds heavier. *This kid must think he has a butt of steel*, I thought as I motioned him over to my desk.

When he put his hands on the desk and bent over, I realized why: He had a wallet about two inches thick in his back pocket. "Take the billfold out, Superman," I ordered him, and his broad smile sagged.

As I swung the narrow oak paddle back, like Mickey Mantle preparing to take a big cut at the ball, all the frustrations of the past three days exploded. I put everything I had into it, hammering his butt so hard that his entire body shot up onto the desk, scattering a stack of books across the floor. The classroom was completely silent for the first time that week. Fred just lay there across the desk, gasping; I could see tears running from the corner of his eyes.

I turned my back and walked to the blackboard. "Okay, open your books to chapter two," I directed the class in a calm voice as Fred struggled to his feet and limped back to his seat. My face was impassive, but inside I felt sick. I never wanted to hurt the kid, just to get his attention. *I guess he's not the only immature asshole in this classroom*, a little voice taunted me from the corner of my brain.

Fortunately, I never had to paddle another kid. I became the most legendary butt-whomper in the history of Bryant Junior High School with that one loud whack. The math teacher who witnessed the paddling was tremendously impressed with the way I could send a teenaged body flying across the room, and word spread. Teachers came calling to ask me to stop by their rooms and look ominous. That's all it took.

Joining Up

**15**

My tough guy reputation kept my classes from deteriorating into a complete zoo. But in terms of real learning, there wasn't much. I barely knew where to begin. Our textbooks were in many cases useless, because a lot of the kids couldn't read them. I sometimes tried to teach English by having them read out of *My Weekly Reader*, which is written for early elementary-school kids. Nobody complained to me that it was too easy.

It was fashionable, then and now, to say that all this was the fault of the educational system, of teachers and administrators who didn't care. Once in a while I found a case that seemed to fill that bill. One girl turned in a test completely blank, without even taking the wild stabs at answers that the rest of the kids did. When I talked to her about it, I discovered she was legally blind—she could barely see the test paper, much less try to read it. I felt like using my paddle on a few of my colleagues over that one.

But that poor little girl was the exception, not the rule. Most of these kids were uneducated because they were rude, rebellious jerks who resisted any attempt to teach them anything. The year I got there, they drove one teacher to such distraction that she went home from school one day and died of an asthma attack. Another teacher who was just marking time until he could retire showed movies nearly every single day of the school year—because that was the only way he could get the kids to shut up.

It was easy to get the movies. It was easy for us to get anything at all; the War on Poverty was in full swing, and Washington was dropping more money on inner cities than it was bombs on Vietnam. Film-strip machines, fancy tape recorders, supplemental textbooks, all we had to do was ask. The only thing the school board couldn't supply us with was students who wanted to learn.

In each of my six classes, there were about ten students who showed an interest in learning. With the rest, I was strictly a baby-sitter. I felt sorry for the teachers who would have to handle them in high school. There were already times when I felt a little nervous

WITH HONOR AND PURPOSE

about confronting some of them. When we did surprise locker inspections, we came away with enough knives and chains to arm a small gang.

A few months into the school year, I was watching a TV documentary on education. To my amazement, it included several interviews with sociologists and psychologists who said that the reason kids in inner-city schools were tough to teach was that they had "low self-esteem." I almost fell off the sofa. My students had *great* self-esteem. When I assigned them to write essays on what they wanted to be when they grew up, almost every single paper said, "president of the United States." They had plenty of ambition; what they lacked was self-discipline.

We tried to impose it. We reasoned with them, bribed them with trips and parties, screamed at them, and of course whacked them with paddles. Nothing worked. (The principal even called a faculty meeting to try to come up with some answers, but he was doomed from the moment he opened the discussion with the line, "We have to remember that discipline is our ace up our holes.") As the year wore on, it was obvious that things were getting worse, not better. Fistfights in the halls weren't common but weren't unusual either. A teacher leaving her classroom at the end of the day found a pile of human excrement outside the door.

Showing up for work began to feel like arriving for the final ten minutes of Custer's Last Stand. Even the most dedicated teachers sometimes threw up their hands in despair. One of the bitterest was the bleeding heart who started the year thinking there were no bad children. I knew the kids were giving him a hard time, but my heart froze as I listened to him one spring afternoon in the teachers' lounge. "Blacks are great," he announced. "Everybody ought to own one."

For me, the final straw came in April, the day after Martin Luther King Jr. was murdered in Memphis. The bell had just rung to mark the start of first-period classes when someone in the back of the room shouted, "Holy shit! Look at that!" Right outside my classroom window, a mob of black students was chasing a terrified white kid. As the kid disappeared around the corner of the gym, several of the students in my class jumped to their feet.

"Nobody in this classroom is going anywhere," I declared. "Now sit down and get out your books." For one taut moment, the kids stayed on their feet, staring at me coldly; then a couple of them shrugged, and everyone sat down. It was the high point of my teaching career—I kept my eighth-graders from joining a mob.

All morning long I watched the bedlam outside that window as riot police tried, with little success, to restore order. One white kid was so badly beaten that he was taken to the hospital. Even so, we were lucky; it could have been so much worse. One kid was seen swinging a hatchet.

I was heartsick. I understood the kids' rage over Dr. King's murder. But what did a thirteen-year-old white child, a thousand miles away from the scene of the crime, have to do with it? The answer was that on that day almost anyone with white skin was the enemy, no matter who he was, what he thought, or how he behaved. I saw some of my own students running around during the riot. Was that what they had been thinking when I was trying to teach them where the capital of Michigan was? *I'd like to beat his head in with a rock?* That was the day I decided to quit teaching.


As it turned out, I quit Michigan, too. I had been dating the same girl for almost six years, ever since I was a senior in high school, and around that same time the relationship went to pieces. Some guys might have joined the French Foreign Legion. I picked California instead. When school was out in June, I moved to San Jose and got into a management training program with the phone company.

It was great. No screaming. No blank stares. No co-workers stopping by to ask me to conk someone with a wooden paddle. I was on the fast track into corporate America, and I couldn't have been happier.

Then my father had a stroke.

It wasn't completely a surprise. Six or seven years earlier, the doctors had warned Dad that one of the valves in his heart was malfunctioning. They could try to replace it, but roughly half the people who had the operation died in surgery. Dad didn't like those odds. Now, however, the bad valve had triggered the stroke.

For a couple of weeks, I tried to carry on in California. But the daily reports from my mother were grim. "He's not himself, Phil," she told me over the phone. "He's not doing very well at all." Even more worrisome than her words was the strain in her voice. My mother had always been the steel backbone of the family. Her anxiety sent a piercing chill through my heart. I decided to pack up my apartment and come home.

But what would I do for a living? It was September; school had been in session for two weeks, and all the teaching contracts were signed months ago. In a matter of days, I had gone from the corporate fast track to being a bum.

I called my old principal to see if he had any suggestions. He did: The physical-education teacher who had been at Bryant since about the time the Earth cooled had transferred to the high school in June, and his replacement hadn't worked out; would I be interested in the job? I drove straight through from San Jose and was in the principal's office a couple of days later, signing a contract. "Did the other gym teacher leave any lesson plans?" I asked innocently.

The principal chuckled mirthlessly. "Lesson plans?" he repeated. "I'll give you your lesson plans for the whole year. When the bell rings to start class, you shut the gym door. When the bell rings to end class, you open it again. If nobody leaves the gym to make trouble, then you're teacher of the year."

I thought he must be exaggerating at least a little, but when I met some of the other teachers after school for a beer, they told me it was a miracle the principal hadn't burst into tears while talking to me. The gym teacher I was replacing had literally run out of the gym and never come back.

My second and final year as an educator began the next morning. I had prepared an eloquent speech for the occasion. "Sit down and shut up!" I bellowed. "Here's the new rules. You come in each day.

I'll throw out a basketball. I don't care if you play with it or sit in the bleachers. I don't care if you put on gym clothes or not. I don't care about anything at all, except nobody's leaving this gym until I blow the whistle at the end of the period. Anybody who tries is getting his butt beat. Is that clear?"

"By you and what army?" a voice called out, half humor and half challenge. I had a sudden mental image of the last coach racing out the door. I took a deep breath.

"Let's settle this right now," I challenged them. "Anybody who thinks he can whip me, line up down here on the gym floor. I'll take you on two at a time—we'll wrestle in the jump-ball circle. If anybody can kick my butt, I'll leave."

I had to wrestle four of the students that period, two the next. By the end of the day, word had gotten around: Kerby is back, and he's even crazier than last year. Nobody tried to leave the gym, that day or the rest of the year.

But I spent the entire school year feeling like a Dutch boy with his finger in a dike. You couldn't staff the entire faculty with slightly nuts ex–football players. More and more often, the principal had to call on the Flint police to keep the school from further deteriorating.

Worse yet, there was nothing unique about Bryant. By the spring of 1969, America looked like it was coming apart at the seams. The mutant offspring of the civil rights and anti-war movements, the Black Panthers and the Weathermen, were spoiling for a fight. Arsons and explosions rocked college campuses. If the president of Columbia University couldn't control his school, how could the principal of Bryant Junior High control his?

My two years of "teaching" had burned the last sociological impulse out of my brain. What I saw all around me was almost criminal, and when you have crime, you need cops. After one particularly rough spring afternoon, I walked over to one of the Flint policemen. "Are you guys doing any hiring? The way my job is going, I might as well have a badge and a gun," I added facetiously. "We have some openings," the policeman replied. "And I hear the FBI does, too."

"Agent Campbell will see you now for your interview," the secretary said in a prim, efficient voice. She set off down the narrow, twisting corridors at a brisk pace. I followed, trying not to stare too obviously at the framed photographs that dotted the institutional-green walls. There was one of a night-firing exercise on a shooting range, a tangle of scarlet traces. Another showed an agent on horseback in a Western landscape, rounding up cattle stolen by an interstate rustler's ring. I could hardly take it all in. *How did I do on that test?* I wondered as we made what seemed like our dozenth turn.

Actually, I had taken two tests in the FBI's old gray building in downtown Detroit. The first one, a multiple-choice exam filled with current-events-type questions, I was pretty certain I had aced. (Although I was starting to have a queasy feeling that the Russian word *pravda* meant "truth," not "people," as I had answered. But maybe that was a good one to miss. Maybe the FBI would be suspicious of somebody who knew too much about the Soviet Union.)

But I didn't have a clue about the second test, which was all essay questions. One was, "Discuss the significance of the Fourth Amendment to the U.S. Constitution." Who the hell knew which one that was? Taking a guess—this was an entrance exam for a police agency, after all—I wrote several paragraphs on the importance of the people being secure from unreasonable search and seizure. Then there was another question about why I wanted to join the FBI. I wrote about how sick I was of riots, demonstrations, and the general breakdown of American society. It was a completely truthful answer, but now I wondered if it would seem fake, like some ass-kisser's idea of what the FBI wanted to hear.

Agent Jim Campbell's stony expression gave me no clue about where I stood, and neither did his questions—mostly resume chitchat stuff about my hobbies, favorite subjects in school, that kind of thing. He asked just one that I had to think about: "If we don't offer you a job as an agent, would you be interested in working as a clerk for a few years and then reapplying?" *He wants me to say I'll eat shit if I have to in order to join the FBI*, I thought as I nodded yes. And I would, too. I really wanted this job. My dad was feeling better, and the idea of another year at Bryant gnarled my stomach like an old root.

Campbell contemplated my answer a moment. "We like to have each applicant meet the special agent in charge, Paul Stoddard," he announced. "Let's stop by his office." He scooped up a pile of file folders in his left hand, and we stepped into the next office.

"Paul, this is Phil Kerby," Campbell said. "He's one of our agent applicants."

"Yes, I know," Stoddard said in a gruff voice. "Now that you've looked around, are you still interested in joining the FBI?"

"Absolutely," I replied, not really trusting myself to say much more. With his horn-rim glasses and combed-back black hair, Stoddard looked disconcertingly like a nearsighted Dick Tracy.

"Well, there's still a lot of paperwork to clear out," Stoddard said. "But I think you'll be hearing from us." He and Campbell smiled. I didn't know it yet, but I was in.


Years later, I ran into Jim Campbell—his nickname, of course, was Soupy—at a meeting of retired agents. "Did that test I took count for anything?" I asked.

"We just wanted to see if you could read and write," he replied. "I was the one who made the decision, during our interview. Remember how I picked up those files before we went in to see Stoddard? That was to hide my right hand. Whenever I took an applicant in there, I gave Stoddard a thumbs-up or a thumbs-down signal with my right hand."

"What did you base it on?" I asked, fascinated.

"Oh, you know," he shrugged. "Whether you would fit in."

An applicant to the FBI these days fills out an application. If he or she fits within the basic guidelines on age, education, and so forth, the next step is a written exam that weeds out most candidates. Then it's on to an interview by a regional board, a drug test, a polygraph, and a fitness test that includes more pushups than I care to think about. A candidate who gets through all that still has to pass a background check.

But in 1969, J. Edgar Hoover was running the FBI. And there was really only one hurdle for an applicant: *Will he fit in?* And I'm not using the word *he* casually; a she, by definition, didn't fit. There were no women agent in Hoover's FBI, almost no blacks or Hispanics, and certainly no one with long hair or a beard. I didn't know it—and, in those days, wouldn't have given it much thought if I had—but I had just joined the country's most exclusive White Boys' Club. (I don't use the word *exclusive* casually, either; the FBI at that time had just five thousand agents. By comparison, New York City's police department has thirty-six thousand officers.)

It took a few weeks, but eventually the official word came in the form of a yellow Western Union telegram:

YOU ARE OFFERED PROBATIONARY APPOINTMENT SPECIAL AGENT GRADE GS TEN SALARY NINETYTWO HUNDRED NINETY-SEVEN DOLLARS PER ANNUM. FOLLOWING ASSIGNMENT TO FIELD OFFICE ADDITIONAL COMPENSATION OF TWENTYTHREE HUNDRED TWENTYNINE DOLLARS PER YEAR MAY BE EARNED FOR OVERTIME PERFORMANCE IN CONNECTION WITH OFFICIAL DUTIES PROVIDED CERTAIN REQUIREMENTS ARE MET. REPORT NINE AM JUNE SIXTEENTH ROOM FIVE TWO THREE ONE JUSTICE BUILDING NINTH STREET AND PENNSYLVANIA AVENUE NORTHWEST WASHINGTON D.C. NO PUBLICITY SHOULD BE GIVEN. . . ."

JOHN EDGAR HOOVER, DIRECTOR,
FEDERAL BUREAU OF INVESTIGATION

My dad drove me to the Western Union office to pick up the telegram. His face, always so tired now, lit up when he read it. My own reaction was mostly astonishment at the salary. With overtime, I would be making $11,626 a year. That was almost double my teaching salary, which had been more than enough for me to live on. Not only was I going to join the FBI and catch Russian spies, I was going to be *rich*. Cool.

It turned out there was one more requirement for me to fulfill. A few days before I headed to Washington, a harried Jack Duvall—the agent who ran Flint's FBI office—called me. "Listen, they've just issued a new regulation," he said. "All recruits have to pull the trigger on a pistol before reporting to Washington. Do you have time to do it tonight?"

"Look, Jack, it's already 7 P.M.," I replied. "There's no need for you to go back into the office just for this. Why don't I come by in the morning?"

"Go back in?" he said in surprise. "I'm still here."

"Well, sure, I'll come in then," I said. After a moment's hesitation, I asked: "Are the triggers on FBI service revolvers, um, especially hard to pull?"

"No," Duvall sighed. "But when they took the last recruiting class out on the academy firing range for the first time, there was some asshole who froze and couldn't pull the trigger. So now there's a rule that everyone has to prove he can pull a trigger before he shows up at the academy. There doesn't have to be a bullet in the gun—you just have to pull the trigger while I watch."

I hopped in my car, drove to the office, and obligingly squeezed the trigger on an empty revolver. In my bemusement, I missed two important clues in Duvall's words about my future. One was that FBI agents worked about twice as many hours a day as I did as a teacher. The other was that, because of a single aberrational screwup, someone at the Bureau had propounded a whole new rule that would affect thousands of people. Not only had I joined the country's most exclusive White Boys' Club, I had just ensnared myself in the country's most maddeningly petty bureaucracy.


The counselor was frowning as he walked toward me, never a good sign. "Well, Kerby, I hope you're enjoying Virginia, because you're not going anywhere tonight," he said. "Your itinerary has been rejected. You'll have to prepare and submit a new one."

"Why?" I asked, befuddled. All I was going to do was spend a sight-seeing weekend in Washington.

"Because when you typed *FBI*, you put periods in it," he replied, his voice stern. "You know we don't use periods."

I managed to stifle my sigh until he was safely across the room, delivering bad news to some other punctuation scofflaw. The first week at the academy, perched on a corner of the U.S. Marine base in rural Quantico, Virginia, had been a long one, and I was looking forward to a couple of days away—or, as one of the other guys had put it, "a trip back to the real world."

It was true: The academy existed in its own little universe, a J. Edgar Hoover fantasyland. In a lot of ways, it was like a summer camp. We bunked eight to the room, wandered to the dorm showers naked if we felt like it, even had a pillow fight one night.

But just as kids often puzzle over the enigmatic rules set by adults, we marveled at the arbitrary regimentation. Losing my Friday night out over the way I wrote the letters *FBI* was nothing compared to what had happened to one poor classmate. He carried a newspaper into the academy's academic wing—not into a classroom, mind you, just into the hallway. That broke one of the academy's most sacred rules, though no one seemed to be too sure who made it or why, and his punishment was swift: a letter of censure for his permanent personnel file. "I am shocked and amazed at your recent misconduct," the letter began; it ended with the initials *JEH*. Nothing like making an enemy of the Director (when our counselors said it, you could hear that capital D) your first week in the FBI.

Some of the guys in my class were chafing quite a bit at all the fine print. I mostly kept my mouth shut, although I did permit myself one small act of rebellion the first night at Quantico. One of the counselors came up to our rooms and announced: "We'll be showing *The FBI Story* downstairs in fifteen minutes." I wanted to groan—watching Jimmy Stewart play an agent was not my idea of a fun way to spend off-hours—but the counselor's face suggested that would be a bad idea. Instead, I simply nodded. But when everybody else went downstairs, I stayed in my room.

Oddly enough, that movie inflicted the first casualty on our training class. When it was over, one of the guys, a deeply religious Mormon from Salt Lake City, was profoundly disturbed. "I never realized that I'd have to kill anybody," he confessed. (So much for the old squeeze-the-trigger test.) The next morning he was gone. I can hardly imagine what he would have done if he'd seen *Silence of the Lambs*.

That dropped New Agent Class 16, as we were known, down to forty-nine men. We looked like we came from the same cookie cutter: White, clean-shaven, short hair, with athletic builds. We even dressed alike, in the approved FBI uniform of dress shoes, business suit, white shirt, and dark tie. A number of the guys had been teachers, like me; several others were ex-military men. One of the great myths about the FBI is that to become an agent, you have to have a degree in law or accounting. In my class, there were only about half a dozen lawyers, including a couple of guys from Mississippi who openly admitted they had signed up in order to avoid getting drafted and sent to Vietnam.

Our days were hectic, shuttling to and fro between classrooms, the laboratory, and the labyrinthine rooms full of files. At the lab, they showed us a thousand ways to link a suspect to a crime. They demonstrated how a little piece of wire at a crime scene could be matched, microscopically, with another fragment found in a suspect's house. They pulled out their vast collection of paint chips from automobiles. They illustrated how an automatic weapon leaves distinctive marks on spent cartridges as it ejects them. They explained all the things you could learn from samples of blood, semen, and hair (which, even in those days before DNA testing, was a lot.)

We spent endless hours learning how to take and match fingerprints. I got the heebie-jeebies from the fingerprint guys, a bunch of little gray men who spent eight hours a day hunched over magnifying glasses counting whorls and loops, lifting their heads only to puff on cigarettes that seemed to have been surgically implanted in their faces.

But I did have some fun wandering around in the fingerprint files. (The FBI has something approaching 200 million sets of prints.) I found Machine Gun Kelly's prints, and John Dillinger's, too. I also looked for a set on my dad's brother Paul, who left his wife and son at home one morning in the 1930s and was never seen again. But there was no trace of him.

The whirlwind tour we were getting was awesome; at times I wondered how anybody could get away with a crime, with all these resources arrayed against him. But I also had some nagging doubts. In murder mysteries, I was always reading about how lividity, the way blood settles in a corpse, can yield clues about time of death and whether a body has been moved. But no one at the lab said a word about that—or about blood-splatter patterns, which I had heard could reveal a good deal about whether a killer was right-or left-handed. Sometimes there was a hit-or-miss feel to the academy.

My concerns crystallized one day at lunch, when a stranger showed up in the cafeteria. "Are you in training?" I asked after he sat down.

"No, I'm an agent," he answered amiably. "I'm assigned to Indianapolis, but I'm here for an in-service class."

"So what kind of a case are you working on?" I asked.

"Well, I've got about five military deserter cases," he replied, mentally ticking them off. "I've got a couple of interstate theft cases. I've got a bank robbery. I've got some civil rights cases."

I thought he must have misunderstood me. Nobody could handle that kind of workload. "How many cases are you working on *right now*?" I interrupted, trying to clarify my question.

"Oh, about forty, I guess," he said.

"Forty?" I blurted. I was wondering how I would handle even *one* case. I had just realized the awful truth: In all these lectures and classes, nobody had said a single word about how you actually went about investigating a case.

It was true: We had classes on how to fill out FBI interview sheets, the ubiquitous FD-302 form—but very little on how to interview a witness. We had classes on the paperwork necessary to forward evidence to the FBI lab—but hardly anything on how to collect evidence from a crime scene.

In fact, most of our time was spent learning how not to run afoul of FBI regulations. Our Bible (or, perhaps, anti-Bible) was something called *The Agent's Handbook*. One of the instructors called it *The Book of Losers*.

"Every stupid thing you read in here is something that some agent actually did and somebody complained to the Director about," he told us. "When it says, 'You may not smoke in someone's house when you're interviewing them,' that's because some agent smoked in somebody's house and Mr. Hoover got a letter about it. When it says, 'You may not walk across someone's lawn when approaching their house,' that's because some agent walked across a lawn and Mr. Hoover got a letter about it."

Even worse than making *The Book of Losers* would be making the list of agents killed in the line of duty, and we spent a lot of time at the firing range to learn how to keep that from happening. We trained with a Smith & Wesson Model 10, a six-shot revolver. To graduate, we had to be able to hit a target from fifty yards away, both right-handed and left-handed. We also practiced with a Thompson submachine gun, just like the ones you see in old gangster movies.

Aside from the firearms training, the most worthwhile courses at the academy were the law classes taught by a veteran agent from Boston named Charlie Donlan. Instead of just droning on about what the Supreme Court had to say about search and seizure law and the ability to detain suspects in *Terry v. Ohio*. Donlan taught by scenario. The stories always revolved around a character called Balls O'Leary. They always took place in Boston, or The Hub of the Universe, as Donlan called it, and often involved the city's Shawmut National Bank:

"Suppose, gentlemen, that you're walking down a street in The Hub of the Universe. You observe the ubiquitous Balls-O exiting the Shawmut National Bank. Your attention is drawn by the fact that he is carrying a paper sack in his hands with money scattering out the top. He has a ski mask on his face, and he's exiting the area rapidly.

"Gentlemen, these are what we call *clues*. If you put clues together, they form something called *probable cause*. In this case, we have a variety of clues that form *probable cause* that Balls-O has just robbed the bank. And what does this prompt you to do? You've seen a felony committed in your presence. So you grab Balls-O, thrust him to the wall, handcuff him, and take him to the seat of government for booking." Remembering, of course, not to step on someone's lawn along the way.

Donlan's lectures were not only entertaining, they were damn instructive about what we could or couldn't do. In all my years in the FBI, I never lost a case to a procedural error.

August slipped into September, and with graduation only a few weeks away, our class was getting fidgety. For one thing, the regimentation was getting on everyone's nerves. Even after we moved out of the dorms at Quantico and into apartments, we had to be available at any hour of the day or night. Spending the night with a woman was expressly forbidden.* One member of the class, a guy from Detroit, decided it wasn't worth it and quit. "Come on, this is just academy bullshit," the counselor implored. "When you get out in the field, it will be different." But he couldn't be convinced, and now we were down to forty-eight.

---

*I suppose spending the night with a male lover would have been against the rules, too, but it didn't come up; in those days, gays were out of sight and out of mind. That doesn't mean that they weren't present, though. One of my contemporaries, Frank Buttino, two decades later, after leaving the bureau, would be the first FBI agent to openly declare himself gay. He was fired, but it wound up costing the government a pretty penny in damages.

We were also on edge about our first office assignment. A few weeks earlier, we had filled out forms listing our top three preferences. All the counselors warned us to lie. "If you list a place, there's no chance you'll wind up there," one told me. "My advice is to list three places you *hate*."

That was a little too Machiavellian for me. Besides, I wasn't too worried about where I was assigned, as long as it wasn't the Deep South. (As a lifelong northern boy, I knew for a fact it was all cotton fields, tarpaper shacks, and Kate Smith records.) Since I had enjoyed my brief stay out in California, I listed San Francisco, Sacramento, and Salt Lake City as my preferences.

My attitude, though, was far from typical. Most of my classmates were absolutely obsessed with the location of their first assignment, even though it would last only a year. Ultimately the most feared destination was New York, because it was so expensive. "You'll eat tomato soup made from ketchup and hot water every night for the whole year," somebody said. Washington had a similar reputation. Miami, with great weather and affordable prices, was considered a dream assignment.*

On the big day, we were called one by one to the front of a classroom. A counselor handed each of us an envelope containing our assignment, and tradition dictated that you opened it right there and called out your city. A good assignment drew cheers and applause, a bad one hooting and catcalls.

Whoever did the assignments had scattered us all over the place: Cleveland, Salt Lake City, Tampa, Sacramento, Albuquerque, Dallas, Houston. Even though I kept telling myself it was no big deal, my stomach started to tighten as my name approached. When I opened my envelope, there were neither cheers nor jeers: Albany, New York. After the roll call, as everybody else traded congratulations and condolences, I slipped out the door to look at a map.

---

*This was in the days before Miami was hip-deep in cocaine. Now new agents practically have to be sent there at gunpoint.

WITH HONOR AND PURPOSE

Three weeks later, we graduated in a ceremony held at the Justice Department in Washington. The two draft-dodging Mississippi lawyers showed up in blue shirts, and our counselors looked like they were on the verge of a stroke. "Are you crazy?" one of them asked. "Didn't you learn anything here?" The lawyers looked confused. "Your shirts are supposed to be *white*, damn it!" the counselor shrieked. "I don't give a shit what happens to *you*, but they'll give *me* a letter of censure, too."

After an emergency consultation, the counselors came up with a solution: They exchanged their shirts with the lawyers, then hid during the ceremony. Albany was sounding better every minute.

Joining Up

## 3

# OUT IN THE STREET

"**H**ey, you doing anything?" The voice came from the desk across the aisle. The agent's eyes (he was a *real* agent, not a bullshit-right-out-of-academy impostor like me) were on a sheaf of yellow teletype messages in his hands. But he had to be talking to me—there was no one else within earshot.

"No, uh, no, I'm not," I replied, choking off the "sir" that instinctively tried to come out of my mouth. For nearly two days now I had been sitting at a desk in the Albany office, doing my best imitation of office furniture, alternately longing for someone to give me an assignment and quailing in terror that they might.

"Well," the agent said, "they've sent us a picture of the suspect in a check forgery case at that camera shop right down the block. Take it over there, would you? See if the clerk can pick her out of a photo spread. There's some other pictures you can use for the spread on the desk in the back of the room."

"I'll get right on it," I replied in a voice that sounded much steadier than I felt. Without even looking up, he handed me a mugshot and a 302 form with a summary of the case.

*Photo spread*. I'd heard the phrase before, and I was pretty sure I knew what he meant: the photographic equivalent of a police lineup. See if the clerk could identify the woman who had passed the bad check. On the desk in back, I found a large stack of photos that had been discarded from case files for one reason or another. I picked up the first four pictures of women I came across and headed out.

Striding down the sidewalk underneath the sunny autumn sky, I glanced through the case summary. Somebody had passed a forged check for about $200 at the camera shop; because it was drawn on a Boston bank, the forgery was an act of interstate theft, and the FBI had jurisdiction. Not exactly Dillingeresque, but it was my first case, and I had goosebumps as I walked into the camera shop.

They faded quickly. The clerk behind the counter could barely conceal her boredom. "I told them before, I don't remember nothing about this check," she complained. She waved her hand at the row of photos I had carefully lined up on the counter. "And I don't know none of them ladies, either." My pace was a bit less brisk on the way back to the office.

"So, how did it go?" the agent greeted me as I entered.

"Not so good," I admitted. "The clerk couldn't pick out the forger."

"Let me see those pictures," the agent said. He leafed through them quickly. "Lucky thing for you she didn't," he announced. "It would never have stood up in court. Who taught you to do a photo spread?"

"Nobody," I answered truthfully.

"Well, next time you do them, make sure the pictures all have at least a general resemblance to the suspect," the agent counseled. "Otherwise the judge is going to toss it." He fanned out the photos, and I saw what he meant. The suspect was a worn-looking, middle-aged woman. Of the four other pictures I used to fill out the spread, two were women half her age.

The agent clapped me on the back. "Don't worry," he consoled me. "You'll learn."

I wondered.


When I recall that first photo spread, two things strike me about it. One is that we actually worked a $200 forged check. These days, an FBI agent wouldn't walk across the room over that amount of money.

A forged check would probably have to be for at least $50,000 to get the Bureau's attention now. It tells you something unpleasant, I'm afraid, about the changes in American society over the past twenty-five years.

The other interesting thing about that photo spread was that, in many ways, it was a sort of metaphor for the year I served in Albany, my first office. I spent a lot of the time tiptoeing away from gargantuan screwups that somehow or other left me unscathed.

The frightening thing is, that was how it was *supposed* to work. The academy taught you how to push FBI paper and avoid finding your way into *The Book of Losers*; then you went to your first office and learned how to be an investigator while hopefully not leaving too much wreckage in your wake.

If I was going to be a loose cannon, I guess the Albany office was a pretty good place to do it. With fifty-five agents, it was small enough so that I didn't get lost, but big enough so that I was able to learn how to work a large variety of cases. (By comparison, the New York and Los Angeles offices have about fifteen hundred agents apiece, while the tiny satellite office in Hyannisport, Massachusetts, had just one.)

The FBI is organized roughly along the lines of federal judicial districts. Most districts have a division headquarters—in this case, Albany—which in addition to the agents in its office controls five or six satellite offices scattered through smaller towns in the territory.

The office is headed by a special agent in charge, or SAC. (And, they warned us at the academy, *never* refer to him as "the sack"— pronounce each letter.) He deals mostly with high-level administrative matters. The guy who actually runs the office day-to-day is the assistant special agent in charge, or ASAC. (And, they warned us at the academy, *never* pronounce each letter—refer to him as "the a-sack.")

The SAC in Albany was a gentlemanly guy named Leo Conroy. The ASAC was a slightly pompous man named Bill Maupai. With his white hair combed back and his tailored suits, Maupai looked more like an English headmaster than a cop. He *acted* a bit like a headmaster too, sitting grandly in an office with windows that looked into the squad room, where the agents huddled like wayward pupils at their desks.

The first thing I learned was that the reassurances the counselors had given us were wrong—the academy was not the only part of the FBI afflicted with a plague of petty bullshit. Agents had to abide by a host of fussy, nit-picking rules. I was astonished to see grown men sneaking out the back door, down four flights of stairs, and through an alley into the rear of a cafe called Basil's in order to have a cup of coffee. No coffee was permitted at our desks, and the Director certainly wasn't paying us to sit around in restaurants, as Maupai never tired of reminding us.

If the agents were treated like children, the support staff was like a pink-collar chain gang. The office had fourteen stenographers (all female, just as the agents were all male) to type up reports we dictated. They had to sign in and out of the office and wear skirts even on the most arctic days of the Albany winter. They weren't allowed to smoke, although agents could. And at the end of each day, they were graded on the number of lines they'd typed.

There were about a dozen first-office agents in Albany. None of us knew our asses from our elbows, but it didn't seem to faze the veterans—who, I suppose, had nursemaided plenty of ignorant rookies into full-fledged agents. Despite all our mistakes, everybody was very patient with us. I don't recall a single time in Albany where another agent yelled at me or called me a blockhead.

Still, it was a process of continual embarrassment for me as I learned the ropes. The first time I worked a bank robbery, I found a witness who gave a good description of the getaway car, including the plate numbers. Self-importantly, I reported to the case agent— the one in charge of the investigation—what I had learned. I expected him to grab a radio to call out an all-points bulletin on the car, but instead he just nodded. "That'll be the switch car," he said.

I chewed my lip for a moment, then asked: "What's a switch car?"

"Nobody robs a bank using their own car," he explained tolerantly, as if I were mildly retarded. "You steal a car, drive it to the bank, then dump it somewhere later and get back in your own car. When we find the switch car, then we'll look around for someone who might have seen the robber change vehicles."

"How the hell do you know this stuff?" I blurted.

"When you've worked about a hundred of these things, you'll pick it up," he replied.

Later, we had a house under surveillance where we thought the suspect might be hiding. There was a car in the driveway. "Okay, Kerby, take a pass by the house," the case agent instructed me over the radio. Obediently, I drove my unmarked Bureau car slowly past the house, watching it from the corner of my eye, then returned to the stakeout point.

"It's all quiet," I reported.

"Well, what's the number?" the case agent inquired.

"The number of what?" I asked innocently.

"The number of the license plate of the car in the driveway," he said, not quite as patiently as before. "Why did you think I told you to take a pass?"

My face burning, I drove by again, then called in the plate numbers.

"Good, Kerby," the case agent purred. "But when you're using the radio, could you please hold the microphone below window level? It's possible that there's *somebody* on this block who hasn't spotted our surveillance yet."


With skills like those, it wasn't entirely surprising that first-office agents didn't work many bank robberies, even as "gowitchas"—as in, I'll go with you to run errands and be the waterboy. We got mostly the bottom-of-the-barrel cases, which, in 1969, meant military deserters. Thousands of young men, faced with shipping out to Vietnam, were peeling off their uniforms and disappearing into the night. It was the FBI's job to find them.

The very first guy I ever arrested, in fact, was an army deserter who had skipped out of a base somewhere in New Jersey. The Bureau forwarded us a military report—a lead, in Bureau parlance—that he was believed to be staying at his parents' home in Champlain, New York, a tiny town right on the Canadian border.

I parked down the street from the house early one October morning, and around 11 A.M. I saw a car pull up outside. A tall, muscular young man got out, carrying a large brown paper bag. In those days of long, flowing hair, his military crewcut stood out a mile away. I floored my accelerator, then had to slam on the brakes almost immediately to get the car to come to a screeching halt in front of the house.

"FBI, you're under arrest for desertion," I announced, popping out of the car. "Lean over the hood of the car."

He just stood there, staring at me dully, until I pulled out my handcuffs. That seemed to trigger something. He reached inside the bag and yanked out a liquor bottle by its neck. *He wants to fight*, I thought in surprise. The other agents had assured me that deserters sometimes ran, but they never fought. Before I even completed my thought, I was lunging for him. I grabbed his arm before he could take a full swing with the bottle, and after a minute or so of grunting and shoving, I had him pinned against the car.

Cuffing his hands behind his back, I shoved him into the passenger seat. I walked around, climbed in, turned the ignition key—and wondered where in the world I was supposed to take him. Nobody had told me what to do if I actually found him.

Trying to look like I knew what I was doing, I drove toward Plattsburgh, a few miles south, where the FBI had a small office. Every minute or two, I radioed the office, but no agents were in. Finally, just about the time I thought I'd have to take the deserter inside the office and handcuff him to a desk, an agent answered my call and told me to take him to a nearby air force base.

The thrill of my first arrest was only slightly diminished a few weeks later when I was in Champlain again, walking down the street, and saw the deserter ambling along as though nothing had happened. I headed right back to the office to report what I'd seen.

"Yeah, he probably deserted again," an agent agreed without rancor. "The military has got so many of these guys it can't keep them all in the brig. They have whole squads made up of nothing but captured deserters, commanded by captured deserters. You think one captured deserter is going to be real careful about watching another captured deserter?"

"Should I go arrest him again?" I wondered.

"For what? I said he's *probably* deserted again. But we don't know that for sure. We don't have any paper on him."

"Well, then, should we call his base in New Jersey?"

The agent looked astonished. "Do you think there's a shortage of these guys? We've got leads on three dozen right now. If they want him back in New Jersey, they'll let us know."

As pointless as it was picking up deserters under these circumstances, I liked the assignment. They weren't dangerous—except for that very first one, no deserter so much as ever raised a fist to me—and chasing them around was actually kind of fun, sort of like going hunting. And I felt good about putting them in jail, even if it was only for a few days. I was sick of hippies and protesters and draft dodgers and deserters.

There were some places that seemed to act as a magnet for deserters. One was Troy, New York, the home of Rensselaer Polytechnic Institute. There was an old deserted observatory in the woods outside of town, where hippies liked to hang out. And anywhere there were hippies, there were deserters. Two or three agents would crawl through the woods to a hilltop overlooking the observatory, then charge down toward the building. Once we had them rounded up, we'd start asking for identification; out of two dozen, there were inevitably one or two deserters.

Oddly enough, despite the fact that everybody was always screaming about civil rights in those days, none of the hippies around the observatory ever refused to show us identification. If they had, we'd have been sunk. We didn't have any legal authority to compel them to show us anything, and they could simply have walked away.

The observatory raids were not really typical. Mostly we caught deserters one at a time. A startling number of them, like the one in Champlain, just went home and didn't try to hide at all. They were playing a waiting game; they knew it would take a few months before the military got around to filing paperwork to have them arrested, a few months more before we got around to looking for them, and another few months more before the arrest paperwork was processed. In the meantime, their chances of an unsolicited trip to Vietnam were dwindling away.

On the other hand, there was the deserter I encountered during a temporary assignment in Syracuse. As a young, single guy, I didn't mind taking road trips out to the satellite offices—resident agencies, the FBI calls them—to cover when someone was sick, vacationing, or just overworked. I probably took twenty-five or thirty road trips of a week or more that first year. I always had to head out Sunday night and return Friday after 5 P.M., because you didn't travel on the Director's time, but I didn't mind. I was getting to see the state, meet new people, and climb out from under the red tape in the Albany office.

When I arrived in Syracuse in early February, the supervisor handed me a stack of withered yellow paper. "We've gotten a little bit behind on deserters," he said. "Work some of these with Whitworth."

Harry Whitworth, like me, had just come over from Albany, where he was also a first-office agent. Whitworth was practically one of a kind in the FBI: He joined the Bureau as a male stenographer and worked his way up to agent. A short, heavyset guy with square features, he spoke in a deep Southern drawl. We ventured out onto the icy streets in search of deserters.

The first couple of leads we checked were so old they were hopeless. "See if you can find one in there that was written *after* the dinosaurs died out," Whitworth directed me as he nursed the Bureau car through an intersection so thick with ice that we could have skated on it. Shuffling through the stack of paper, I found one that was only four years old. "Great, we're moving into the Stone Age,"

Whitworth snorted. But he turned the car and headed for the last known address of the deserter's wife.

The place was in a part of Syracuse that had once been grand but was edging toward seedy. The big old houses had been divided up into cheap, overcrowded apartments. In one of them, on the third floor of a fading Victorian house, we found the wife—a pretty but washed-out little girl in her early twenties. "Bobby hasn't been here," she assured us earnestly at the door.

"Would you mind if we had a look around?" Whitworth asked. She shook her head in polite agreement and waddled ahead of us into the apartment.

It took us only a few minutes to go through the dwarf apartment's closets and check under the only bed. Our man was nowhere in sight. "You know, this isn't going to go away," I warned the wife as we got ready to leave. "We're just going to keep coming back. It's in your husband's interest to get this situation settled and put it behind him."

"I know, I know," she agreed solemnly. "I'd like to see him, too. I'm worried about him."

On our way downstairs, we knocked on doors of other apartments, but the neighbors all insisted they knew nothing. Inside the car, Whitworth turned to me. "See anything odd in the apartment?"

"The cigarette in the toilet," I nodded. "Did you notice anything about it."

"Non-filter," Whitworth said, nodding his own head. "When was the last time you saw a woman smoking one of those?"

"He's around here somewhere. You think he's in one of the other apartments?"

"Maybe. Didn't the lead say his grandparents lived around here? Let's talk to them, then maybe come back here."

The grandparents were just two blocks away, and it was quickly apparent we weren't going to get anything out of them. We turned around and parked a few hundred feet down the street from the deserter's apartment. If we were right and he really was inside, our earlier visit might prod him into moving.

We hadn't been there ten minutes when an old red Ford Falcon roared to life in the driveway of the Victorian house. I watched as it rolled into the street. The car had been fitted with big tires, and the engine sounded like it had been installed at Indianapolis. And at the wheel sat the deserter's wife. She gave us a big smile and wave as she passed.

"Well, so much for our vaunted powers of concealment," Whitworth observed dryly. "Look, let's pull her over and ask her about that cigarette. If he's inside the house, no way he's coming out now."

I reached out the window to put the portable police light on the roof, and Whitworth plugged it in to signal her to stop. To our astonishment, a head popped up in her passenger seat. Two beady, close-set eyes fixed us with a stare. "It's him!" I said excitedly. "She had him lying down in the car!"

The car slowed a bit, but there was no sign it was pulling over. The couple seemed to lean toward one another. "Son of a bitch!" Whitworth roared. "He's getting behind the wheel. Get ready for a ride!"

Sure enough, the Falcon's engine gave a shriek and the car peeled around a corner. We followed a few seconds later, the Bureau car fishtailing madly on the icy pavement. Whitworth kept the accelerator to the floor as the speedometer passed forty, fifty, sixty. I kept my vision fixed on the Falcon as it blasted through a series of ragged, fishtailing turns along the snow-covered streets, but from the corner of my eyes I could see houses flash by like the herky-jerky frames of an old movie.

"This bastard is never going to stop on his own!" shouted Whitworth. "Get on the radio, see if we can get some help from the local cops."

I picked up the microphone with one hand, using the other to brace myself against the dashboard, and silently cursed the Washington bean-counter who had decided to save a few nickels by not equipping Bureau cars with radios that could reach local police frequencies. This was going to be like Indians relaying smoke signals.

"We're in a high-speed pursuit and we need some assistance from

Syracuse PD," I told the Bureau office, concentrating on keeping my voice calm as we slid into another turn.

"Ten-four," the agent on the other end acknowledged. A few moments later, his voice returned. "Okay, I've got the police dispatcher on the other line. What's your twenty?" he asked, radio code for location.

I glanced around, but my tiny storehouse of geographical knowledge of Syracuse had been laid waste by our frantic, twisting pursuit of the red Falcon. "Where are we?" I asked Whitworth.

"Beats the hell out of me," he barked, struggling to keep the car from slipping off the road. "I've never been in this part of town before."

I tried to catch a glimpse of a street sign, but they zipped past like bullets. It was useless to ask Whitworth to slow down; we were barely keeping the Falcon in sight as it was.

"Tell them we're somewhere on the east side of town, in an older residential neighborhood," I finally said into the mike.

"*That* really narrows it down," the other agent replied. I started my own sarcastic retort, but bit it off as I saw our speedometer edge past eighty. Instead, I said a silent prayer that the bitter cold would keep kids inside in front of the television. One child on a bicycle could turn this into a bloodbath.

Ahead, the Falcon braked hard, its back end swerving crazily from side to side, and then made a hard right turn. Its two right tires reared into the air, and the left wheels were barely clinging to the street. For a moment it looked like the car was doing a high-wire act; then the right side slammed back down onto the road and the Falcon shot forward as the deserter hit his accelerator again.

Whitworth's face pinched into an unearthly grimace as he crushed the brake pedal of our Bureau car. I grabbed the dashboard with both hands as he wheeled the car right. There was a sickening floating sensation as our wheels went up, a bone-jarring crash as they came back down. Somehow we were still on the street. The houses were thinning out now, and up ahead I could see the street turned into a freeway access road.

Out in the Street

The radio crackled to life again. "Have you got a twenty yet?" the office asked. As I raised the mike to my mouth, Whitworth cried out: "Oh, shit! Look what he's doing!" I watched in horror as the Falcon thundered the wrong way up a freeway exit ramp. We followed seconds later.

"We're on a freeway now," I reported to the office. "It looks like we're headed out of town—lots of trees, few buildings."

"Look at a sign, any sign," the agent answered. "Any kind of an exit sign and we'll know where you are."

"All we can see are the backs of signs," I admitted. "We're going the wrong way." The office had no answer to that.

Actually, the chase was slightly less terrifying up here on the freeway. Luck was with us—we hadn't seen a single vehicle on our side of the divided highway—and the broad, straight freeway was a much better place to stage a high-speed chase than the narrow, twisting residential streets. But the Falcon was still outrunning us; we couldn't catch it and try to force it over. As the cars zoomed along the snow-covered concrete at sixty miles an hour, I wondered how long we had until we faced oncoming cars.

Maybe the deserter was wondering, too. At the first opportunity, he veered across three lanes and jetted down an entrance ramp. With another "oh, shit," Whitworth did the same. At the bottom of the ramp, the Falcon did another death-defying right turn and zipped off along a two-lane highway into the countryside.

Whitworth, stamping on the brake pedal, jerked the steering wheel to the right. This time the tires didn't bite on the icy surface. The car spun loonily in a clockwise circle, like a carnival ride gone amok, and plowed into a snowdrift. The soft, powdery snow sucked us in like mud and the car came to a shuddering halt.

"You okay?" Whitworth asked. I nodded, not quite able to speak. "That guy is *definitely* going to Vietnam," he snarled, and gunned the engine. The wheels spun for a moment, caught, and wrenched us back onto the road. Twisting the wheel again, Whitworth raced us down the same road the Falcon had taken.

The deserter must have had his own problems on the slippery asphalt, because it was only a minute or two before we topped a small rise and had him in sight again. The narrow road stretched straight ahead of us for miles. To the right was an open farm field, to the left a dense forest of pine trees. The snow had drifted three or four feet high along parts of the treeline.

The Falcon was slowing down. Suddenly it darted across the road and skidded to a halt in front of the woods. The deserter jumped out of the car and began fighting his way through the snow toward the treeline. As he staggered through the drifts, the car pulled out again.

"What's this idiot doing?" Whitworth wondered. "Is there a road back in there somewhere?"

"Who knows?" I replied. "I'll hop out here and chase him on foot, and you follow the woman. We'll be covered either way."

"I hope you brought your snowshoes," he grunted, pulling the Bureau car over.

They certainly would have helped. Even where it hadn't piled into drifts, the snow was up to my knees. It was like trying to chase someone through a pond of molasses, except molasses would have been a lot warmer. Within a minute or two, everything below my hips was a block of ice. *I will not think about my suit*, I commanded myself. *I will not think about my shoes*.

The deserter wasn't having any better luck than I was, but he did have a head start. Soon he disappeared into the woods. But he must have skipped out of the army before the course on cold-weather camouflage; his deep trail through the snow was easy to follow. For ten or fifteen minutes I huffed and puffed in circles through the dark woods, flailing at the snow and wondering what his plan was. Then, suddenly, the trail pivoted and led straight out of the forest.

Just before I emerged from the treeline, I could hear the woman screaming. "You no-good motherfuckers, you cocksuckers, why don't you just leave us alone?" she howled. As I struggled out of the woods, I could see Whitworth's car at the side of the road, the deserter spread-eagled over the trunk, his hands cuffed behind his back. Even from this distance, I could see his chest heaving. The snow hadn't been any easier on him than on me.

"She doubled back, I guess to see what was happening," Whitworth explained. "I followed her, and just as we got here, he came out of the woods. He was too tired to run. You really wore him out."

"Right, that was my strategy," I replied between gasps. "I just didn't know it."

"Handcuff her, too," Whitworth said, gesturing at the wife, who was in the middle of a long, loud discourse on assholes and sons of bitches. "Harboring a fugitive."

"Can we get her for having a dirty mouth, too?" I asked as I pulled the handcuffs from my pocket.

As it turned out, we couldn't even get her on the harboring charge. When we marched her into the Syracuse office in handcuffs, the other agents looked like someone had just farted. One of the older guys took us aside.

"Jesus Christ, are you guys crazy?" he demanded. "If we start arresting the wives of deserters, we'll all be lynched. And if you ever arrest a *pregnant* wife again, the rest of us will buy the rope."

"But she was hiding the guy," Whitworth protested. "She even tried to smuggle him past us in the car."

"No jury is going to convict a deserter's wife for wanting to keep him out of Vietnam," the other agent declared flatly. "And the U.S. attorney isn't even going to try."

He was right—the prosecutors were even angrier when they heard what we had done, and Whitworth and I had to sit through a long lecture on discretion. But nobody ever said a word to us about roaring around residential neighborhoods at ninety miles an hour. Lucky for us the local cops never caught up with us that day; if they had found out we were staging our own private Le Mans over a deserter, they might have arrested *us*.

———

They didn't teach it at the academy, but the first FBI rule I learned in the street was: Don't rat out another agent.

I probably encountered a dozen examples of this during my first three or four months, ranging from the agents who snuck down the back alley for coffee to a couple who helped cover up a minor auto accident with a Bureau car.

But none of them could top an agent I'll call Freddie. He was an older guy, about fifty, with a well-deserved reputation as an ace on bank robberies. I worked as a gowitcha on a couple of robberies, and it was amazing the way he could sniff out leads. He had some kind of mystical mind-meld with bank robbers.

So when Freddie asked me if I would help him set up a meeting with a confidential informant, the adrenaline rush nearly blew the top of my head off. CIs, as they're called, are the lifeblood of law enforcement. All the forensic science stuff with microscopes and paraffin tests is great for proving guilt once you have a suspect, but first you have to find one. And probably 90 percent of the time, it will be a CI who tells you where to look.

"Look, this is a top-echelon informant," Freddie murmured to me in a back corner of the office on the day he asked for my help. "You can't tell *anybody* here about this. If it gets messed up, somebody could die."

I nodded wisely. "What do you want me to do?" I whispered.

"Tomorrow we'll take a Bucar," he explained, using agent jargon for a Bureau car. "We'll pick up the CI and take her to a restaurant. I'll go inside to debrief her. You park a little ways down the street and keep an eye out for anybody suspicious. When I come out of the restaurant, if everything's okay, I'll give a wave with my left hand. When you see it, you drive over and pick us up."

I was dying to ask what kind of a case we were working and what the CI knew, but I knew I couldn't. You don't ask for details about another agent's CI any more than you would ask for details about how he has sex with his wife.

The next morning was cold and gray. "Drive over to Latham Circle," Freddie directed me, piquing my curiosity even more. That was Albany's high-rent district. Not the kind of place you'd expect to find a desperate junkie or a bank robber's hooker girlfriend. This case must be even more important than I had thought.

Freddie guided me to a fancy women's gym. Instantly a woman dressed in a purple leotard and a fur coat stepped out and slipped into the car. As we pulled away, I eyed her clandestinely in the rearview mirror. Tall and sleek, with luxuriant dark hair framing big brown eyes, she was a traffic stopper.

Freddie and the woman talked in low voices as I drove to a restaurant a few blocks away. Although I strained to hear, I couldn't pick up anything they said. "Remember, the left hand," Freddie reminded me as they got out.

I parked two blocks down the street, tugged up my overcoat, and settled in to watch. For what? Not too clear. "Anything suspicious," Freddie had said. An hour and a half later, I'd seen a couple of businessmen I suspected had downed more than three martinis at lunch, but nothing more. Freddie emerged from the restaurant, waved with his left hand, and I headed for the door. The CI joined us a moment later. We dropped her off at the gym after a brief ride filled with more backseat whispers. "Thanks, that worked out pretty well," Freddie said when we got back to the office, and that was it.

The next morning two snickering agents passed by my desk. "I heard you took the old man to see his *informant*," said one with a leer. Added the other: "Do you know if she *came across* with anything?" the other cackled.

I listened to similar cracks all day. Apparently everybody in the office—except me—knew that Freddie was banging the aerobics lady on the Director's time. The only thing she was disclosing to him was the contents of her leotard. My job was to make him look important to his girl ("Gosh, Freddie, your own chauffeur and everything!") and keep the Bucar from sitting around unattended in front of a restaurant and attracting questions.

After that I noticed that when Freddie worked bank robberies outside Albany, he spent about an hour coming up with leads. Then

With Honor and Purpose

he assigned younger agents to do all the legwork, while he went back to the motel to make sure the beer was iced down and taste-tested. He was a funny, smart guy, and I never stopped liking him. I did start avoiding assignments with him. But I never turned him in.


"All first-office agents report back here immediately," crackled the radio. The dispatcher's voice was stoic, but I knew something big must have happened. I'd never heard a call like that before.

At the office, Maupai gave us the story quickly: A Mohawk Airlines plane with fourteen people aboard had crashed near Lake George, about seventy-five miles north of Albany.

"The FBI Disaster Team is flying in from Washington right now," Maupai said. "I want all of you to report to the hospital in Glens Falls—that's where the team will set up headquarters."

"What do we do?" asked one of the agents.

"Whatever they tell you, Maupai said, his face grim.

The hospital, when I arrived two hours later, was a scene out of hell. They had set up a temporary morgue in a conference room just inside the front door. Plastic garbage bags had been spread out on the floor, and the bodies were lying on them.

I say bodies, but only the shapes were human. Flying at night during a fierce thunderstorm, the plane had dipped too low and slammed full-speed into the top of a mountain. The fire afterward had burned every recognizable feature off the corpses. They looked blank, like store mannequins made out of charcoal.

But even the flames hadn't been able to erase the signs of their horror. Every body was contorted, as if the passengers had been shrinking away in fear as the plane closed in on the mountain.

"Some of that is from the fire—it twists the bodies," said one of the Disaster Team technicians as he handed me a wad of cotton soaked in menthol to shield my nose from the acrid stench of seared flesh and aviation fuel. "But some of it really is fear. When people see they're about to crash, they clench their fists like vises. Good thing, too."

"Why do you say that?" I asked, trying to turn away from the bodies without being too obvious about it. "It doesn't look like it did any of these people any good."

"Good thing for *us*, I meant," the technician said. "It means the fingerprints are preserved. That's going to make identifying them a lot easier." He turned and picked up what looked like a stainless steel set of hedge clippers. "Here, go to work on the fingers, will you? Bring them over here and I'll take the prints."

"What do you mean?" I asked blankly.

"Cut the fingers off," he said matter-of-factly as he pulled on a pair of rubber gloves. "Snip them off and bring them over here. It's too hard to move their arms."

"You want me to *cut their fingers off?*" I repeated helplessly.

"Well, you can cut their lower jaws off for the dental specialist if you'd rather do that instead," he said. "But that's a little trickier."

I looked at the technician. He was a neat, trim man with a touch of gray in his perfectly clipped hair, sort of like a middle-aged Ken doll. There was not a trace of malice or morbidity on his face. Just another day at the office.

"No thanks," I said, laying the bone-cutters down on the table. "I'm not doing this."

As I turned to walk out, I started to drop the cotton from my nose, too, but the odor immediately staggered me. I clapped it back over my nostrils and lurched toward the door. I wondered if I should turn in my badge here, or go back to Albany and give it to Leo Conroy. I wanted to spare everyone the indignity of having to fire me for my gross insubordination.

As I reached the door, I felt a hand on my shoulder. I turned to see an agent named John Levan, an accountant who specialized in white-collar crime.

"Phil, don't worry about this," he said. "I'll handle it, I don't mind. Just go on back to the hotel."

"I just refused an order," I replied. "I'm going to be fired. I might as well go back to Albany and get it over with."

"Nothing's going to happen to you," Levan reassured me. "Some people can do this, and some can't. Have a couple of beers, go back to the hotel, and we'll see you in the morning."

I took his advice, but I was certain I was doomed. Not only had I refused an order, I had refused it from a *headquarters* guy. In an organization where you got in trouble for mispunctuating FBI, this was certain death.

The next morning, my memory of the bodies slightly dimmed by several Budweisers, I heard a knock on the door. I opened it to see the technician and another Disaster Team agent. "Come on, let's get some breakfast, you pussy," the technician said with a smile. "You younger guys can't cut it, but that's fine. It just means they can't retire the rest of us."

We had a friendly breakfast, talking about football and politics and anything but the plane crash, and it began to dawn on me that nobody was mad, nobody was going to report me. But when breakfast was over and the other agents got up, I wondered what to do. I couldn't go back to that morgue again.

Levan read my mind. "Come on, Phil," he said. "Somebody else will work the morgue today. You have an assignment that's even worse."

One of the passengers had been a young woman from Glens Falls. With a veteran agent, I drove to the house where she lived with her family.

The family came to the door, and I had the feeling they might have been sitting up all night, waiting for us to knock. They were a very mom-and-pop type couple in their late fifties, the kind of small-town people who probably would have offered us pie and coffee if we'd come for any reason except to tell them their daughter had in all probability been roasted alive.

The other agent took the lead. "I'm sure you know about the plane crash," he said gently. "Your daughter's name was on the passenger manifest, and she was probably aboard."

They nodded. Both of them looked infinitely sad, certain their daughter was dead, but afraid to say it for fear of extinguishing that one in a zillion chance they were wrong.

"The victims are going to be very difficult to identify," he continued. "We'd like to know the name of your daughter's dentist"—I admired the way he had avoided saying the word *was*—"so that we can obtain her dental records. And we'd also like to take some fingerprints from her room."

The lady of the house led us into the bedroom, a prim little alcove in the back. A brush and a handheld mirror were neatly arranged on her dresser. As I carefully spread a light coating of graphite over the handles, looking for fingerprints, I wondered what she thought as she sat here each morning brushing her hair. The boy she would meet—or, maybe, already had—who would be her husband? The babies they would have? In her daydreams, had she already picked out their names? One minute, your future is spread out in front of you, stretching to the horizon; the next, it's all blank. *What could her parents be thinking?* I wondered. You spend twenty years raising a child, making your contribution to the future, fitting yourself into the natural pattern of the universe. And then a plane is a few hundred feet out of its way and all the patterns go bust.

The prints I lifted from the brush and mirror looked pretty good, but just to be safe, I took some from the handle of the girl's toothbrush, too. I was careful, but I worked quickly. I didn't want them to think too much about fingerprints, about how you might collect fingerprints from a corpse. I didn't want them to start imagining a pair of stainless steel hedge clippers. On the way out, I saw tears trickling silently down the lady's cheeks. In the car, they ran down mine, too.

# 4

# KILL WHITEY!

There was something about the way he walked that caught your eye: a stride that seemed casual and purposeful at the same time, like a tough cat on his way home after a hard night at work in the alleys. Other people noticed it, too. The hookers and junkies who dotted the sidewalks on the hard-bitten east side of Columbus stepped out of the way as the tall, muscular black man with the short Afro passed.

"That's gotta be him, don't you think?" my partner Paul Miller asked as he eased the Bucar up the street in the same direction the man was walking.

"Nommo X himself," I agreed. "The exalted leader of the Columbus Afro Set." Miller and I had just come from a meeting with the Columbus Police Department intelligence unit, which considered Afro Set the city's most dangerous black militant organization. The cops had shown us a photo of Nommo X, a guy who worried them a lot.

It wasn't hard to figure out why. "Do you see what he's got in his right hand?" I asked Miller.

"Holy shit!" he exclaimed. There were probably other people on this street packing .45 automatics, but at least they had the good sense to keep them covered up. Nommo X, though, carried his openly, letting it dangle loosely in his hand.

"What do you think?" I asked Miller. "You wanna try to talk to him? See where he's coming from?"

"Sure," he replied, gunning the engine slightly. In a few seconds, we were right alongside Nommo, who shot us a quick glance and then shifted his eyes forward again. I was certain he'd been aware of us for some time.

"Hi, Nommo," Miller said, flashing his boyish Philadelphia grin. "We're agents Miller and Kerby of the FBI. We wondered if you have a few minutes to talk to us."

"About what?" Nommo asked, not even looking our way. He kept walking; we kept rolling along.

"About guns," Miller replied. "And philosophy," I quickly added, thinking that sounded more like a chat (which it was supposed to be) and less like an interrogation. It at least got his attention. He swiveled his head toward us. "Since when does the FBI have a philosophy beat?" he quizzed us.

"I think it could do a lot of good for you and us both," I said. "Come on, hop in the car and we'll go get a cup of coffee."

"Hell no, I'm not getting in a car with you," Nommo cried out, finally halting. "What are you, crazy? Even if I *wanted* to, you think I'd do it out here where everyone can see me?"

"I think it would do a lot of good," I repeated.

"No good is going to come out of my getting in a car with you," he said, his voice calmer and not unkind. "Now why don't you do both you and me a favor and just get the hell out of here?"

I shrugged at Miller, who pressed the gas pedal. I watched Nommo shrink in the rear-view mirror, though the .45 in his right hand seemed mysteriously to grow larger as we pulled away. In my memory, it looms larger still. Afro Set, at least the Cleveland branch, would turn out to be worse than anybody over at the Columbus Police Department believed. And Miller and I had breezed right up to the leader in the middle of a ghetto street, not a care in our heads that he had his finger on the trigger of an automatic pistol. God, I guess, protects fools, little children, and dumb young FBI agents. I was twenty-five years old.

That warm Ohio evening in the spring of 1971 was my introduction to one of the FBI's most controversial investigative classifications: "racial matters." For nearly forty years, the Bureau probed the internal affairs of various black groups and leaders. In the 1940s, when this started out, the investigations centered around Communist Party influence in civil rights organizations; by the late 1960s, the focus had shifted to trying to forestall violence by black groups associated with the New Left.

To say the "racial matters" investigations have critics is like saying the Sahara has sand. A lot of people believe the program was nothing more than spying. And they consider one of its cousins—COINTEL-PRO, a sort of Bureau dirty tricks campaign aimed at extremist groups—as downright criminal.

It isn't easy to argue with them. For one thing, they have a lot of legitimate ammunition, including J. Edgar Hoover's blindness to the institutional racism of the agency he created. I cringe when I hear Hoover's former subordinates explain that the only reason the Bureau was so lily-white during his tenure was that they couldn't find any qualified black agents. In forty years? Come on. And some FBI officials certainly seem to have seen Soviet fingerprints just about anytime a black sharecropper in Alabama wanted to register to vote.

But I also think some of the criticism is unfair hindsight. It's easy, in the 1990s, to scoff at the idea that the Communist Party was in secret control of the NAACP. But that wasn't necessarily so clear in the 1940s, when the Communists were an aggressive, growing force, funded and directed by Moscow, that sought to exploit every rift in domestic American politics. Even NAACP officials themselves worried about it. Documents recently declassified under the Freedom of Information Act show that no less than Thurgood Marshall, the NAACP's chief counsel and a future Supreme Court justice, was passing information to the Bureau about Communist infiltration of his organization.

There's no question that the FBI's investigations of Martin Luther King eventually mutated into ugly and senseless harassment. But the Bureau's original concern—that King was falling under Communist influence—was well-founded. Two of the top officials in the American Communist Party, the brothers Morris and Jack Childs, were actually working for the FBI during their last twenty years in the party. They warned the Bureau that Stanley Levison, one of King's top advisers, was the man in charge of the secret funds that Moscow sent to the American Communists. It was Levison's presence in King's braintrust, not racist paranoia, that triggered the FBI's interest.

The story of Levison and his links to Moscow is well-known to historians. But it's rarely mentioned in newspaper stories or books about the FBI's racial investigations. Likewise, when you read accounts of how Bureau officials ordered break-ins as part of the pursuit of Weather Underground fugitives, it's usually portrayed as government persecution of an innocent flower-power group whose only crime was opposing the Vietnam War. In reality, the Weather Underground was a pack of terrorist bombers that dallied with intelligence agencies in Cuba and North Vietnam. They set off explosions at the Detroit Police Department, the New York Police Department, the U.S. Capitol, and the Pentagon, just to name a few places.

A big part of the problem is that much of American history of the 1950s and 1960s is being written by the people who stood on the other side of the police line at demonstrations. Like the party-line journalists in George Orwell's *1984*, they spend a lot of their time dropping things down the memory hole. A few years ago, when the old New Lefty Abbie Hoffman died, I was astonished to read an editorial in the *Miami Herald* calling him "a true American patriot" who spent his life "struggling to raise the nation's moral standards." Moral standards? He was a cocaine trafficker who wrote a book explaining to kids how to make pipe bombs and advising them which ammo was best for killing cops. Imagine what the obituaries will make of Charles Manson.

In Columbus, I never heard of "racial matters" investigations veering off into the COINTELPRO dirty tricks. (Although I did hear rumors of agents going down to the airport on the day the bundles of Black Panther newspapers arrived to make sure they were "accidentally" soaked by firehoses.) Headquarters wanted regular reports on any marches or demonstrations, which were used to prepare a weekly assessment of the potential for civil unrest. And Washington also expected us to investigate any black group judged to have the potential for *violence*.

Most of the agents in the Columbus office would have stood on their heads naked eating bugs if that was what it took to stay away from racial matters. In a way, that was rather odd. Most FBI agents were political conservatives—in my whole career in the Bureau, I only met one agent who could be called a liberal—who had little sympathy with the NAACP, much less the Black Panthers. Moreover, there was a certain amount of racism in the air, not virulent, not blatant, but there nonetheless.

How could there not have been? The Bureau was composed almost exclusively of white men who lived in white neighborhoods and worked and socialized with other white people. The only black people they met were pimps and bank robbers. That's going to have a corrosive effect on the most open-minded guy in the world after a while, and not just in the FBI. Lots of criminologists have observed the same thing in police departments where the force is overwhelmingly white.

So you'd think there would have been no shortage of agents volunteering to work on racial matters, but it was quite the opposite. Some guys probably sensed it was a political hot potato that would eventually explode in everybody's face. And for others, it just wasn't what they had joined the FBI for. For them, law enforcement meant catching bank robbers and kidnappers, not poring over membership lists and propaganda tracts.

But when I heard the office brass was looking for someone to work racial matters, I jumped at the chance. After spending what I thought was a pretty productive year in Albany—I left with a half-dozen commendations and good marks from all my supervisors—I discovered I was right back at the bottom of the heap in Columbus, a rookie assigned to nothing but dog cases.

Mostly I was doing background checks on applicants for federal jobs and working civil rights cases. That didn't mean chasing the Ku Klux Klan. Civil rights cases in Columbus were almost always allegations of guard brutality at the state penitentiary downtown. I hated those cases with a passion. Each one started with an inmate claiming a guard whacked him one for no reason. The inmate names ten other witnesses, all of them inmates too. So you start interviewing them:

Witness No. 1. *Yeah, I saw it. Right out of the blue, the guard slugged Joe for no reason.*

Witness No. 2. *Yeah, with both fists, hit him three or four times.*

Witness No. 3. *No, it was with a baseball bat.*

Witness No. 4. *No, it was a baseball bat and a bicycle chain.*

Witness No. 5. *Yeah, and after that, he held Joe down while the entire Chinese army came into the cell and sodomized him with laser beams.*

There were probably some valid cases in there, but they were buried under an avalanche of unmitigated horseshit. Next to civil rights cases, almost anything would have looked good.

But when I volunteered for racial matters, it was more than just trying to get out from under a crummy caseload. My two years of teaching were still fresh in my mind. To me, at least, it was apparent that there was a criminal element in the black community, a wolf covering itself with the sheep's clothing of politics: *Selling drugs is revolutionary. Bank robbery is an act of liberation. Anybody who gets in your way is a pig, and offing pigs isn't crime but self-defense.* The victims of this doublespeak were black much more often than they were white.

I suppose there are people who will see that all as rationalization for racism, that anyone who volunteered to work racial matters must have been a stone racist. They're wrong. I was as horrified as anyone when the news surfaced that somebody at FBI headquarters had mailed out tapes of Martin Luther King's bedroom encounters. I have always regarded King as a hero, a once-in-a-lifetime inspirational leader who provided an eloquent voice for people who otherwise had none. During my junior year of college, a bunch of us jumped in a car and drove down to Fort Lauderdale for spring break. I still remember the bathrooms we saw in Georgia marked WHITE and COL-ORED. As far as I'm concerned, if it hadn't been for Martin Luther

King, we probably would have had a widespread armed revolution in this country.

We had arrived in Ohio in late 1970 and fell in love with it almost instantly. Yes, we—one of the last things I did in Albany was marry Debbie Smith, a Bureau stenographer. I met her at an office clambake my very first weekend in Albany. After we were married, she confessed she'd had her eye on me even earlier. The steno pool had a rotating system of first dibs on new agents, and she happened to be at the top of the list when I arrived. Wisely, Debbie exercised her option, and I was off-limits. I was, of course, shocked and appalled to hear that these women treated us as little more than slabs of meat for their personal gratification, but I guess it worked out okay in the end.

Ohio-bashing is one of America's leading national sports; you always hear jokes about the Rust Belt and rivers catching on fire. But we thought it was great, at least our corner of it. Intellectually and culturally, Columbus bubbled; it had all the advantages that go with being a state capital and the home of a big university. At the same time, you could still afford to buy a house, and in most of the city's neighborhoods you could let your children play in the front yard without worrying that they'd be missing an arm or a leg when it was time to come in.

The Columbus office was a great place to work, too. A lot of the agents were in their twenties and early thirties, part of the same late-'60s hiring burst that brought me into the Bureau, and it was like an instant social club. We all lived in Westerville, on the north side of the city, where we barbecued together, drank beer together, played football, basketball, and softball together.

In our sunny new life in Columbus, there was only one cloud. It was in early June of 1971 when my Bucar radio sputtered to life. "Three nine-two to CI-75," office to Kerby. "Go ahead," I answered, expecting a routine message about some new civil rights case. "Call home immediately," the dispatcher said. Dread pierced my heart as swiftly and sharply as an icepick. They never did that, told you to call home immediately.

I found a pay phone and called Debbie. My father had just suffered another stroke, this one big enough to leave him in a coma.

We went to Michigan, sat at his bedside. We put cold cloths on his forehead, suctioned out his throat, hugged him, told him that we loved him. Nothing worked. A week later, we buried him.

Afterward, I went up to the bedroom. His wallet was on the dresser. Opening it, I found no money or credit cards. Just a Social Security card and a photo of the family. It was so typical of my dad. He lived his life for us. I went in the closet. I looked at his shoes, smelled his jacket, brushed his shirts across my cheek. But he wouldn't come back.


Among the group of agents who lived out in Westerville was Paul Miller, who would become the only real partner I ever had in the Bureau, as well as my best friend. I have no earthly idea why. I was a Midwestern meat-and-potatoes boy, deeply suspicious of everything and everyone on either coast. Paul was a Jewish lawyer suffering a painful exile from Philadelphia who grieved three times a week at the lack of tasty cakes and hoagies in Columbus. He tried hard to adapt a protective Middle American covering, but it always slipped. One day he was proudly showing us tomato plants he was growing on his patio. A farmer! Growing his own food! He wasn't even suspicious when one of the other agents, deadpan, told him you have to pinch those nasty yellow buds off the plant as soon as they appear. Miller industriously plucked them all, then wondered why the stubborn plants wouldn't bear fruit.

The FBI, though, wasn't paying Paul to grow tomatoes, but to investigate. And at that, I never met anyone better in all my years in the Bureau. Paul once got a case where two unexploded homemade bombs had been found in unclaimed luggage at the Buffalo airport. That was it: two bombs, nothing else. No witnesses, no suspect, no motive, no nothing. By tracing the empty beer bottles in one of the bombs back through the brewery, he started an investigative chain that ended in the conviction of two brothers who were working a complicated insurance scam.

Miller was twenty-eight when I arrived in Columbus and already a three-year FBI veteran with some big cases under his belt. He even worked the murder of Martin Luther King, doing surveillance on an Atlanta boardinghouse where the assassin, James Earl Ray, sometimes stayed under an alias. One thing he had not learned to do in that time was handle a gun. We used to have an office pool on which one of us would be his first accidental victim. One agent told me of creeping through a darkened basement in search of a suspect, Miller behind, covering him with a shotgun: "All of a sudden, in the dead silence, Miller says out loud, 'Hey, where's the safety on this thing?' "

In fact, he could be almost as dangerous with a briefcase. When we went on interviews, I took a notebook and sometimes a photo or a couple of documents. Miller packed half the Library of Congress, and it could take him what seemed like days to decide which ones he wanted to take inside and which ones to leave in the car.

Once, when we were out looking for a guy who was supposedly a heavy-duty gun-runner, Miller simply could not get his files straight. Finally I was afraid if I watched him for one more minute, I would have to choke him to death. "While you finish extricating your head from your ass, I'm going to look for the apartment," I advised him. He shook his head and kept furiously shuffling through papers.

The apartment was in a long, dim hall where several lights had burned out. I made my way to the door, which was cracked open, revealing the place was vacant—our man had moved on. I walked back down to the hall's entryway and crouched there, out of sight. A couple of minutes later, I heard footsteps. As Miller rounded the corner, I jumped up and screamed. He jumped up and screamed. His briefcase flew open, and all of a sudden we were buried in the middle of a ticker-tape parade.

Of course, if I'd been wrong—if the gun-runner was still

around—we'd have been *corpses* buried in the middle of a blizzard of paper. But I think I've already offered my theory on fools, little children, and dumb young FBI agents.

It took about two seconds for my offer to work on racial matters to be accepted. My first assignment was to look into Afro Set, a new black nationalist organization that had recently set up shop in Columbus. Originally known as the Afro American Sect, the group was founded in Cleveland, where it was at least as strong as the Black Panthers. There was also a much smaller fledgling chapter in Wheeling, West Virginia.

We didn't know much about Afro Set's activities in Columbus. But in Cleveland, they had a reputation as the most vicious gang roaming the streets of the city's east side. In a crime that more or less typified how far off shore certain elements of the east side had drifted from civilization, a sidewalk hot dog peddler had recently been shot dead by a customer who snarled, "I told you no mustard, motherfucker!" before pulling the trigger. Phone repairmen wouldn't go to the east side at all for fear of snipers, and firemen would enter only with police escorts— not that cops offered much protection. Some of them had been killed while sitting in their cars at traffic lights.

Nothing like that was going on in Columbus, at least not yet. But the rhetoric in Afro Set flyers we found around town was chilling. "We want all *whites* out of our community. . . . As long as we are not allowed to establish a state of our own, we will fight and kill anyone who gets in our way," read one typical leaflet. (Like all Afro Set material, it bore the group's slogans in big letters: WAKE UP NIGGER! and NIGGERS ARE SCARED OF REVOLUTION.)

Afro Set was by no means the only radical group that had caught the FBI's eye in Columbus. We were keeping an eye on white extremists, too—particularly the Weather Underground, which had deep roots on the Ohio State campus in Columbus, and the Ku Klux Klan, which had support in the southern part of the state. And when the revolutionary black separatist Stokely Carmichael came to Columbus, we searched his motel room after he checked out. There were a lot of discarded notes and phone messages indicating that he was in close touch with Pan-African advocates. They were dutifully forwarded to Washington.

Some of the investigations made me a little uneasy. The office spent months digging into the Nation of Islam before concluding it was just what it said it was: a religion. I understood the rationale for that investigation—the Black Muslims attracted a lot of ex-convicts, which seemed fishy—but the reasoning behind the probe of a campus group called Afro Am struck me as completely far-fetched, and I refused to get involved in it.

Afro Am was an ordinary student political group, not much more radical than the Young Democrats. But the masthead of the group's newspaper said it was a member of the Revolutionary People's Communication Network, a radical news service set up by Kathleen Cleaver of the Black Panthers. On the basis of that single slender thread of evidence—if you can even call it evidence—agents in our office opened case files on every single member of Afro Am. Eventually the files were closed because about the most sinister activity Afro Am engaged in was organizing voter registration drives. Nonetheless, the names of all those kids remained in the FBI indices, as we called the massive Bureau card file in Washington. If any of them ever applied for a sensitive federal job, bingo! The name would come up.

But I didn't have any qualms about the Afro Set assignment. My job was to identify the members and learn if they were stockpiling weapons or showing other tendencies to violence. And if they were committing crimes, I was supposed to put them in jail.

To get things under way, Miller and I visited the Columbus Police Department's intelligence unit. They're mostly gone now, done in by lawsuits and media scandals, but back then almost every big-city police department had a squad that monitored potentially troublesome radical groups. These so-called Red Squads often were better informed than the FBI. Often they had information about SDS which, we speculated, could have have come from hidden microphones—which the Justice Department would never have given us permission to install. If anyone knew anything about Afro Set, it would be Tom Waters, the lieutenant who ran the intelligence unit.

"They worry us a lot," confessed Waters as we sipped coffee in his office. "All they talk about is killing whites. Practically all of them are armed—they don't make any secret about that, they carry guns around in public all the time—and the few members we've been able to identify have rap sheets that make us think they're capable of carrying out their threats."

"Have they done anything?" I asked.

"Not that we can prove," Waters said. "We've busted a few of them for stickups, but then the leaders say the guys were just operating on their own and it didn't have anything to do with the group. I don't believe it, but we haven't been able to prove it. They've roughed up some hookers and junkies on the east side, but try to get those kind of cases into court."

"Hookers and junkies?" Miller asked, perplexed.

"They claim they're cleaning up the neighborhood," Waters said. "Personally, I think it's a shakedown scheme, but even if you could get the hookers and junkies to testify about it, who'd believe them?"

The leader of the Columbus Afro Set, Waters said, was this tall, slick-tongued guy known as Nommo X. Nommo had proven kind of elusive to the cops; about all they had found out about him was his real name, James Edward Brown. Miller and I promptly drove to East Main Street to find him.

Looking back twenty-five years later, we were silly and naive to think Nommo would voluntarily get into a Bucar while half of east Columbus watched. Everyone in Afro Set would have known about it in a flash, and no matter what Nommo said later, some of them would have suspected he was a snitch. The way groups like Afro Set dealt with snitches was not pretty.

That's not the way Miller and I saw it that day in 1971, though. We were actually a bit crestfallen as we drove away. (In fact we were never able to develop information that Nommo was involved in any criminal act. Nevertheless, we plugged away.)

Then Miller brightened. "I think I might have another way to get inside the group," he said.

"I'm listening."

"I've got an informant, a black guy," Miller explained. "He's been pretty good at ferreting stuff out in the past. Of course, it's always been ordinary crimes—bank robberies, mostly. But I think it would be worth giving him a try."

"Sure, can't hurt," I agreed. "How soon can we see him?"

"It takes a couple of days to get in touch with him. And I might as well warn you, he'll want to do it at midnight in some kind of a shitty back alley."

I thought Miller was kidding about the dark alley, but that was exactly where we met the snitch (nobody in Columbus called them CIs) three nights later. I felt a little foolish—and a little edgy, too—as we crept along, picking our way through broken bottles and piles of trash. The alley looked empty and I was about to suggest to Miller that we'd been stood up when Robbie, as we'll call him, stepped out of the shadow of a garbage Dumpster.

"Anybody see you come in here?" he whispered.

"I don't think so, Robbie," Paul whispered back. "We were very careful."

"Good," Robbie said, solemnly nodding his head. " 'Cause you know I'd get in trouble if folks knew I was talking to the police."

Snitches come in all shapes and sizes, but as I looked at Robbie, I had to wonder if he could be as good as Paul said he was. Probably fifty or so, with a weatherbeaten face that made him look older, Robbie had a physical deformity (I'm not going to say what it was) that made him look slightly comical. His clothing was ragged and stained, and when we walked down the alley a ways, I realized that pungent odor came from him, not the Dumpster. To top it all off, his language was simple, almost childlike. He seemed like a guy Fred Sanford would have kicked out of the junkyard.

"Robbie, have you heard of this group Afro Set?" Miller asked. Robbie screwed up his face in puzzlement. "You know, they have an office over on East Main?"

This time, his eyes lit in recognition. "Sure, they're always threatening to hurt people. I don't like them, no sir."

"Do you think you could hang around over there?" Miller said. "Could you find out the names of some of the members? Find out what they do inside that building."

"Sure, I can do that easy," Robbie agreed. "Sure, easy."

"Okay, then we'll meet here in two weeks," Miller said. He slipped a twenty-dollar bill into Robbie's hand, and we headed for the Bucar, hoping its wheels were still attached.

"You really think this is going to work?" I asked on the way home.

"I know he doesn't look like much," Miller said. "But he's given me a lot of good information. Sometimes I've even shown him photos of bank robbers, and he wanders in and out of the bars until he finds them and IDs them. And he's never been wrong."

"I guess we'll see," I said, trying to conceal the doubt in my voice.


Two weeks later: same alley, same Dumpster, and, I'm almost certain, same ratty shirt and pants on Robbie. "Were you able to find out anything?" Miller asked him.

"Some things," nodded Robbie. "And I brought you these papers." He pulled a sheaf of typewritten sheets from underneath his shirt. Looking over Miller's shoulder, I saw a long list of names and addresses. Robbie had just handed us the whole membership list of Afro Set.

"How did you get this?" Miller asked in astonishment.

"Sometimes when I'm working in the office, no one watches me," Robbie said. "So I made copies."

"Working in the office? Working in the *Afro Set* office? How do you do that?"

"I joined," Robbie said simply.

For the next six months, Robbie continued to feed us a continuous stream of documents: Afro Set rules and regulations, charts matching "slave names" (say, Joe Smith) with "African names" (say,

Kenyatta X), phone numbers, updated membership lists. Nobody at Afro Set suspected a thing. All the things about Robbie that made me doubt he could perform as a snitch—his raggedness, his simplicity—were actually the perfect camouflage for an informant.

Once we had the membership lists, Miller and I went right to work. We just started showing up at the homes of members and asking if we could talk about Afro Set. (We supplemented the list by watching Afro Set headquarters, recording license plates, and then checking the auto registration. That gave us names of people who flirted with the group but didn't actually join.) We had no warrants, no legal artillery at our command, but almost all of them agreed at least to talk to us.

It may sound a little crazy that black nationalists would voluntarily sit down for chitchat with people whom they regarded as little better than the Gestapo. But they did, and I wasn't surprised. During my career in the Bureau, I encountered very few people who flat-out refused to speak to me. A lot of them didn't tell me much, and a lot of them lied their asses off. But even among its sworn enemies, there's a mixture of fear and fascination for the FBI that makes it hard to walk away without a word, no matter how crooked or communist they are. Even Nommo X talked to us once he could do it in private, though the interview was a complete stonewall on his part.*

But not everyone was so close-mouthed—especially among the few people against whom we could turn some legal screws. Whenever an Afro Set member or a close relative got arrested on minor charges, Lieutenant Waters would call us from the police department. Miller or I would trot over to the jail and suggest the charges might disappear if we got some good information in return. Eventually we had

---

*Nommo got a little skittish as the investigation continued. One night Miller and his wife went to the movies. (The picture, ironically, was *The Great White Hope*.) Afterward, Paul went into the bathroom. Nommo came charging in thirty seconds later, followed by half a dozen of his punks. "I'm getting sick of you motherfuckers following me everywhere!" he shouted. A long, tense, and loud discussion ensued, but there was no way Miller could convince Nommo that their presence at the same film was a coincidence.

half a dozen sources inside Afro Set reporting to us on a relatively regular basis. And we got bits and pieces from scores of others. We were beginning to assemble a picture of what went on inside the group.

Afro Set had about one hundred members in Columbus, a slightly larger number in Cleveland. (The Wheeling chapter was pretty Mickey Mouse, everyone agreed.) That didn't count the hundreds of young kids the group could bring out to strut around in black leather jackets and parachute boots when Afro Set leaders wanted to intimidate someone with a public display of force.

The police department felt intimidation was what Afro Set was all about. They saw the group was essentially a big extortion ring— although Lieutenant Waters had gotten the equation slightly wrong. The hookers and junkies weren't the targets. Instead, Afro Set offered what amounted to a protection racket to the mom-and-pop businesses struggling to survive in the increasingly blighted black neighborhoods of Columbus and Cleveland: You pay us, and we keep the riffraff away from your place. You don't pay, and the junkies will stack up like cordwood in front of your store.

As for their promises to clean up the streets—well, Afro Set delivered. Of course, their methods were a little crude. Forty shots were fired one night at a bar on Main Street in Columbus that catered to pimps and whores. My guess was that the Columbus cops could get rid of prostitution and drugs, too, if they were allowed to shoot at anything that moved.

A more sophisticated variation of the protection scheme was targeted on all the nonprofit antipoverty agencies in the cities' ghettos. Afro Set leaders approached them all, demanding grants and even seats on their boards of directors. Nobody had to be so crude as to discuss the consequences of a refusal.

Afro Set had amazing success with this. A Presbyterian church in my own neighborhood (where, incidentally, I'm fairly certain no black person had ever set foot) coughed up $10,000, saying with a straight face that Afro Set would use it to buy African art. And the federally funded Model Cities program was on the verge of giving

Nommo and his thugs $160,000 to fund their "security" program. Sources reported that Carl Stokes, the mayor of Cleveland, had already channeled some federal money by Afro Set, although the FBI's Cleveland office wasn't able to nail that down.

For all Afro Set's rhetoric in Columbus, we couldn't find any evidence that the local chapter compared to the one in Cleveland, which was almost a black version of the Mafia. The Columbus chapter was almost like kids playing cops and robbers—or cops and revolutionaries—by contrast. We never took a single one of the Columbus group's members to court.

Miller and I wrote report after report on the structure and organization of Afro Set. These so-called letterhead memorandums were forwarded to headquarters, where, I'm pretty certain, they were used to insulate walls and ceilings. There sure wasn't any evidence anybody was reading them. In one of them, we inserted a paragraph-long discussion of the merits of drinking Coca-Cola. Headquarters didn't say a word.

But I wasn't discouraged. For one thing, I was convinced Afro Set was a dangerous group and the trail we were following would lead somewhere useful. For another, the investigation was spinning off a wealth of leads on conventional crime.


"Phil Kerby? This is Eddie Jackson. Do you remember talking to me a few months ago and giving me your card?"

Of course I did. His name (which, by the way, is not really Eddie Jackson) had come up during a check of license plates seen outside Afro Set headquarters a few weeks earlier, and I went by to interview him. It was obvious when I pulled up outside the house where he lived with his mother—it was neat as a pin—that Eddie couldn't be your typical Afro Set bullyboy. He turned out to be a handsome and well-spoken kid of twenty-five whose eyes danced with humor and intelligence. Why he wasn't in college instead of hanging around with Afro Set goons was beyond me.

We talked for an hour that day, a couple of hours the next week.

It was obvious he wasn't a major player in Afro Set, just a guy who dabbled around the edges, and I should have cut it short and moved on. But I really liked him. We discussed everything from W. E. B. Du Bois to Crispus Attucks, and we debated whether there were really any political answers for American blacks to be found on the African continent. It was one of those conversations that are entirely too rare between black and white Americans, honest and stimulating without any name-calling or guilt trips. He enjoyed it, I'm positive, as much as I did. At the end of the second conversation, I gave him a card and told him to call me if he ever had anything. And now here he was on the phone.

"Hey, Eddie, it's good to hear from you," I said. "How are you?"

"I've been okay, man," he replied. "But I have kind of a problem."

"What's that? Anything I can help with?"

"Maybe," he said hesitantly. "It's like this. I'm going to rob a bank today."

He'd been going to drink beer now and again with some guys he'd met on the street. Somehow one night the talk had turned to how easy it would be to rob banks, and then before he really knew what he was doing, Eddie was part of a gang. Three guys were on their way to his house right now with sawed-off shotguns and masks, which they were going to use to rob the bank branch on the campus of Capital University, an expensive and exclusive liberal-arts school in downtown Columbus.

"Man, I have really screwed up," Eddie admitted. "I don't want to do this. But I'm afraid if I try to back out now, they're going to kill me. They're really serious about it."

"You say they're coming right now?" I asked, my heart pounding. In the FBI, in those days, nothing was a bigger deal than a bank robbery.

"They'll be here in fifteen minutes," he confirmed.

"Eddie, I'm going to put you on hold for just a minute," I told him. "Please, please don't hang up." I dashed across the office to the supervisor's desk. "I've got a snitch on the phone," I explained breathlessly. "He and some friends are about to rob the bank over at Capital University."

"Have they left yet?" the supervisor demanded.

"No, but any minute."

"Give me his address and we'll get some agents over there right now," he said.

As I stood there, the supervisor coolly scrambled every agent in the whole office. Fifteen Bucars poured onto the street, half of them to watch Eddie's house and follow him, half to stake out the bank in case we lost him. Miller and I were sent to the bank—but as we scurried out the door, I halted dead in my tracks.

"Holy shit, I can't believe it!" I told Miller as I ran back to my desk. "I left Eddie on hold!" When I picked the phone up, it was dead. I tried dialing his house, but the line was busy. There was nothing to do but head for the bank and hope he was managing okay.

Luckily, one of our Bucars reached Eddie's street just as an old green Oldsmobile with four black men in it pulled out of the driveway. The agent got close enough to radio a description, and I confirmed one of them was Eddie. "Good, we're in business," the agent said. Then he called other cars to join the surveillance.

What followed was a guided excursion of every black residential area in Columbus. The Oldsmobile would pull up at a house and one of the guys would go inside carrying a paper bag. A few minutes later, he'd come back out with the same paper bag. This went on for hours. Later we found out they had been swapping guns around, connoisseur bank robbers in search of the perfect tools. But while it was happening, we couldn't figure out what the hell they were doing. And we couldn't stop them, either. Until they committed an overt act—say, driving up to the bank with ski masks on—there would be no way to make charges stick. So we stayed on the scenic tour. The miraculous thing was that they didn't spot the surveillance: eight Bucars full of spic-and-span white guys trailing them through one black neighborhood after another.

I got the call from Eddie around 8 A.M. It was about 1 P.M. when the reports from surveillance cars started indicating that the Oldsmobile was finally headed for the bank. An agent stationed at an intersection a mile away called in with the final alert: "Gentlemen, this is a bombing run. They just put on ski masks and sunglasses."

We had decided the arrests had to be made in the parking lot; the bank itself was inside the student union building where, if a shootout erupted, the potential for casualties was enormous. Five Bucars were positioned around the big lot, waiting for the Oldsmobile. Moments later, when it rolled to a stop, all five roared to life, skidding through the parking lot to pin the Oldsmobile in. We scrambled from our cars, ten FBI guns trained on the flabbergasted robbers.

The day's second miracle: They dropped their guns and gave up without a fight. If they hadn't, some agents surely would have been killed. We had instinctively arranged ourselves in a circle, great for playing dodgeball and just terrible for shooting at bank robbers: You'll hit each other. These days, the academy teaches young agents how to form an L ambush, so they'll live longer.

"Looks like this is the place," Miller said, pointing at the two-story town houses that comprised the grimy housing project in northeast Columbus.

"Yeah," I agreed. "Let's get this over with and get out of here. I want to get home before my brain fries like an egg."

It was a brutally hot August day when nothing had gone right. We were working our way through a list of Afro Set members, trying to interview them, but every one of them had either moved or wasn't home. The last name on the list was Robert Emerson Perry. One of our snitches told us Perry had recently left the Cleveland chapter and moved to Columbus. Supposedly he was disillusioned with the group. But neither Miller nor I had any hope Perry would talk. Afro Set's Cleveland chapter was another world, meaner and tougher than the one in Columbus—there were even rumors of murders up there—and we practically never got anything useful out of the Cleveland people. Even if Perry was home (and the way this day was going, that didn't seem likely), this would be a five-minute conversation consisting mostly of sullen *I dunnos*.

I rapped on the door of the town house. "It's open, come on in," called a female voice. I pushed the door open and Miller and I stepped into an apartment that was even more sweltering than the pavement outside. A pretty young black woman with a towering Afro glanced up at us from the ironing board where she was pressing shirts. "Can I help y'all?" she asked politely.

"We're agents Kerby and Miller from the FBI," I said. "We're looking for Robert Emerson Perry. Is he here?"

"Bobby," she called over her shoulder, "you've got company." A moment later, a short, thick man with coal-black skin walked out of the back. "You must be the FBI," he said before I could speak. "I heard you guys have been shakin' the bushes, talking about Afro Set. I wondered how long it would take before you got here." He smiled at us, and it was like somebody had switched on the lights. The man just glowed. I liked him instantly. And all my pessimism of five minutes ago vanished. I sensed instinctively, from the way he greeted us and the way he smiled, that he wanted to talk.

"Sounds like we don't have to give you the speech," I said. "We think Afro Set is dangerous, to white people and black people alike. And from what we've heard, you had some problems with the group, too. That's why you're back here from Cleveland."

He motioned for us to sit down. "That's Johnnie Mae, my girl-friend," he said, gesturing toward the young woman who continued her ironing. She glanced up and flashed a smile, then looked down again at her shirts. "Johnnie Mae's a nurse's aide," he explained. "Regular job, with a paycheck. Don't smoke, don't drink. Not the kind of girl I'm used to." He paused, and Miller and I shot one another glances. This sounded like a stream of aimless non sequiturs, but we were both certain it was going somewhere important.

"We met a few months ago," Perry continued in his rich baritone voice. "We been pretty happy together. Like it to stay that way. It makes me think I need to get my life arranged. But I'm not sure how easy that's going to be. Some things, it's hard to take back."

"Robert," I began, but he interrupted.

"Bob," he corrected me, and the smile glowed again for a couple of seconds.

"Bob," I tried again, "if you want to put your life in order, this is your chance. You can put your old life behind you. And you can keep some other people from living that same life. You've seen those young kids Afro Set brings out to demonstrations. Ten, eleven years old, learning to be gangsters. That's not the right way."

He rubbed his face with his fists, stared up at the ceiling for a minute. "If I've done something, can you help me?" he finally asked.

I chose my words carefully. Bob Perry was telling me, in effect, he had committed crimes, but not what they were. I didn't have the moral or legal authority to write him a blank check. Nor did I want to screw up a budding relationship by promising more than I could deliver. At the same time, I had to say *something* encouraging; you can't just tell somebody, hey, spill your guts for the sheer pleasure of it, never mind that you might get reamed later.

"Bob, I don't know what it is you might have done," I said, looking directly into his eyes. "My guess is that whatever it is, it involves state charges, not federal. I can't make any promises at all when it comes to those, except that if you're square with us, we'll make sure the state prosecutors are aware of it. Of course, if you lie, all bets are off."

Bob looked back over his shoulder. "Watcha think, Johnnie Mae? Should I do it? Should I talk to them?"

"It's the Christian thing to do, Bobby," she replied quietly, without taking her eyes off the ironing.

"The Christian thing to do," he echoed. I didn't detect any irony. It was more like he was recognizing something from a long time ago. For a couple of minutes, he seemed to be drifting. Then he snapped back.

"Well, where should I begin? What do you want to hear about first?"

"Tell us the biggest thing you know first," I suggested.

"The biggest thing I know? The biggest thing I know? Guess that would be about Harllel. You know who Harllel is, doncha?"

Harllel X—he used to be Harllel Jones—was in the Cleveland chapter of Afro Set. Like Nommo X in Columbus, Jones was a smooth talker capable of tying white liberals in all kinds of guilty knots.

"Yeah, we know who Harllel is," I said. "What about him?"

"Bet you didn't know he killed a man."

In the silence that followed, the hissing of Johnnie Mae's steam iron sounded like a locomotive.

"Oh, he didn't pull the trigger," Bob resumed, breaking the hush. "But he gave the orders. He told us, go out and kill a man, it doesn't matter who, as long as he's white. So some old man, wasn't doing anything but driving the interstate, got shot dead. Ask the Cleveland police, they'll know about that old man." He gave us another smile, but this one was bleak and icy. "Oh, I'll give you a bunch of things to ask the Cleveland police."


What followed was the most amazing interview of my career in the FBI. In the next half hour, Bob Perry told us about four unsolved murders he claimed were committed by Afro Set in Cleveland. What he described was a group addicted to murder. Killing was the solution to any and every problem, from insubordination to hurt pride, from sexual frustration to low pocket change. That leaflet warning that "we will fight and kill anyone who gets in our way" was not mere rhetoric, but a statement of policy.

At the center of it all, according to Bob, was Harllel X. "Harllel acts like he's the black Messiah," Bob said, "but the people in Afro Set don't look like the apostles to me." Yet they were faithful. They had proved it, Bob told us, the night in August 1970 that Harllel sent them out to kill a man at random.

It all started when an Afro Set member named Willie Lofton went to a McDonald's on Cleveland's east side. There was some kind of a hassle with a white security guard in the parking lot, and Lofton got shot dead. Within hours, there was an emergency meeting at Afro Set headquarters. "Harllel was really mad," Bob recalled, a cloud falling over the big brown cow eyes that were usually so friendly. "At the end of the meeting he screamed, 'Go out and kill white people!' Just like that. 'Go out and kill white people!'

"Three or four cars went out full of Afro Set members with guns. One group was picked up by the police after they stopped to rob some whores and wound up in a shootout. A couple of cars just kind of faded into the night. But the fourth car went ahead. Up on the Inner Belt Freeway, it pulled up alongside an old man. Just driving along. Nobody knew him. He didn't have anything to do with McDonald's or Willie Lofton or Afro Set or anything at all. But he was white. So they shot him."

"How certain are you about this?" I asked. "How do you know the guys in the car didn't just make up this story to be big shots?"

"I'm sure about it," Bob said quietly, looking away. "I was in the car."

Obviously, we had to have Bob's story checked out. The responsibility for this investigation moved north. We called the Cleveland FBI immediately after Bob told us the tale. A quick look at the records showed that a sixty-eight-year-old man named John Smith was shot in the head while driving home from work around 1 A.M. on August 7, 1970. Bob told us that they shot a second elderly white man a few minutes later—he even fired some of the shots, missing on purpose—but that man was only slightly wounded. The police had records of that, too: sixty-eight-year-old Harlow Tate, who survived. And Bob's story about the carload of Afro Set members being stopped that night also checked out. I sent the first of many teletypes to the FBI's Cleveland office on Bob's revelations.

The Smith murder was the only one Bob had personally witnessed and it was the only one he tied to Harllel X. But as Afro Set's "minister of defense," Bob presumably was privy to all the group's best gossip, and he offered detailed accounts of three other killings.

Over the span of a dozen meetings in back alleys and shopping center parking lots over the next couple of months, he fleshed out the details of a tale so harrowing and lurid that it sounded like a Ku Klux Klan fantasy—a tale that had never been told before outside Afro Set.

According to Bob, two killings were linked to the so-called Queen Mother of Afro Set, a woman named Esther Hazel and known within the group as Tyenetha Bey. A big woman who weighed nearly three hundred pounds, Tyenetha fancied daishikis, turbans, and slim young girls. As the chief of Afro Set's female cadres, she often ordered the group's women to have sex with her. Those who resisted were accused of violating Afro Set's code of conduct and "tried" by a kangaroo court in the basement of the group's headquarters on Hough Street in Cleveland. The guilty verdict that quickly followed could result in anything from a vicious beating to an unspeakable death. A teenager named Alice Wilson had been strangled after Tyenetha failed in an attempt to push her out a fourth-story window. Another woman—Bob didn't know her name—had been tortured and mutilated for hours, with a coke bottle jammed up her vagina and an American flag down her throat, before she was thrown off the second story of a building. Afterward, her body was sawed into pieces and stuffed into a fifty-five-gallon drum of lye.

The fourth murder Bob described came at the hands of a man named Marvin Bobo who now went by the name Bo X. "He's one of the scariest dudes in Afro Set," Bob told us. "He's a stone killer, a man who'll snuff you out soon as he'll look at you." We were able to come up with a picture of Bo X; he reminded me of Luca Brazi, the fat, balding killer in the movie *The Godfather*. His eyes were empty and savage.

Bo X was the triggerman in the freeway murder of John Smith. And, Bob told us, he had at least one other murder to his credit. He spotted a white hooker working near a bus stop on Cleveland's east side. "He dragged her into an alley to rob her," Bob told us. "But she only had six cents in her pocket. Bo X shook her and he said, 'Shit, bitch, somebody with only six cents don't deserve to live.' And he stomped her to death right there in the alley."

It was hard for me to imagine Bob Perry running with these people. Talking to Miller and me, he was gentle and intelligent. But I knew there had to be a darker side to Bob. Perhaps his romance with Johnnie Mae had washed it away. But Bob hadn't been made Afro Set's minister of defense because he had the soul of a poet. If we'd had any doubts, his description of the current defense minister, who called himself Gitu Ali Bey, put them to rest.

"There's a cat that people fear," Bob told us. "He's a real trip for anyone who crosses him. A tall, thin dude with beady eyes and a big puffy Afro. He never goes anywhere without a gun. You know how he makes his money? He robs bank robbers. When he hears about a bank being knocked off, he asks around till he finds out who did it. Then he tracks them down and beats their ass till they give him the money. Afterward, he ties the guy up and calls the FBI, tells them where to come pick up the robber. That way he collects the reward money, too. I told you, he's a cat that people fear."

As much as I trusted and liked Bob, the story of Gitu Ali Bey and the bank robbers gave me pause. Much as we might like to at times, the FBI doesn't beat up suspects and it doesn't cooperate with people who do. So I called Bill Green, an agent working the Afro Set in Cleveland, to check the story with him.

"It's pretty much true, I think," Green confirmed. "We carry Gitu Ali Bey as an informant, and he's given us a bunch of bank robbers. We've always suspected he beats the shit out of them. But we can never prove it because they'll never testify—they're too scared of him. Hell, you should see them when we arrive to pick them up. They're so terrified of Gitu, they're actually happy to be arrested."

Green, a University of South Carolina grad with just over a year in the FBI, was running the Afro Set investigation in Cleveland. Like me, he had sort of happened into it. When he arrived in Cleveland after doing his first-office year in Indianapolis, he was given the dregs of the cases. That included running over to the city jail whenever some inmate said he wanted to talk to an FBI agent. Those almost always turn out to be bullshit—a guy wants to beat a shoplifting rap by claiming he saw somebody on the grassy knoll shoot Kennedy, or something like that.

So when an inmate calling himself Wayouci Ali Moyou asked to see an agent, Green got the call. Moyou told Green he knew about some murders committed by this group called Afro Set. One was an old man shot on the freeway. Another was a girl Moyou had been dating who had been chopped up and put inside a fifty-five-gallon drum of lye. This was just about the same time Bob Perry started talking to me, and it didn't take long before Cleveland and Columbus were exchanging flurries of teletypes.

Moyou didn't know as much about Afro Set as Perry did, but his independent verification of some of the stories was important in building our confidence in Bob. And Moyou did move the investigation forward in a couple of important ways. Most notably, he was able to direct the Cleveland cops to the drum full of lye. Unfortunately, two years had passed, and while the gelatinous mess the cops found inside the drum was provably human, it was way beyond identification. And Moyou didn't know the girl's real name, only her Afro Set alias.

The Bureau office in Cleveland had teamed up with the police in a task force to investigate Afro Set, and Green was developing new sources all the time. Their stories were just as horrifying as the ones we heard from Bob Perry.

One Afro Set member had said something disrespectful to a leader. He was taken out one night and tied across a railroad track. After a train ran over him, the other members picked up his head and stored it in a pickle jar. They brought it out at meetings once in a while to remind everyone of the high price of disobedience. Another time, a couple of black guys unknowingly wandered into George's Bar, an Afro Set hangout at East 55th Street and Woodland Avenue, the heart of the ghetto. They were drinking beer, dancing with some of the girls, and generally having a good time. But one of them was very light-skinned, and some of the Afro Set members thought he was white. His buddy went to the bathroom, and when he came back, the light-skinned guy was gone. At first the buddy thought he might have gone outside with one of the girls, but after a couple of hours he got worried. "Have you seen that man in the yellow shirt who was here earlier?" he asked someone at the bar. "Yeah, the white motherfucker," the man—an Afro Set member—replied. "We offed him."

"You *what?*" the friend asked in horror.

"We offed him. White motherfuck come in here, mess with our women. We shot him in the alley and stuffed him down a sewer over on Woodland."

The police, when they heard the story, searched the sewer. But it emptied right into the main line, which quickly spilled into a sewage processor plant. The body had been ground into a million pieces and lost forever.

Between what Bob was telling us in Columbus and the work of Green's task force in Cleveland, they opened thirteen murder investigations against Cleveland Afro Set members.

Late in the year, Cleveland detectives came to escort Bob Perry up there to testify to a state grand jury. The detectives, who had never before known Perry's identity, were amazed. "We had a list of half a dozen names who we thought it might be," one of the cops told me. "But we never guessed you might have gotten somebody who was defense minister. What did you have on him to make him turn?"

"His conscience," I said.


Early in the year, the grand jury issued indictments against Afro Set members. Harllel X was charged with the freeway murder of John Smith. So was the infamous Bo X, Marvin Bobo, who pulled the trigger. He was also indicted for stomping the hooker to death. Tyenetha Bey, aka Queen Mother, aka Esther Hazel, was charged with strangling Alice Wilson. No charges were brought in the George's Bar case, where we didn't have a witness or a body, or the lye drum case, where we weren't even certain who had been killed.

Gitu Ali Bey wasn't charged with anything, but it didn't matter. One night when he was asleep, a girlfriend who he'd hit one time too often put five slugs in his head. As a man who prided himself for the rough justice he dispensed to bank robbers, I am sure he appreciates the irony, wherever he is.

Several of the defendants pled guilty—including Bo X, whose attorneys thought they had bargained for a relatively light sentence on second-degree murder in the freeway killing. But at the sentencing, when the judge asked Bo X if it was true he had shot John Smith just because he was white, Bo replied: No, I didn't care if he was green, yellow, black, or white. If I want to kill somebody, I'll kill 'em. I'll kill you, too, if you don't like it. In the blink of an eye, the light sentence turned into life.

Tyenetha Bey was convicted of manslaughter and got life, too. Harllel X was convicted of second-degree murder after a trial in which Bob Perry testified calmly despite the best efforts of the defense to make him look like an FBI provocateur—which was nonsense, of course; we didn't talk to him until a year after the killing. Because he rode along the night John Smith was killed, Bob was indicted for murder, but the charges were dropped after he testified against Harllel. I wasn't a member of the prosecution team on any of these cases—my role ended when I handed Bob over the Cleveland detectives. I saw him once or twice after that, but he soon dropped from view.

I wish this chapter ended with that last sentence. Unfortunately, it doesn't, and the story gets much shabbier. The attorney for Harllel X, assisted by the ACLU, filed suit in federal court to set aside the conviction and succeeded in getting a new trial. The main thrust of his case was that the Cleveland police failed to give the defense copies of a statement by one of the gunmen in the car that didn't mention anything about Harllel ordering the shooting.

The U.S. attorney's office in Cleveland at that time seemed to run from controversy, and Harllel's suit was no exception. When I went up to Cleveland to testify, the government lawyer whispered to me,

"We don't want to look heavy-handed on this thing," leaving me by myself to argue the finer points of constitutional law based on a couple of courses at the FBI academy. Small wonder we lost.

I was plenty pissed off about the way the U.S. attorney's office left me dangling in the wind, but it was nothing compared with what happened to Bill Green. Harllel X sued Green for several million bucks, accusing him of withholding evidence. Although the suit involved actions Green had taken in performance of his duties as an FBI agent, the U.S. attorney's office refused to defend him. It was only when a former head of the office threw a public fit and offered to take the case for free that the Justice Department relented. The suit dragged on for years—and would surely have bankrupted Green—before it was thrown out.

Harllel X never was retried. By the time the judge ordered a new trial, five years had passed, and Bob Perry couldn't be located. Without him, the prosecutors threw in the towel. Afro Set, however, was shattered, and Harllel made no attempt to pick up the pieces. Harllel became sort of a professional civil rights advocate in Cleveland, a role he plays until this very day. He even won a big award from the NAACP in 1993 for his community work.

A few years ago, Harllel's twenty-five-year-old son was shot to death, apparently a gang-related murder. The heartbreak that showed through in newspaper stories quoting Harllel was unquestionably authentic. "It's our job in the community to say, wait a minute!" the Cleveland *Plain Dealer* quoted him. "We're going down there and we want that judge to know that this was a cold-blooded, premeditated murder. That we don't want this man out there killing anybody else."

Bill Green and I couldn't have said it any better.

# 5

# AGENTS
# ON PARADE

It was nearly 6 P.M. when John Fisher got home, a little later than usual, and the phone was ringing as he walked into the house. Leaving the keys in the door, he picked up the receiver. "Hello?" he said, wondering if something had happened back at the office.

"Have you checked the mail yet?" asked a voice Fisher didn't recognize.

"No, I just got home," he answered, puzzled.

"You better go see what's in your mailbox, right now," the voice commanded.

Abruptly the connection broke off, leaving the phone buzzing in Fisher's ear.

He walked outside, where the last rays of an October sunset were being swallowed by the dusk. Inside the mailbox, under the usual stack of bills and catalogs, Fisher found an envelope with his name typed on it. No address, no stamp. It hadn't been left by the mailman.

His curiosity mounting, Fisher tore it open. Inside was a single typewritten sheet. He read for a few moments, then walked quickly back into the house. He picked up a phone book and opened it to the government listings, looking for the number for the FBI.

"Have you searched the building yet?" I asked. "Have you made any attempt to see if there's really a bomb?"

"Bombs, not bomb," Fisher said. "And when you read the letter, you'll see how difficult that would be to do." He pushed the letter across his dining room table. "He doesn't say where he's put them. Nationwide Insurance's national headquarters is here in Columbus. But we've got large regional offices around the country, and smaller offices in practically every medium-sized city in America. Altogether, we're talking about more than one hundred buildings. We can't possibly search them all without tipping our hand."

Fisher handed us the letter. Neatly typed, each block-style paragraph numbered, it was simple, clear, and chilling: The author wanted $280,000. If he didn't get it, Nationwide Insurance was going to suffer a terrible calamity. "There are devices already in place in many offices throughout the country," the letter said. The word *bomb* wasn't used, but none of us had any doubt what he was talking about.

The money was to be delivered at seven the next morning by a company official named Don Fossellman. He was to drive to a phone booth at a gas station in downtown Columbus—the letter even specified which company car he should use—and wait for a phone call with further instructions. Cryptically, the letter directed him to bring a screwdriver and pair of pliers.

I felt an icy finger on my heart when I read the final sentence: "If you alert law enforcement, you will be responsible for the consequences." Maybe meeting at Fisher's home hadn't been such a great idea. If the house was being watched, the arrival of FBI agents had surely been noticed. But I didn't say anything. The damage, if any, was already done.

When Fisher called half an hour earlier to report the extortion note, he hadn't had to explain who he was. Nationwide was among the largest employers in Columbus, and as its president, Fisher made frequent appearances in the newspapers.

It had only taken us a few minutes to drive to his home in the posh northern suburb of Worthington. The colonial-style house looked big enough to hold a small shopping mall. When Fisher had parties, I wondered, did he issue maps at the front door?

But I pushed the thought out of my mind. With just twelve hours before the ransom was to be delivered, a lot of decisions had to be made. "Do you have any idea who sent the note?" I asked. "It's got to be someone who works at Nationwide, or used to. Who else would know the details of the company motor pool? Maybe there's a clue in the ransom demand. That's an odd amount, $280,000."

"I thought about that," Fisher agreed. "But I don't know of anyone who's been arguing with us about $280,000. And even if it is an employee, that doesn't narrow it down enough to do anything between now and tomorrow morning. We have thousands of them."

"What about this guy Don Fossellman, the one who's supposed to deliver the money? Is he a senior official? Has he had to fire anyone recently?"

"No, he's just an underwriter," Fisher said. "He hasn't even been in Columbus that long—he was working in one of our offices in Pennsylvania. He doesn't have any idea what this is all about."

"What about the ransom? What do you think about paying it?" I inquired. This was a delicate moment. The FBI normally argues against paying ransoms to extortionists or kidnappers. But, in the end, the decision would be up to Fisher. He was the one, after all, who would have to answer to employees and stockholders if a bomb went off.

"I doubt if we can even get that kind of cash at this time of night," he mused. "Earlier this year, when there was a wave of executive kidnappings, we worked out a deal with a bank where we could get $100,000 in an emergency. I don't know what they would say to this." He looked up, and his eyes seemed to flash. "But I'm not going to ask them. Hell no, we're not going to pay it."

There were barely perceptible sighs of relief from around the table. Fisher's tough-it-out attitude would make what came next much easier.

We had a plan. First, the telephone company would be asked to do what's called a trap-and-trace on the pay phone where the ransom call was supposed to come in. If the call lasted long enough, we would be able to find the extortionist and arrest him before he got off the telephone.

If that didn't work, we had a second line of defense. Instead of Fossellman, the Nationwide underwriter, the ransom package would be carried by an FBI agent wired for sound. When he received the call, he would repeat the instructions, as though he were making sure he'd heard them correctly. That would broadcast them to twenty agents waiting in cars around the area. We would all convene on the ransom drop and arrest the extortionist there.

"It sounds good to me," Fisher said after we finished describing it. The agents felt another wave of relief. We were going to go ahead with the plan whether he liked it or not. We didn't need Fisher's permission to enforce the law. But the operation would be much easier with his cooperation.

With nothing more to discuss, the meeting broke up. A couple of agents went back to the office to talk to the phone company and put together a ransom package full of stuffed newspaper. The rest of us went home to get a good night's sleep before what we hoped would be a quick, simple arrest.


We should have known better. Extortion cases always seem to go off the rails in some weird, unexpected way. Even the concept of the crime can get a little cloudy at times.

The legal definition of extortion is the giving up of one's property, willingly or unwillingly, in response to a threat to ruin one's reputation or inflict physical harm. (It turns into a federal crime if the extortionist uses the U.S. Postal Service to deliver his threats. In the Nationwide case, we were using federal laws on bombing as our initial reason to get involved.)

The Nationwide case—a threat to blow up a building unless ransom was paid—was about as clear-cut as you can get. But I once watched local police work a case in Michigan where a developer, angry at a ruling in a zoning case, threatened to reveal that the judge allegedly visited hookers. The developer awaiting trial for extortion. His attorney argued that he wasn't guilty of anything but good citizenship, that the public had a right to know what kind of

WITH HONOR AND PURPOSE

a man the judge was. The judge bought it, and the developer went free.

Typically extortionists are among the cruelest criminals. Lots of crooks scare their victims, but only kidnappers and extortionists cultivate fear, nurturing it like an evil flower. A bank robber might point a gun at a teller and yell, "Give me the money or I'll blow your head off!" But he doesn't hang around to watch his victims squirm; he doesn't feed on their fright for days or weeks or months the way an extortionist does.

But common wisdom gets proven wrong all the time on extortions, including that little bit I just recited. I once had a case in Michigan where the president of a small-town bank was getting threats signed by a group calling itself the New Republicans. The letters said his children would be killed if he didn't leave $200,000 out in the woods. They included terrifyingly accurate descriptions of his home, where the kids went to school, and their daily routine.

Twice the president made ransom drops while we watched from planes, waiting to make an arrest, but the money wasn't retrieved. The third one took place in a rainstorm that threatened to ruin our surveillance. Finally pilot Paul Koch defied orders and took off despite the rain. He spotted someone picking up the money, trailed him, and directed us to a house where he holed up.

When we walked in to arrest him, I couldn't believe it. The author of all those cold-blooded threats turned out to be a wizened little old man of seventy or so who barely looked capable of opening his Geritol bottles by himself. "Why did you do it?" I demanded, truly outraged. "My wife's got cancer, and I couldn't afford to get her a doctor," he said meekly.

"Yeah, right," I scoffed. You get so tired of hearing these bullshit tales.

But when we searched the house, we found her lying in bed, so thin you could count all her bones, every raspy breath sounding like it might be her last. The bullshit tale was true: The fabled New Republicans were an old man and his dying wife. Nothing could have justified the weeks of dread he inflicted on the banker. But when the old man got a suspended sentence, I can't say I cursed the judge as a bubble-headed liberal.

We were putting most of our faith in the trap-and-trace. The Bureau doesn't like its bag of telephone tricks opened to public eyes. But in an age when any customer with caller ID service can see the phone number where the call is originating, it's hardly news that the FBI can trace numbers almost instantaneously.

That's been true for some time. Even on that morning in October 1973, the days of "Keep him talking, Charlie, we've almost got it," the way movie cops always talked about phone traces, were long gone. We knew the trap-and-trace would tell us within moments where the extortionist was calling from. The only reason we needed to stall him and keep him on the line was to give our agents time to arrive and arrest him. To make sure we could pounce on him quickly, we had ten Bucars positioned around downtown. Orchestrating them would be Dick Cleary, the wiry, soft-spoken Ivy Leaguer who was the "case agent," Bureau parlance for the head of the investigation.

The job of taking the phone call fell to Bob Horel, a big, soft-spoken agent who was approximately the same height and weight as Fossellman, the Nationwide underwriter who was supposed to make the ransom drop. Horel's physique would probably fool the extortionist if he was watching us from hiding, but we worried that his voice would give away our deception. We told him to keep his answers terse. Horel usually worked fraud, embezzlement, and other cases where the investigation consisted mostly of juggling long columns of numbers. He didn't look altogether happy about the new direction of his career.

The phone booth where Horel went to await the call, ironically enough, was within blocks of the Ohio State Penitentiary. A few minutes before 7 A.M., the Bucars began rolling into position along nearby streets. My car was stationed serendipitously alongside a donut shop.

"I'm gonna grab something here," I told Flint Gabelman, my partner for the day. "You want me to bring you anything?"

Gabelman yawned. "No thanks," he said. "I'm going to get some breakfast as soon as we arrest this asshole."

I trotted inside and ordered a cup of coffee and a jelly donut. Back in the car, I took a bite out of the donut—and recoiled as bright red strawberry filling splashed down the front of my white shirt.

"Oh, *shit*," I groaned.

"Look on the bright side," Gabelman counseled. "If there's any shooting, you can say you were hit. You'll get a medal."

I laughed, but I was unconsoled. It might be a couple of hours before I could get home to change shirts.

The radio crackled to life. "I'm standing at the phone, waiting," Horel said into the small transmitter concealed inside his coat. A moment later, we could clearly hear the sound of a phone ringing. "Hello?" Horel answered. There was a moment of silence, then we heard him say, "Yes, this is Fossellman. I got the money. What do you want me to do with it?"

There was a longer pause, then Horel's voice again. "Let me read that back. Go over to the east side of town and get on Highway 204. Go east toward Zanesville."

"Sounds like the caller has bought it," I said to Gabelman.

"Go about twelve miles, till you get to Millersport," Horel said.

"This is going to work," I told Gabelman excitedly. "They'll have the trace any second."

"Go past Millersport one-quarter mile until you see a tree," Horel continued. "Take a left. Go three miles until you see a barn at an intersection."

"When is the office going to tell us where this guy is?" Gabelman complained. "They've gotta have the location by now."

"Go one-quarter of a mile and turn right. Start counting the utility poles. Stop when you get to the fifth one."

"Count the utility poles?" I blurted. "Is this guy anal, or what?"

*"Where's the damn office?"* Gabelman screamed. "If the trace isn't working, why don't they say so?"

"On the fifth pole, I'll see a little numeral one, cut from tin," Horel said. "Use the screwdriver to remove it. Underneath, a small glass eyedropper has been inserted into a hole drilled in the wood. Remove the eyedropper. Inside, I'll find further instructions."

There was a longer pause, punctuated by Gabelman's cursing, and then Horel returned to the air one last time. "He's hung up," Horel reported."

The instant he stopped speaking, a dispatcher's voice broke in. "The call came from a phone booth at Veterans Memorial," he said urgently, referring to an office building across the Olentangy River, about a mile away. "All units proceed there immediately."

"Why did you wait so long to tell us?" an angry voice asked over the radio as I wheeled the car around.

"I've been trying to give instructions for ten minutes," the dispatcher said, an edge in his voice. "But all the radios locked onto the channel Horel's microphone is on. I haven't been able to get through."

In less than three minutes, half a dozen Bucars converged on Veterans Memorial. But to no one's surprise, it was too late. The caller had simply melted into the pedestrian traffic along Broad Street, where early-bird groups of office workers were already starting to arrive. Since we had no idea what he looked like, our only hope had been to catch him on the telephone.

"All right," Cleary said over the radio, "we're going to have to proceed to the location the caller gave Horel over the phone. Did everyone write it down?" I was relieved when Gabelman's grunted "no" was quickly echoed by the rest of the cars. No one had expected such an elaborate set of instructions—and no one really expected to have to make the ransom drop, anyway. We had been banking on the phone trace.

"Well, Horel's got it," Cleary said. "I'll keep him in visual contact, and we'll be in touch by radio, too. Federspiel, you follow me." One by one, he reeled off our call signs, forging a long chain of pursuit.

"This sounds like the Macy's Thanksgiving Day parade," Gabelman fumed as we headed east.

"Yeah, and the way I look, I guess we're the clown float," I said, peering down at the jelly stain on my shirt. "Well, the phone call wasn't a total loss. At least we know what the damn screwdriver and pliers are for."

When an FBI operation goes wrong, it's almost always due to a communications screwup. That was especially true twenty years ago, when we used radios that couldn't even communicate with local cops or sheriffs.

But even today communications are the Bureau's Achilles' heel. A radio is always locking onto the wrong channel or going mysteriously silent at the exact wrong moment.

One of the most unfortunate mishaps is for an agent's knee to hit the radio mike and open it inadvertently, putting what he thinks is a private conversation onto the air for everyone to hear. This particular problem rarely compromises an operation, but it almost never boosts your career when your SAC suddenly learns your candid opinion of him.

One of the most hilarious microphone lapses in Bureau history involved an agent in Chicago with a strong, distinctive Boston accent. He accidentally opened his mike just as his partner suggested that they debrief a hooker.

"I'm gonna get in the back seat with her," the partner said. "Don't turn around, she gets embarrassed easily."

For the next three or four minutes, there was only silence. "Can we hurry this up?" the Boston agent finally asked. "Give me another minute," his partner pleaded.

Another long silence. "Come on, let's get a move on," the Boston agent complained. "Just another minute," his partner pled.

"Sure, sure," the Boston agent snapped. "Go ahead, take an hour for all I care. I'll just stay up here and drum on my nuts." For the rest of his career, no matter where he transferred, no one ever called him anything but The Drummer.

It took nearly forty-five minutes for Horel, meandering along the back roads, to reach the utility pole he was looking for. Gabelman and I were a mile away when Horel spoke into his body mike again.

"I think I'm at the right place," he said. "And I'm pretty sure I'm alone. I'm out in the middle of a field—there's no place anyone could hide. I'm going to approach the pole." A moment later: "The tin piece he told me about is here. This is definitely the pole." A few grunts as he struggled with the screws. "There's a glass tube—it looks like the stem of an eyedropper—with a piece of paper inside." Then: "Oh, shit. Listen to this. *Turn around and go back one mile. Turn left. Continue about five miles until you see a red barn. Then take the second road to the right. Stop at the eighth utility pole. Look for more instructions under the piece of tin.*"

I could almost hear the cries of "Oh, shit" echoing along Highway 220. In fact, I *could* hear them, because Gabelman was staging a one-man cursing festival right beside me. "Does this shithead think he's going to get a mileage bonus?" he complained.

"Maybe it's the guy who has the contract to sell tires to the FBI," I suggested. "Or maybe somebody at AAA has gone over the edge from too many years of drawing route maps."

Half an hour later, Horel found the next utility pole. Again he fished a glass tube out of a hole drilled in the wood. Nobody was surprised when he started reading: *"Go two miles until you see a farmhouse with a stone fence. Turn right . . ."*

It continued like that all day, zigzagging northeast across Ohio. Seven or eight times Horel stopped to retrieve the glass tubes from utility poles, and it seemed each set of directions was more complex than the last. Some even came with friendly travel tips. *"Better urinate here, it's a long way to the next stop,"* said one. Another noted the presence of a convenience store nearby and suggested: *"You might want to get a sandwich, there won't be another chance for several hours."*

As the countryside turned hillier, our radios started to fade, and some Bucars would be out of touch for twenty or thirty minutes at a time. Some got lost; others nearly collided as the route doubled back on itself. Pretty soon, we were all bunched together, trying to keep Horel in sight, because it was the only way to avoid losing the trail. If the extortionist was watching, he'd have to be an idiot to miss us. We looked like a train: ten plain four-door sedans with matching black-wall tires bunched within a mile of each other. All we needed was a caboose.

"This is the biggest goat-rope I've ever seen in my life," I moaned to Gabelman in midafternoon after what seemed like our 115th stop.

"Well, I was in Vietnam, so I've seen some major goat-ropes," he said. "But this certainly ranks up there near the top."

"For Christ's sake, we're almost to Stupidville," I grumbled, using our pet name for Steubenville, the grimy little industrial town perched on the border with West Virginia.

"Did you know Robert Frost wrote a poem about Steubenville?" Gabelman asked.

"Get out of here."

"No, really," he said earnestly. "I couldn't believe it either. I even memorized a little bit of it. You want to hear it?"

"Sure," I said, intrigued. "I didn't figure you for the poetry type."

Gabelman cleared his throat. " 'I shot an arrow into the air and it stuck.' "

I groaned, feigning despair, but made a mental note of the poem. Persecution of Stupidville was a favorite pastime in the Columbus office.


Near Steubenville, the directions sent us due north for a while. Then we started going east again, crossing into Pennsylvania, which put us in the Pittsburgh FBI office's jurisdiction. The Pittsburgh SAC demanded that his agents take over the pursuit. We all went home—including Horel, whose stage career was ending before he got to the final act. A Pittsburgh agent took over the role of Fossellman.

By the time we got back to Columbus, it was late at night. As I got ready for bed, I wondered about the progress of the ransom convoy, which was probably halfway across Pennsylvania. I sighed; all I had to show for the day was a hopelessly stained shirt. If there was any consolation, it was that no bombs had gone off at Nationwide offices. But to that had to be added the word: *yet*.

Shortly after dark, the caravan of FBI vehicles approached the New York State line somewhere south of Buffalo. There was another jurisdiction change, but the Buffalo SAC decided not to change horses in midstream. He added a couple of agents to the caravan as liaison, but left Pittsburgh in charge.

With darkness falling, the Pittsburgh SAC was worried that the extortionist might make a move. Gordon McNeill, the new agent playing Fossellman, was ordered to take an intentional wrong turn as he drove through a small Pennsylvania town. He drove a few blocks, pulled into a parking lot, and waited. Moments later one of the Bucars arrived. Two agents carrying shotguns jumped out, dived into the back seat of the "Fossellman" car, and crouched down. McNeill drove off again. With any luck, the backups hadn't been seen slipping into his car.

A couple of hours later, the car stopped at a utility pole to pick up the gazillionth glass tube of the day. The next leg of the trip would take them into the Allegheny National Forest. The directions were to travel several miles along a side road, then stop to look for new instructions.

Inside the park, the Bucars drifted back a little bit. The road was a straight, narrow ribbon of asphalt, and there was no chance anyone would get lost. Maps showed the road went straight through the park and exited somewhere near Buffalo.

Watching his odometer, McNeill stopped his car; it was time to check for another eyedropper. As he climbed out, he noticed a barrier in the road up ahead; park rangers had sealed it off for some reason.

Suddenly there was a shout from the woods. Before he could even react, hands came out of the gloom to snatch at the bag. McNeill jerked it back, and there was a scuffle in the darkness. A bullet whizzed past McNeill's ear as he broke free.

The two backup agents came scrambling from the car, looking for someone to shoot back at, but they couldn't see a thing in the murky night. Then they heard the sound of a motorbike from up ahead, on the other side of the barrier. The extortionist, whoever he was, was making his getaway, and there was nothing they could do about it. These days, an airplane would have been part of the surveillance right from the start, and would be able to surreptitiously track the motorbike, but back then the Bureau didn't have them.

We had used a helicopter, borrowed from the Columbus police, during the morning—a fairly stupid idea, since choppers sound like flying train wrecks and are just about as inconspicuous. It was piloted by a Columbus police officer whose copilot was an agent named George Murray, who'd flown helicopter gunships in Vietnam. Murray was having a great time, reliving the old days, until the chopper neared Zanesville. "Say, what's the range on these things, anyway?" he asked his pilot.

The answer was: "You're past it." Moments later, they were making an emergency landing.

Gordon McNeill and the other agents, though they couldn't follow the extortionist, did search the area just beyond the roadblock. They found a .22 rifle lying on the road. After that, there was nothing to do but get back into the car and make the long drive home. They were going home empty-handed, just like we had; but anytime someone shoots at you and misses, you have to count yourself lucky.

McNeill, a few years down the road, would learn that lesson well. He eventually transferred to Miami. In 1986, he was supervising a team staking out banks in hopes of catching a team of bank robbers plaguing the city.

During the stakeout, the agents spotted the two robbers. There was a high-speed chase, collisions, and a Rambo-like rain of bullets, all the stuff that you see in cop movies that never happens in real life. When it was over, 140 shots had been fired. The two robbers were dead. So were two agents. Five others were wounded—including McNeill. The doctors pulled fifty-two bullet fragments out of his body.

Miraculously, McNeill survived. Even more miraculously, to my way of thinking, he came back to work. As I write this, he's a supervisor in the FBI's San Francisco office.

The next morning, Cleary sent me over to Nationwide to talk to a man named Jim Marion. "He's got some ideas on how to develop suspects within the company," Cleary said.

"Is he the corporate security director?" I asked.

"Not exactly," Cleary said. "He seems to be in charge of anything that might get messy. He's the company personnel director, and he's the guy they call when anything gets stolen."

*Great job*, I thought. *Corporate vice president for getting struck by lightning.* I couldn't believe that a company as big as Nationwide didn't have a full-time security director.

Marion was a kindly-faced man in his fifties who was absolutely enthralled to be talking to an FBI agent. He had been a cop himself for a few years in Pennsylvania around the time of World War II, and it was obvious that, however much more he was making as a corporate troubleshooter, his heart was back in the patrol car. He wanted to know what kind of gun I used, what kind of radios we had in FBI cars (a subject I wasn't too thrilled to discuss that morning), and the mechanics of placing a wiretap. It took a while to gently steer the conversation back to the extortion.

"My office tells me you have some good ideas about the case," I said, not mentioning that nobody had told me what they were.

"Well, it seems to me that the letter must have come from someone who has a beef against us," Marion said. "And because of my personnel job I pretty much know everyone at Nationwide who's at odds with the company. This morning I had my secretary pull the personnel files of the last ten people who left here under less-than-pleasant circumstances. As well as several years of crank mail.

"In a company with a hundred offices, you know the names of the last ten people fired?" I asked in amazement.

"Pretty much," he said. "Plus, I restricted it to people who have worked, at one time or another, in the Columbus area. After all, this man knew where Mr. Fisher lived and had his home telephone number. He picked a particular car out of our Columbus motor pool."

I wasn't completely convinced, but at least it was a way to start. And I thought anybody who underestimated Marion was making a mistake. His eyes were friendly, but they held a hint of caginess, too. He couldn't possibly have survived in that dump-all-the-messes-on-me job of his without some canny instincts. Knowing where all the corporate bodies were buried was probably part of his portfolio.

"Are those the files?" I asked, pointing at a stack of folders on his desk.

He nodded. "I've already started going through them," he said.

"Do you mind if I take a look at a few of them?" I asked. "We could get through this faster."

The first file I looked at, about an inch thick, was mostly the routine paper droppings we all leave along our trails through life: flimsy carbon copies of letters announcing raises, transfers, changes in insurance. Scattered through it was a series of increasingly florid letters complaining about a Nationwide supervisor, several of which suggested that he was descended from female dogs.

It was those letters that drew my attention. Beside the file, I had a copy of the extortionist's letter to Fisher. Every time I came across a letter in the file, I glanced over at the extortion note to see if they had any resemblance. In particular, I looked for a couple of distinctive things we had noticed in the extortionist's letter. One was the way each paragraph had been numbered. Another was the odd punctuation of the salutation. *Dear Mr. Fisher:–*

It took half an hour to work my way through the file and I didn't find anything that remotely linked it to the extortion. I picked up the next one and winced at the weight: It was double the size of the first file. Looking again at the stack, I saw some folders that were three or four inches thick. Apparently nobody ever got fired at Nationwide during their first six months, or even their first six years.

For nearly two hours we trudged through the files, silent except for an occasional clicking of tongue against teeth from Marion as he stumbled across some new, undetected sin against the corporation. I was on the verge of suggesting we break for coffee when he exclaimed: "Damn! I think I've found it!"

I hurried around the desk. The file was opened to a letter that began, *Nationwide Industries:*–Underneath were three neat box-style paragraphs, each one numbered. Although the lab would have to run tests to be sure, the paper and the style of the typewriter looked to me like they were the same as those used by the extortionist.

"Who is this guy?" I asked.

"Schubert, Glen Schubert," Marion said excitedly. "Damn it, I knew we should never have taken that guy back. He was never anything but trouble around here."

Schubert, it seemed, had been a district claims manager, supervising eleven claims adjustors. "As a worker, he was really pretty good," Marion recalled. "He was really good at investigating claims, he knew how to get them settled quickly and without a fuss, and he was good at training other people. But personally—"

Personally, he was an asshole, to use an FBI technical term. He argued bitterly with his bosses, harangued co-workers, and generally disrupted things. "And even though he was a member of management," Marion said, voice low and eyes wide, "even though he was management, *he wanted to organize a union.*" He looked like he wanted to wash his own mouth out with soap.

A couple of years ago, Schubert had asked for a year's leave of absence to go join some off-brand religious sect in California which, among other things, preached wife-swapping. Nationwide quickly granted the request, certain he'd be swallowed up in the nut culture of the coast and never seen again.

But when the year was over, he turned up again. "I said all along we shouldn't rehire him," Marion said. "But somehow it happened anyway. And a *lot* of people were angry. It really put some noses out of joint among people who had to work with him. I couldn't blame them. He was nuts."

Almost as soon as he was reinstated, Schubert started writing a series of vitriolic letters complaining about Nationwide's job-training program and the company's benefits. Finally, just a few months before the extortion attempt, his insults had gone over the top, and Nationwide fired him. The letters were all right there in his personnel file, each bearing the telltale salutation and numbered paragraphs.

"Do you know where he lives now?" I asked.

"Yeah, I noticed there was some correspondence about a problem with his last check," Marion said. "Here it is—White Plains, New York. What will you do now?"

"Get a search warrant," I said over my shoulder as I walked out the door.


By the time I got back to the office, the noose around Schubert's neck had pulled a little tighter. The Buffalo office had discovered that the rifle found out in the national forest had once been repaired at a shop in Yonkers, New York. The customer's name was Glen Schubert.

An arrest warrant was issued that evening, though some sort of technical problem stopped the agents from going to Schubert's home that night. He wasn't home—but while they were chatting with his wife, he walked in. If there was the slightest doubt we had the right man, it ended when we searched his home, car, and another house where he sometimes stayed. We found a case of glass eyedroppers identical to the ones we pulled out of utility poles, the sheet of tin from which all the markers had been clipped, a pair of shears that had probably been used to cut them. (I could hardly wait to hear Schubert explain that sheet of tin.) We also seized a typewriter from the house which, the lab later proved, had been used to write the extortion note and all the directions.

What we *didn't* find was significant, too. There were no blasting caps or detonator cord or anything to do with explosives at all. Although we'll never be certain, it didn't appear that he really knew anything about building bombs or had any intention of trying it. The threat against Nationwide had been the act of a man long on imagination, but luckily short on capabilities.

The evidence against him was so overwhelming that, when the case went to trial a few months later, none of us could figure what Schubert was going to offer as a defense. Apparently he couldn't, either. Three days into the trial, he switched his plea to guilty. He was sentenced to fifteen years in prison.

For everybody else, the case had a much happier ending. Nationwide executives were so impressed with the way their cop wannabe Jim Marion outperformed the FBI that they made him vice president for corporate security. Fifteen years later he retired, and Bob Federspiel—one of the agents who worked the case—retired from the Bureau and took his place.

Who knows? Maybe the case ultimately had a happy ending for Schubert, too. He was released after serving about half his sentence. Last I heard, he was working as a counselor in a halfway house for parolees in the Albany area. I hope he isn't trying to organize a union; he doesn't want Jim Marion on his trail. One thing's for sure: Schubert wasn't cut out to be an extortionist. Using the same typewriter for both his signed letters of complaint and his unsigned blackmail attempt was just flat dumb. Unfortunately for the FBI, not every extortionist is such a blockhead.

Certainly the guy the FBI came up against some years later in Michigan was a lot more clever. He ordered the agents to leave the ransom money in the back seat of a car parked on a downtown street. Then they were supposed to beat it. Of course, they didn't; there were agents all over the place. The vigil went on all day, but no one approached the car, and finally the SAC called it a day. The agents walked over to the car to pull the ransom money out—and it was gone.

A quick search of the car revealed that under the rear floor mat, a six-inch-square hole had been cut in the car. The hole was situated directly over a manhole, which led into the storm sewer system, which emptied out into the Flint River. The money had been picked up right under our noses, and we didn't even get a chance to wave good-bye.

# 6

# DOG FERGUSON

The November rain drizzled against the office windows with a monotonous hiss, reminding me just how wet and cold it was outside. *A good day for catching up on paperwork*, I thought, shuffling through a stack of teletypes. *A good day for staying indoors.* I wasn't the only one who had suddenly discovered a good reason to stay off the streets. The office was bustling, the staccato clatter of typewriters punctuating the steady hum of a dozen phone conversations. Behind me somewhere, two older agents were reliving the good old days, which—as near as I could tell from the snatches of conversation I overheard—had ended when the Pony Express came and ruined everything.

"Did you hear Dog is back in town?" one of them asked, apparently changing the subject.

"Yeah, I heard he was over at East High last night," the other replied. "He walked into the gym during a basketball game, wearing one of those fur coats, trailing all those babes behind him."

"Another standing ovation?"

"Of course," the other agent snorted in disgust. "The biggest pimp in America, how could the kids not clap?"

"Yeah, he's a real role model. A constant reminder to those kids that they don't have to be worthless little pieces of shit. With some hard work, they can grow up to be *really big* pieces of shit."

"What the hell are you guys talking about?" I interrupted, intrigued in spite of myself. "There's a pimp working high school basketball games?"

They both chortled. "He wasn't working, just showing off," one answered. "He struts in there, lets everybody get a load of all the diamond rings and fur coats he's earned peddling pussy. It's like the class nerd showing up at homecoming ten years later with a wad of cash and a flashy blonde."

"He walks right into the high school? And nobody does anything?" The image pissed me off.

"What's to do? The guy hasn't been convicted of anything."

"Why doesn't somebody make a case on him?" I demanded.

"You don't think we've tried?" one of the agents retorted. "You don't think *everybody's* tried? This office has had an open case on Dog Ferguson since Kennedy was president." He shook his head, then added derisively: "But of course, we never had the advice of a young hotshot like you. Why don't you take it over?"

"Maybe I will," I sneered back. "Where can I get the case number?"

"Thirty-one seven-o-six-one," the two agents said in unison, like schoolboys chanting their times tables.

A couple of days later, I drove over to the division headquarters in Cincinnati where case files were kept. It took me all day to read the two-volume file on William Gaither Ferguson, and at the end I still didn't have the answer to my most nagging question: How did he get the nickname Dog?

But that may have been just about the only subject that hadn't been covered. This guy was much more than a pimp, he was a one-man crime wave. The file was full of interviews with informants alleging his involvement with drug trafficking, fraud, and every form of theft ever enshrined in the criminal code.

The other agents hadn't been exaggerating; since 1963, Dog Ferguson had been investigated almost constantly by the FBI, the DEA, the IRS, and the New York City police. But nobody had ever convicted him of anything. I peered at the stack of surveillance photos that had accumulated in the file over the years. It was hard to believe that the man in the pictures—a dainty, dudish little black fellow in his late thirties with a wreath of delicate curls—had defeated all those agencies.

Part of the problem, I knew, was the inherent difficulty of making cases related to prostitution and drugs. In most crimes, you have a complaining victim who tells you what happened to him and offers some clues to help you pin it on the bad guy. In prostitution and drug cases, that doesn't happen. The hooker and her john, the dope dealer and his junkie, they're all wrapped up in the same conspiracy. Nobody's dialing 911.

Even so, as I worked my way through the file, it was obvious that there had been some botched opportunities on Dog Ferguson. Dozens of promising leads hadn't been followed up. Potential informants hadn't been contacted. Nobody had ever asked for a wiretap, even though it was obvious that Dog conducted a lot of business over the phone.

The more I read, the more the thought of Dog Ferguson sauntering through a high school gym made me grit my teeth. The only thing an FBI agent hates worse than a criminal who gets away with something is a criminal who gets away with something and then flaunts it. In the 1930s, when John Dillinger and Pretty Boy Floyd and Ma Barker taunted us, Hoover went after them with a terrible vengeance. Fifty years later, John Gotti, the so-called Teflon Don, made the same mistake, rubbing the Justice Department's nose in it every time he won a case in court. After a while, it seemed like half the FBI was assigned to getting him. And, eventually, we did.

Dog Ferguson wasn't in Pretty Boy Floyd's league. But he was a miserable shitty little parasite, a guy who'd never done an honest day's work in his life and lived off the misery of others. He was the local boy gone bad, not made good, and he didn't have any right to parade through the city's schools.

I was going to stop him.


Ordinarily the FBI doesn't chase pimps or whores; they aren't committing federal crimes. But as Dog's empire grew, he had expanded outside Columbus. He had contacts in New York, Los Angeles, Atlanta, and several other cities. That ran him afoul of ITAR, the Interstate Transportation in Aid of Racketeering statute. ITAR makes it a federal crime to use telephones or any other forms of interstate travel or communication to carry out certain designated crimes—one of them being prostitution.

For the first few days that I worked on Dog's case, I was on the telephone constantly with police department vice squads in those cities. Using a subpoena, I had gotten copies of the long distance telephone bills for the apartment Dog used on visits to Columbus— for the past six years, he had really been living in New York—as well as those of a couple of his top lieutenants. There were a couple of dozen different numbers that were listed over and over. I passed the numbers along to agents in those cities; they checked to see if they belonged to people who were suspected of involvement in prostitution. If so, the agents used a subpoena to get the long distance bills for these new suspects. Within a couple of months, we developed a skeletal model of Dog's organization.

Meanwhile, I went into the streets. The file was full of names of women who had worked for Dog at one time or another; although many of the names and addresses turned out to be phonies, I managed to find a few of them, who in turn sent me to others. Even more fruitful was the Franklin County jail. Every time a hooker who worked for Dog got busted, I went to see the arresting officer.

"Does this bust mean a lot to you?" I would ask. Almost inevitably the answer was no. Arresting hookers is usually more a matter of public order—getting a nuisance off the street temporarily—than criminal law enforcement. If it was okay with the cop, then I'd tell the woman I had a deal for her: The charges would be dropped if she would agree to talk to me about Dog.

That was how I met my first important snitch, a skinny black woman in her early thirties (I'll call her Amber), whose sister, I'd heard, was a longtime member of Dog's stable.

"Hell yes, I'll talk to you, if you get me out of here," she told me in the jail's interrogation room. "Man, this is some shit luck, getting arrested like this. I don't even *do* this shit anymore."

"The police officer seemed to think that, when you mentioned fifty dollars, it was a little high to be talking about bus fare," I observed.

"Oh, he nailed me," she agreed. "I don't mean he's lying. But really, I'm not in the life anymore. I just needed some quick cash."

"Yeah?" I replied skeptically. "So what line of work are you in now?"

"I boost."

"Boost?"

"You know, steal," she explained. "I steal things. Pays a lot better than hooking, baby. And you can't stay out on that street forever."

The longer we talked, the more convinced I was that Amber was telling the truth: She was no longer working as a whore. But even though her information on Dog was a bit dated, she was sharp and articulate. Her descriptions of the hooker hierarchy were well worth the price of a misdemeanor prostitution bust.

At the bottom of the pyramid, Amber said, were the street whores who prowled around the Columbus bus station. For ten or fifteen dollars a shot, they provided oral sex in the back seats of cars or in the doorways of downtown's grim back alleys. These were mostly young runaways recruited as they got off the buses, or old, broken-down whores, half-crazed on drugs. Dog kept all their money; in return, he gave them a place to stay, something to eat, and bailed them out after their frequent arrests.

A woman who showed some earnings potential on the street could get promoted to an apartment whore. Dog had two or three flats in upscale buildings around New York, each staffed by half a dozen or so women. They worked by appointment, mostly with visiting businessmen, and had a lot of repeat customers. The pay scale was secretive—"every one of those dumb bitches thinks she's Dog's *special lady*," sneered Amber—but the women mostly charged between fifty and one hundred dollars a pop and kept perhaps 20 percent of what they made, depending on how Dog was feeling that day.

Apartment whores who showed a real aptitude for dishonesty, and who also managed to keep their heads above water when it came to drugs, became boosters. Boosters roamed the country like hordes of voracious locusts, stealing anything that wasn't nailed down and a lot of stuff that was. They used fake identification and stolen cars that could be easily abandoned if necessary.

"Mostly what we do is shoplift," Amber said. "But this ain't like a kid stuffing a candy bar in his pocket. This is some *major* stealing. Some of the girls wear maternity clothes that are empty when they go into the store and full when they come out. Some use a booster girdle, a thing you wear under your clothes that has pockets that you can slip stuff into. Then there's the booster shopping bags. They've got false bottoms. You just put them down on the counter—say, on top of a piece of jewelry or a bottle of expensive perfume—and when you pick the box up, the jewelry or perfume goes with it."

Amber's favorite trick was what she called "salt and pepper."

"I team up with a white girl," she said. "She dresses up real conservative and elegant, like she's from the Junior League or some shit like that. I dress like the worst, low-down kind of street whore, with my tits hanging out and a skirt that barely covers my ass.

"The white girl will go into a place—a jewelry store, or maybe a fancy department store—by herself. She asks to see the pearl neck-laces, or the gold bracelets, or something like that. A minute later, I walk in. I start picking up everything real fast and looking at it. I say 'fuck' a few times. Pretty soon every salesman in the store is hanging on my ass, watching me to make sure I don't steal something. If anybody says anything to me, or even if they look at me funny, I start screaming: 'You racist motherfuckers! You hate black people!' They call the police. I get searched. But they don't find nothing—I ain't taken one goddamn thing—so they gotta let me go.

"And maybe that's about the time that somebody realizes that Blondie has disappeared, along with a few thousand dollars worth of pearls."

———

I spent a lot of time talking to whores over the next few months. Few were as lucid or as cooperative as Amber. Some were not too bright; many had brains that had been turned inside out by pills or booze. Some simply didn't know much about Dog Ferguson. But almost all of them told me something, even if it was just a little bit. Hookers, I found, were like Persian rug merchants—always ready to make a deal. If they could save themselves a little bit of hassle by answering a few questions, they'd do it.

There was a lot of snorting and hoo-hahing around the office about Kerby's "sources." And it caused a certain amount of friction at home, too. One night around 2 A.M. Amber called to tell me some hooker I'd been looking for was back in town. "Yeah, yeah, right, see you tomorrow," I grunted, and hung up.

"Who was that?" Debbie asked sleepily.

"Amber," I mumbled.

"Who's Amber?" Debbie asked, her voice sharper.

"A whore," I replied slurredly. The bedroom's temperature dropped about 20 degrees.

I hated to disappoint everybody, but nothing untoward ever took place during any of these sessions. Only once did a whore try to sweeten the deal with a freebie. She was a cute little girl named Josie, who had been hooking since she ran away from home at age sixteen. Now, at twenty, she was working her way through Ohio State on her back.

I had met with her a couple of times, picking her brain about various elements of the case against Dog, and one afternoon I stopped by her apartment on the north end of town. "Who is it?" she called out when I knocked. When I answered, she yelled back, "I'm in the shower, but the front door's unlocked. Come on in and wait."

Five minutes later she came out the bathroom door, wearing nothing but a T-shirt that failed to reach the Promised Land. "Whatcha thinking?" she asked, her eyes bright.

"I'm thinking you better go put something on," I said.

"Oh, you think you're too good for a girl who's been a hooker," she pouted.

"No," I answered, "I think I'm an FBI agent, and I think I'd like to stay one. So go put something on."

About a week later, an agent, whose name will remain private as an act of mercy, wandered by my desk and saw a photo of Josie I had pulled out of a file.

"Is that one of your hookers?" he asked in astonishment. "Gee, she looks like a college coed."

"She *is* a college coed," I confirmed. "But she's also a hooker."

Agent anonymous rubbed his chin. "Hey Phil, you know I'm trying to get some snitches into the SDS chapter over at Ohio State," he said. I nodded. SDS was one of the more violent campus leftist groups. And two of the nuttiest and most dangerous SDS fugitives, Mark Rudd and Bernardine Dohrn,* had been seen around Ohio State. "Do you think this girl would be willing to join SDS and work as an informant? There'd be some money in it for her."

I suspected Josie could make more in an afternoon from sex than Tom could pay her in a year for politics, but you never know. She might just do it for the excitement. "We can ask her," I said. "Let's go on over to her apartment."

When we arrived, it was the same drill: "I'm in the shower, but the front door is open." We waited in the living room, while I struggled to keep a straight face. This agent was near retirement and acted twenty years older than that, the perfect Victorian gentleman. I couldn't wait to see what he thought of the T-shirt.

Josie came bouncing out of the bathroom in a shirt that was, to my utter incredulity, *shorter* than the one I'd seen last week. "Hi, Phil," she purred. The agent's eyes were like balloons, getting bigger every second.

---

*The high spot of Dohrn's tenure came during one of the group's "war councils," when she actually praised Charles Manson. "Dig it!" she exulted. "First they killed those pigs, then they ate dinner in the same room with them. They even shoved a fork in a victim's stomach. Wild!"

"This is my colleague," I said, wondering if his eyeballs were going to explode.

Josie made sort of a little curtsy. "Pleased to meet you," she said politely. "Won't you please have a seat?" She gestured at a couple of cane rocking chairs behind us. I sat down, but my fellow agent didn't move. And he still hadn't said a word.

I gently nodded toward the rocker.

He glanced at me, then locked his gaze back on Josie. He took a shuffling step backward toward the rocker, then another. But his eyes never left Josie.

Finally he stopped, his back to the chair, and sat down. But he hadn't gone back far enough. His rear barely clipped the front of the chair, which shot backward into the wall and bounced clattering away. Meanwhile he crashed into the floor like a man dropped butt-first from the Eiffel Tower. He sat there amid the wreckage for a moment, blinking, and finally offered: "Pleased to meet you." That was the last time Josie came out of the bathroom in a T-shirt.

Josie's after-school activities gave new meaning to the term "work-study program." But she wasn't the only one. I met half a dozen Ohio State coeds who were hooking their way through school. And I'm not sure all of them intended to stop once they had their diplomas. One whore I talked to had a degree from the University of Toledo. What that suggested to me was that the sociological explanations about women being forced into prostitution by broken homes and poverty are—surprise!—not always true.

Certainly I met plenty of hookers who grew up in homes that were little better than cesspools, including a couple who were second-generation whores, turned out by their own mothers. But I also met one whose father owned a major industrial company. He could have, and would have, put her through Harvard fifty times. Instead, she chose to work for a smarmy little pimp in north Columbus.

In fact, one of my best snitches was a woman who could easily have led a better life. A tall blonde whose body curved at truly stunning angles, she was studying for an art degree at Ohio State. She had been a model, but decided that hooking paid better.

My first encounter with the art student—let's call her Ashley—was an ambush interview. I just showed up unannounced at her house, an old Victorian place near the campus, to ask if she'd talk to me.

"FBI, huh?" she said, shaking her shimmering mane of hair. "I don't know what we could talk about. But come on in."

We walked inside, through a hanging screen of beads, into a small living room dotted with big throw pillows. Fragrant smoke wafted from a small brass incense-burner on an end table. I could hear Bob Dylan droning from a stereo somewhere. Who said the sixties were over?

"So what does the FBI want to talk to me about?" she asked, sitting cross-legged on one of the pillows.

"I know you've been working as a prostitute," I said bluntly. "I'm not interested in you, but I'm building a case against Dog Ferguson. And I know you've worked for him in the past."

"*Prostitution*?" she said, her voice tremulous. "What are you talking about? Just because I have a sex life, that makes me a whore? Wake up, man, it's the twentieth century."

For about a zillionth of a second, I wondered if I had made a mistake. This Bohemian house certainly didn't fit the glittery, disco style of Dog Ferguson's other women. On the other hand, half a dozen other hookers had told me stories about Ashley.

"Look, this will go a lot faster if we cut all the bullshit," I said sharply. "Just go get your book, because I want to go over it with you and ask some questions."

She gave me a startled look. How did I know about the book? Whom had I talked to? Without a word, she rose from the pillow and padded into a room in the back. She returned a moment later with a small appointment book covered in black vinyl. She handed it to me and sat back on the pillow, waiting.

In truth, nobody had told me about Ashley's book. But after talking to numerous hookers, I was certain every whore in America had one. It's a coded list of clients and their favorite sexual hijinks, along with phone numbers of pimps and other hookers. It's usually a hooker's most precious possession.

"You've got a listing here for Leg Man," I said, flipping through the pages. "Who's that?"

"A client, a businessman from Cleveland," she said, biting her lip. "I think his name is Bill. But I don't know anything else about him. He calls when he's in town."

"Okay. Fast Black. Who's that?"

"A pimp from Columbus who's out in L.A. now. He tried to get me to choose him a while back, but I didn't do it. It would have cost too much."

"What do you mean, choose?" I asked in confusion.

"Choosing is when you hook up with a pimp," Ashley explained. "But, with the top guys, you have to buy your way into the family. It's a down payment to prove you're going to be able to earn."

"How much?" I asked.

"It depends on the pimp's status. One of Dog's girls moved to Los Angeles last year and chose a guy out there named Black Jesus. I heard it cost her twenty-five thousand dollars."

I shook my head. The more I learned about whores, the less I understood them. Giving a pimp most of the money you earned was bad enough. But paying him thousands of dollars up front for the privilege of being exploited?

"Didn't Dog object to losing a girl?" I asked.

"There's a kind of an understanding among these guys—players, they like to call themselves," Ashley said. "It's like a fraternity or something. Last year they even had a big costume party, just for players and their ladies. Dog went as the Scarlet Pimpernel, and Black Jesus was one of the Three Musketeers. Sweet Mel was there, too. You know him? He's headquartered on the West Coast, even has some girls working in Hawaii."

"How can he collect the money from girls working all the way in Hawaii?" I interrupted.

"Western Union," she said. "That's how Dog gets his money in

New York, too. Western Union doesn't even use names, just passwords provided by the people who are sending and receiving the money. It's the perfect way to pass around money from dope and hookers."

We kept running through Ashley's book until I hit the initials C. C. It was followed by a series of phone numbers in various area codes, all crossed out. "What's this all about?" I asked, pointing to the entry.

"That's Canada Candy," Ashley said. "She's one of Dog's best boosters. She's been at it for years, stealing all over the country. They say that once at Thanksgiving, she walked out of a supermarket with a frozen turkey stuffed between her legs."

This wasn't the first time I'd heard of Canada Candy, or even the twentieth. She was legendary, both among whores and vice squad detectives. Over the past ten years, she had been arrested in thirty-five or forty cities across the United States, every time under a different name.

Because the charge was always either shoplifting or prostitution, and because she always used a different ID, she usually was out on bail in a few hours. She never stuck around for trials, just hit the road to a different city under a different name. It was only weeks later, when the FBI matched her fingerprints, that the local police department would discover they had been holding a celebrity.

In fact, no one was even certain who Canada Candy really was. Her first arrest was under a similar nom de plume, and the booking form showed that she was born in Canada. But whether that was her real name, or just the first of her assumed identities, no one really knew.

I never laid eyes on Canada Candy, but I saw dozens of the mug shots she left behind in local jails. She was in her late twenties, getting a little plump, with dark hair and impenetrable black eyes. I studied them, wondering why a woman clever enough to outwit half the cops in America wasn't clever enough to see that she was leading a life with a dead end.

The Ferguson investigation spun off in all kinds of odd directions. Going through one whore's book—she was the Toledo grad, a truly beautiful black woman—I found a Washington, D.C., phone listing. "Who does this belong to?" I asked. When she answered with a name, I almost fell out of my chair. Her client was the well-known administrative assistant of a congressman. To me, it was an obvious national security issue; this man was open to blackmail at any time. I sent a teletype off to headquarters, describing what I had found. I never heard anything back.

Not surprisingly, I came across a good deal of pornography during the investigation—some of it clearly obscene even on a bad day at the Supreme Court. The very worst were the snuff films where a girl's breast is actually cut off on camera or a person is killed. I know everybody says these so-called snuff films are fakes, and most of them undoubtedly are. But some of these films were incredibly realistic, and they seemed to have been made on a budget of $1.98. No way had the director been able to afford some fancy Hollywood special effects man.

Most of the truly sick pornography we came across, including the stuff with children, was distributed by a shady outfit located in Cleveland. Wanting to know a little more about it, I decided to visit a man who owned two Columbus adult bookstores.*

I found him behind the counter in one of the stores. "Phil Kerby, FBI," I introduced myself, flashing my FBI credentials.

"Yes, can I help you?" he replied nervously.

"Oh, I just thought I'd stop by to arrest you," I joked—badly, as it turned out. He fainted dead away.

---

*I first encountered the stores during routine surveillance of Soviet diplomats while working on counterintelligence cases. They *loved* those stores. The joke among agents was that, if you were following a Soviet and lost him in traffic, there was no need to worry; just head for the nearest dirty bookstore.

Another name that interested us a lot was Larry Flynt's. Flynt, who lived in Columbus, for years had operated a sleazy chain of establishments called the Hustler Clubs, a sort of low-rent version of the Playboy Clubs. Recently he had started publishing a graphic girlie magazine by the same name.

We didn't think there was much we could do about the magazine, which lay within Supreme Court guidelines on pornography. But there were constant stories about prostitution inside the clubs. If Flynt was moving women around from club to club for the purposes of prostitution, we could probably get him on an ITAR charge.

But nothing ever came of it. Flynt's wife, Althea, the former topless dancer who managed the clubs, had come up with the perfect way to keep us from planting undercover agents inside. Word was, every new employee, male or female, was required to have sex with someone already on board. That was beyond the pale for an FBI agent, even in the post-Hoover era.

Flynt knew we were chasing him, and knew we weren't getting anywhere. To prove there were no hard feelings, he sent a few free issues of *Hustler* to the Columbus FBI office. During the day, those magazines just sat there like dead cockroaches, too vile even to pick up and throw away. But sometimes in the morning, we'd find they had moved from one table to another. The agents who worked in the office late at night, monitoring wiretaps, responded with injured dignity when asked about it. I guess the office just had unusually large and horny mice.

At one point, I thought I had opened a whole new front for the Ferguson investigation. Several of my snitches told me about an apartment house full of hookers near the state capitol, run by an elderly white pimp we'll call Antoin.

But as I checked around the office, it turned out Antoin's operation was no secret. Quite the contrary: It was a cherished Ohio tradition. Half the men in the state, it seemed, had lost their virginity there. But since there was no evidence that interstate commerce was involved, there was no way for the FBI to get a handle on the case.

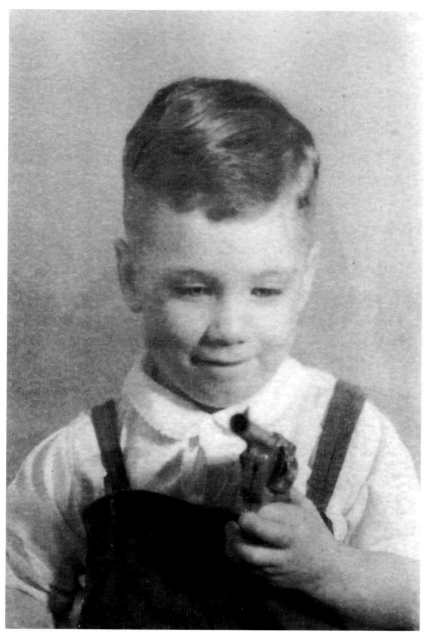

Phil Kerby as a child: a tale of things to come.

Phil Kerby as a varsity football player at Central Michigan University, Mt. Pleasant, Michigan.

Joe Koletar and Phil Kerby. Firing Range, FBI Academy, Quantico, Virginia.

Phil Kerby on the firing line at the FBI Academy.

Loading my Smith & Wesson Model 10 handgun, Firing Range, FBI Academy.

My new agents class, 6/16/69. Note white shirts and white people.

Louis "Louie" Freeh, director of the FBI.

After assaulting his hideout, the Detroit FBI SWAT Team
with Colombian drug suspect in custody.

"Spoon" Thompson poses for a bank surveillance camera.

Harllel Jones (AKA Harllel X) of the Cleveland Afro Set.
(Reprinted with permission from The Plain Dealer @ 1970)

Jimmy Shipman, second from the right, enjoys a cigarette
as his fate is decided by a lineup.

Detroit mob figure Anthony "Tony Jack" Giacalone, on right.

J. Edgar Hoover, "The Director."

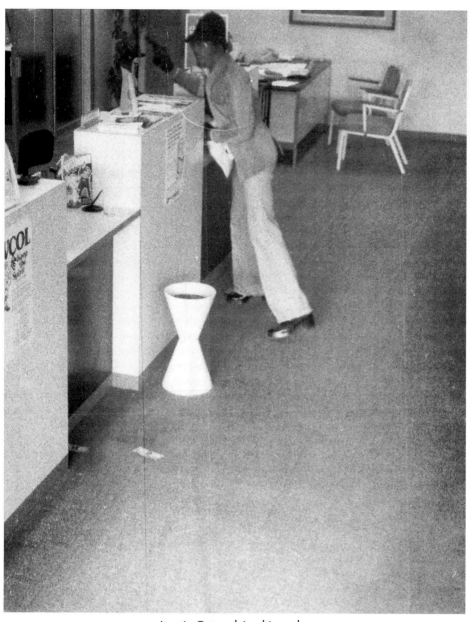

Lonnie Gates plying his trade.

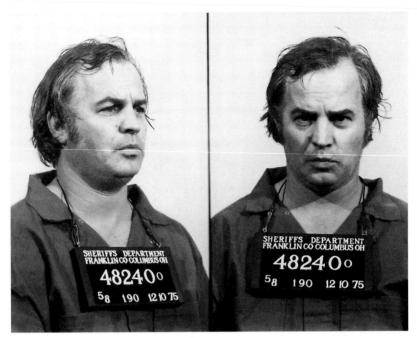

Convicted kidnapper John Garsides.

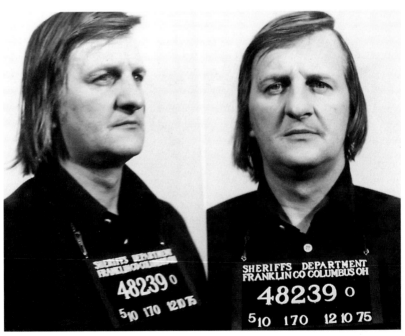

Convicted kidnapper Nabozny.

Glen Schubert pleaded guilty to extorting the Nationwide Insurance Company.

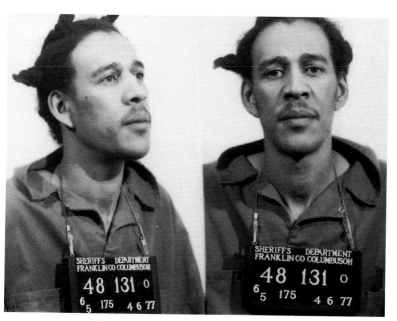

Jimmy Shipman. He kept cropping up like a bad penny.

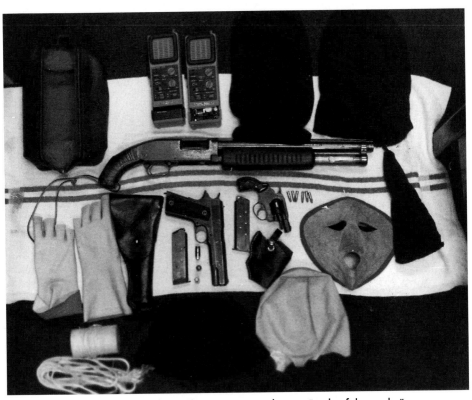

Bank robbery kit from Clare County, Michigan: "tools of the trade."

One of the agents in the office, a former Ivy League football player named Bob Federspiel, had decided to make the best of a bad situation. He had approached Antoin and asked him to become an informant. "No way," Antoin snapped, walking away.

"Yeah?" yelled Federspiel. "Well, who needs you anyway? I've heard you're a thief, a pimp, a scumbag, and a queer!"

Federspiel stormed off. When he got back to the office, half an hour later, the phone was ringing. He picked it up. "Goddamn it, I'm certainly not a queer!" Antoin yelled.

"It was the beginning of a long and beautiful friendship," Federspiel told me.

There was another skirmish between the forces of good and evil that we did win, although I actually felt a little bad about it. Several hookers told me about what they called The Tour. It started in Wheeling, West Virginia, headed north through several Ohio towns, and ended in Cleveland. In each stop, the hookers said, there was a whorehouse where they worked for a few days before moving on.

One of the stops on The Tour was a little town named Newark, twenty miles east of Columbus. None of the hookers I talked to had ever actually worked in Newark, but they all knew the name of the lady who ran the whorehouse there. We'll call her Louise Smith.

Hoping to get a lead on her, I called the FBI agent who ran the one-man office in nearby Zanesville. "You ever heard of Louise Smith?" I asked him.

"Oh, sure," he replied. "She runs the whorehouse over in Newark."

"What?" I sputtered. The agent, apparently worried that I thought he had gone overboard in using the word "whorehouse," defended himself. "Gee, Phil, it's a known whorehouse. Everybody knows about it."

"If everybody knows about it," I said, at last in control of my tongue, "why the hell hasn't it been shut down?" To that there was only silence.

Paul Miller and I drove over there the next afternoon. I was just amazed. The only word that fit this place was *bordello*. It was a gingerbready, two-story house, complete with cupola, right in the middle of town. Inside, everything was red velvet and polished wood.

Louise Smith met us at the door. She looked like the sweetest grandma in eastern Ohio. And she had absolutely no fear of us. "Now, Mr. Kerby, I'm very glad to meet you, but I'm afraid you're quite mistaken," she said, ushering us into a parlor. "No one is violating federal law here, oh no. But you go ahead and talk to my girls and make sure."

Over the settee was a row of five fringed silk pull-ropes. She gave one a delicate, ladylike tug, and a moment later a young woman wearing a satin robe came down the stairs.

"Ruthie, dear, this is Mr. Kerby and Mr. Miller," Louise Smith told her. "They'd like to ask you some questions. I know you'll be truthful with them." She gave me a little wave: *Fire away*.

"What do you for a living, Ruthie?" I asked.

"Well, sir, I guess you could say I'm a whore," she replied politely. "Men have sex with me for money."

"Where did you work before this?" I asked, hoping she'd say West Virginia and give me jurisdiction.

"Nowhere, sir," she said. "I'm a local girl, from right here in Newark."

One by one, Louise Smith's ladies paraded downstairs and admitted to breaking half a dozen state laws every night. But each of them adamantly denied knowing anything about The Tour. Half an hour later, after a cup of Louise Smith's tea, Miller and I were on our way home.

I pulled Louise Smith's rap sheet before we came over here," I said. "It goes back forever, something needs to be done."

"You think if we passed the word to the local cops that we knew about it, they'd do something?"

"It's worth a try."

The next morning I called the agent in Zanesville and suggested he pay a visit to the authorities. He called back: The best little whorehouse in Ohio had been shut down and the girls sent packing.

When I stopped by Miller's desk to give him the news, he looked sad. "I almost wish they would have turned it into a museum or something," he said. "Christ, I feel like we just shot the last buffalo."

Despite all the other leads we generated, I remained fixed like a laser on Dog Ferguson. Nothing his hookers told me lessened my determination to put him in jail.

A lot of them adored him, no question about that. Like any good pimp, Dog had a charming and generous side that he used to manipulate his women. Every single one of them mentioned the time he came to Columbus and bought seven pink Mustangs for his favorite whores. Then, in his pink Cadillac, he led them on caravans around the city.

But Dog used fear to keep his women in line, too. Several hookers told me that women who balked at turning over all their earnings, or wanted to leave when it didn't suit Dog, were branded on their backs or butts with a red-hot wire hanger. To be perfectly fair, the stories were always second- or third-hand; I never talked with anyone who claimed to have seen it happen, much less experienced it. But the mere fact that so many of the hookers believed it told me something about Dog's dark side.

I remembered that dark side every time I thought about what happened to Toby DeShong. Toby DeShong was Dog's very first whore, an exotic mixture of black and Asian blood that still made men tingle years after they had seen her. Talk to Toby, everyone said, Toby can serve up Dog to you with an apple in his mouth.

The problem was that Toby was long gone. No one had seen her in Columbus in years. There were rumors that she was in New York, and I passed some leads to the Bureau office there, but nothing came of it. I carried an old black-and-white snapshot of her in my coat pocket, a grudging gift from a hooker, and sometimes I pulled it out to show around in bars where the whores gathered, to no avail.

One evening Miller and I were driving downtown, through an area where some of Dog's girls worked the streets, when I saw a woman duck into a bar. "It's her!" I chattered excitedly. "Miller, it's Toby DeShong! We gotta go back there."

"Give me a break, Kerby," he replied, making no effort to stop the car. "You've never even laid eyes on her. You wouldn't know Toby DeShong from Lily Langtry."

"I'm telling you, that was her," I insisted. But his (highly scatological) skepticism made me start doubting myself. It was probably just wishful thinking. The bar's lights grew dim in the rear-view mirror, and I didn't insist that we go back.

But about a week later, one of my hooker snitches called me. "Toby DeShong's back in town," she said. "She's got an apartment and some kind of a legit job. Looks like she's here to stay. I got her home phone number if you want it."

I called her that night to tell her I wanted to talk. "All I'm asking is ten minutes," I told her. "If you'll agree to see me, we can do it in private, at your apartment. If you won't agree, I'll show up where you work and embarrass the hell out of you." It was a little white lie—I didn't know where she worked—but it was effective. She agreed to see me the next day.

Whatever Toby had been doing the past few years, it had paid well. Her northside apartment was right out of *Architectural Digest*, lots of blond wood and rich leather. She didn't look bad, either: In her early forties, her once-spectacular figure was turning slightly matronly, but her cinnamon skin and obsidian eyes had lost nothing to time.

Those eyes had a frightened look as I explained that I needed her help on Dog. And her voice wavered when she spoke. "I've got to think about it," she said haltingly. I had the feeling she was choosing her words carefully, trying not to commit to anything, but trying even harder not to make me mad. "It's been a long time, and I have to collect my thoughts. It's a very complicated situation."

I shook my head sympathetically. After chasing her for so long, I was determined to take it slow. If she knew even half as much as everybody said, I'd be able to put Dog not just *in* prison but *under* it. "Take a few days, Toby," I urged her. "Think it over. I'm sure you'll see it's the best thing. Why don't I come back in a week?" She nodded, and I was on my way.

Three days later, I got a call from the same hooker who had tipped me off that Toby was in town. "Did you go talk to her?" the woman asked nervously.

"You know I'm not going to answer that," I said. "You want me to tell people I've been talking to *you*? Anyway, why are you asking?"

"Because Toby's dead," the woman said, her voice a mixture of anger and fear. "They say she fell down the stairs of her apartment and broke her neck. Sure be kind of funny if she all of a sudden became accident-prone after meeting with you, wouldn't it?"

I called the Columbus PD's homicide squad. It was true: Toby had died in a fall. The police were treating it as an accident.

I told them who she was and that she had been thinking of co-operating with me. They took another look around, but came to the same conclusion. There just wasn't any evidence of foul play, a homicide detective told me.

And probably there wasn't. But out on the street, the hookers always doubted that it was an accident. I guess, deep in my heart, I did, too.


With so much of Dog's business centered in New York, I decided to go have a look myself. Since I didn't know the city, the New York office assigned two agents, Phil Reilly and Eddie Ancin, to help me cover leads.

The first day, I had an interview scheduled at 10 A.M. with a former hooker at her apartment in Manhattan. Reilly looked at the address and nodded. "Great," he said. "Eddie will go over at nine. Then you and I can follow at ten."

"Why does Eddie have to get there so early?" I asked, confused. "This girl is willing to see us—she's not going to run. And even if she did, Eddie doesn't know what she looks like."

"He's not standing guard," Reilly explained. "He's going to look for a parking space. Then, when we get there, he'll give us the space and he'll go on to the site of the next interview."

"You're shitting me," I said flatly, certain that these big-city agents were having fun with the Midwestern hick. But they weren't. We used a talented and college-educated, $40,000-a-year FBI agent as a parking attendant. And every night, I got down on my knees and said effusive thanks to God for keeping me out of a New York assignment.

One of the most important contacts I made in New York was the head of the NYPD vice squad, Bob Rothstein. German-born, he was a classic tough-guy cop, the kind you see in old gangster pictures. How tough? His hobbies were shark-fishing and he spoke admiringly of German thumbscrews. As much as he admired the thumbscrews, he did concede the benefits of modern technology.

"We had some great success with our first Xerox machine," he recalled. "I would get pimps up here, and they'd be sitting right there in that chair, lying their asses off: 'No, Mr. Rothstein, I don't even *know* any prostitutes.'

"I'd say: 'Okay, Velvet, we're gonna give you a lie-detector test with our new polygraph machine. And if you're telling the truth, fine, but if you're not, I'm going to cut your balls off.'

"One of the detectives would hold the guy's hand over the screen of the Xerox machine. When he answered the question again, the detective would punch the copy button and make a photocopy of the pimp's hand. Then another guy would come in and study the photocopy, like he was reading it. After a minute, he'd say: 'He's lying.' You should have heard them scream. We actually got some confessions that way."

Rothstein had been following Dog Ferguson ever since the Earth cooled, and he had an encyclopedic knowledge of Dog's operations. "This guy is the biggest pimp in America, no question," he told me. After a week in New York, I didn't doubt it. Dog had four or five apartments in a luxurious high-rise building in the east seventies. The complex doubled as a setup for a cluster of apartment whores as well as Dog's corporate headquarters. From here he moved hookers, con artists, and booster squads around the U.S. like malign chess pieces.

My last day in New York, Rothstein took me over to see what the vice squad called The Stroll. It was a couple of blocks in mid-town Manhattan near a grand old hotel, now turning seedy. Though it was the middle of the afternoon, a dozen haggard, empty-eyed women plodded up and down the street, croaking "hey, baby" in a pathetic burlesque of a hooker's come-on. "A bunch of them work for Dog," Rothstein murmured in disgust.

I watched them for a long time, wishing the high school kids who applauded him could be here. This, not the fur coats and gold chains, was Dog's real legacy.


Soon after my return from New York, I visited the U.S. attorney's office in Columbus to talk to Bob Zitko, the chief assistant U.S. attorney in Columbus, who, while well-educated and brilliant, came across as imperious. "Forget it," he said, shoving the investigative files back over the desk to me. "We're not going into court with this."

"What are you talking about?" I asked, stunned. I had been afraid he might ask for six months' more work. I never *dreamed* he would pitch the whole case out.

"What I'm talking about is, you don't have a winnable case here," he said, acid dripping from his voice. "There's not enough hard evidence."

"What do you mean, hard evidence?" I demanded. "We've got hotel records, bank records, phone records, arrest records . . ."

"Barely a handful. Mostly what you've got is the word of a bunch of whores. Half of them won't show up to testify at all, half of those who do will change their story on the witness stand, and no juror will believe the rest."

My jaw clenched to keep from screaming, I stomped out of Zitko's office. There was some truth in what he said, I knew that. Whores *were* unreliable, crummy witnesses. But a couple of them, I felt, could hold their own, and I thought we had enough paper to flesh out the case and make it stick.

For a couple of weeks I pondered what it would take to change Zitko's mind. We weren't going to find much more in the way of records; prostitution is mostly a cash business. I could search for more whores, hoping sheer numbers might persuade him, but that didn't seem likely.

Then it occurred to me. What if we could use Dog's own words against him? What if we could record him on a wiretap?

The FBI had been tapping telephones in national security cases (as defined, rather flexibly, by J. Edgar Hoover) for years, but wiretap evidence became admissable in regular criminal trials only in 1968. And, six years later, we still weren't doing many of them.* The main reason was the truly awesome amount of documentation the Justice Department wanted on a case before it would ask a federal judge to approve the tap. (The complexity of operating the taps didn't help, either.)

I wasn't sure a tap would work against Dog. Veteran criminals, especially those who've been investigated over and over again, are usually smart enough to speak only in code over the telephone. Sometimes you don't even hear code words, just: I'm going to a phone booth, call me at such and such a number.

But, from the long-distance records we had collected, we knew that Dog spent hours and hours on the phone with his Columbus associates. They couldn't be talking code all the time, could they? Maybe Dog had beaten law enforcement so many times that he had grown overconfident. It was worth a try.

It took me days to organize my evidence into an affidavit that was so long I just about gave up counting the pages and just weighed it

---

*The real growth in criminal wiretaps, ironically, didn't begin until Janet Reno— supposedly a bona fide liberal—became attorney general. In 1993, her first year in office, the number increased 32 percent. In 1994, it jumped another 23 percent. Even so, in 1995—the year I retired from the FBI—fewer than four hundred criminal wiretaps were approved.

instead. I wanted to place the tap on the telephone of Dog's top lieutenant in Columbus. Long-distance records showed hundreds of calls every month from his apartment to Dog's headquarters in New York, and I was sure there were an equal number going the other way.

The application for the tap would have to be approved by Leonard Sands, a federal prosecutor with the Organized Crime Strike Force headquartered in Cleveland. Lugging a large cardboard box that contained my affidavit, I arrived a few minutes early for our appointment and took a seat in the small reception area outside his office. Another agent from the Columbus office, one of the guys marking time for retirement, was sitting there too.

"What's in the box, Kerby?" he snickered. "You got Dog Ferguson in there?"

I managed a tiny smile, but not easily. I knew some of the older agents in Columbus, the same ones who dared me to take the case, were beginning to talk. I had been on the case for nearly a year and a half, and Dog was still on the streets. Ha ha, guess you stepped on your dick, youngster. Guess you don't fly around in a cape after all.

I didn't feel any better after talking to Sands. He was a tiny, dapper man with wavy black hair who spoke in such precise sentences that they sometimes sounded rehearsed. We went over the evidence for a couple of hours, but he wasn't persuaded.

"Your informants aren't good enough," he said. "A judge isn't going to let you secretly listen in on private conversations based on what you've got here. A wiretap is the most intrusive thing we do, much more serious than a search warrant."

"Damn it, Leonard, you guys are much tougher than the judges," I complained. "They approve almost every application."

"And the reason they do is that we screen out all the weak ones," he replied, a gentle reproof in his voice.

It was a long drive back to Columbus. I felt I'd gotten a fair hearing, and Sands's decision was based on his reading of the evidence, not his concern for his image. But I still didn't like it.

*Ichabod Crane*, I thought, *that's who it is! He looks like Ichabod Crane.* I had been sitting across a desk from the U.S. attorney for half an hour, making a last desperate plea to revive the Dog Ferguson case, but my concentration kept breaking. He reminded me of someone, but I just couldn't put my finger on it. Now that I had the name, I wondered why it took me so long to think of it. Tall, thin, and stooped, an unruly mop of white hair and a bobbing Adam's apple: William Milligan was a dead ringer for Ichabod Crane.

Coming to see him had probably used up my testosterone for the next six months. Going over the chief assistant U.S. attorney's head to his boss was an incredibly risky political ploy. If it made Milligan angry, I'd be back to chasing military deserters next week, because I'd never get another case into federal court.

But Milligan had a reputation as both a gentleman and a smart, tough prosecutor. The more I thought about it, the more I couldn't believe he was the kind of guy who tiptoed away from tough cases.

The meeting had been okay so far. I'd been half-afraid he'd agreed to see me just to dress me down for questioning his assistant's judgment. But that wasn't the case; he was open and friendly, but noncommittal. I marshaled my arguments for one final thrust.

"I think one of the problems I've had getting anyone to give this case a shot is that everybody thinks whores and pimps are small-time, vice squad stuff," I said as we locked eyes. "But there's nothing small-time about Dog Ferguson. He's running a coast-to-coast network of whores and drug dealers, and he's rubbing our nose in it. How can we let him do that? How can we let him tell every high school kid in Columbus that dirty money is easy money? Why shouldn't they all become pimps and dope dealers, too, if we're not going to say any differently?"

"Do you have anything more, anything at all." Milligan asked.

"I might," I said. "An idea, at least. 'Diamond' Darryl Agers is in federal prison now on a drug charge. Why don't we put him in front of a grand jury and immunize him?"

Milligan's face lit up. I allowed myself a small, proud smile. It *was* a good idea. Diamond Darryl was a New York pimp who did a lot of business with Dog. A few months earlier, he had been caught red-handed with a couple of kilos of cocaine that federal drug agents believed belonged to Dog. But Diamond Darryl loyally took the rap and pled guilty.

What I was proposing was to grant him immunity from further prosecution and then question him in front of a grand jury about his business with Dog. If he refused to answer, the judge could jail him for contempt for the full term of the grand jury, up to eighteen months. And then we could do it all over again.

Ordinarily prosecutors are stingy about granting immunity. I don't blame them. It's like a get-out-of-jail-free card that means they can never be punished for any of the crimes that you force them to testify to. But Diamond Darryl was already in jail; we wouldn't be letting him ride off into the sunset.

"Do you think it will work?" Milligan asked. "This cuts both ways, you know. Since he's already in jail, maybe he'll figure he has nothing to lose if he refuses to testify."

"I'm not sure," I admitted. "But if he starts thinking that we're going to do this every eighteen months for the rest of his life, and he'll never get out, I think we've got a good chance. He's already looking at a couple of years for the cocaine beef. There's no such thing as honor among pimps—if they were honorable, they wouldn't *be* pimps. If we put enough pressure on Diamond Darryl, I think he'll roll over."

Milligan sat quietly for a moment, his narrow chin resting on his hand. "All right," he said. "This is worth a shot." As I stepped into the hallway, I wanted to sing and shout. Dog Ferguson was going to jail.


Diamond Darryl's attorney warned us that he wouldn't speak to the grand jury. He didn't. He was a good-looking guy; his ebony skin set off his big smile, which he flashed often, even at cops. But there was something cold about it. Watching him, I felt that if I turned my head, he'd slit my throat.

Despite his refusal to testify, we got the grand jury to indict Dog on a violation of the Mann Act, the old law about transporting a woman across state lines for immoral purposes. That was no great achievement. Many grand juries will indict a cigar-store Indian if the prosecutor asks them to. A trial would be another matter. Despite my bravado with the prosecutors, I was nervous. The whores really might crumble on the witness stand, and without them there was no case at all.

The trial was set for March 31, 1975, more than sixteen months since the November morning I pulled Dog's file. We immunized Diamond Darryl again and transferred him to the Franklin County jail in Columbus, hoping to get across the idea that the contempt citations were going to keep rolling in.

I had also brought in Bob Rothstein from New York to testify as an expert witness on prostitution. We chatted a little bit about a few of his newest thumbscrew acquisitions. "Too bad you didn't bring some along. We could take them in and then discuss the concept of immunity with Diamond Darryl." I joked the day before the trial began. "Maybe he'd start seeing things our way."

"That's not a bad idea," Rothstein said, standing up. "Where's his cell?"

"No thumbscrews," I laughed.

"No thumbscrews," Rothstein agreed. "But let me talk to the guy. I know him. I'll bet I can talk some sense into him."

I had Diamond Darryl brought to an interrogation room. Rothstein went in, minus his hardware, and shut the door. Half an hour later, he came out smiling. "I believe Darryl is in the grips of a seizure of good citizenship," he said. "I believe you'll find he's willing to discuss his business associates with the jurors." I glanced inside the room; a sullen Diamond Darryl nodded a grudging "yes."

"What did you tell him?" I asked Rothstein, genuinely curious.

"I told him that he's a player," Rothstein said, "and for a player, New York is the major leagues. I told him that one of these days he would be out of jail, and he would want to come back to New York. And I told him New York is my turf, and if he ever expected to come back there again without me being all over his ass all day, every day, he'd better tell the truth on the stand tomorrow."

The next day, when the defense found out Darryl was going to testify, Dog Ferguson pled guilty in exchange for a three-year prison sentence. In the blink of an eye, a criminal career that flourished under the frustrated eyes of the biggest law enforcement agencies in America was over. He sent a long row of dominoes toppling. Eventually we got convictions against four other pimps.

I have often thought about that chat between Rothstein and Diamond Darryl. Knowing Rothstein, I wondered if they discussed any adventurous practices like swimming in the East River or hanging out skyscraper windows. But Diamond Darryl never complained. And when he came out of the interrogation room, his thumbs were still firmly attached to his hands. I checked.

# 7

# MONK

I could feel it as soon as I opened the door, like a crackle of static electricity running up my fingers. Something was up. The Columbus office of the FBI was never slow—contrary to what they thought in New York and Los Angeles, the Midwest had its fair share of kidnappers, extortionists, and bank robbers—but something special must have come in by teletype from another office that needed our help. As I walked to my desk, I heard the indistinct buzz of a dozen murmured conversations around the room. "What's going on?" I asked one of the other agents as I flipped through my phone messages.

"Cleary's got something about a fugitive 91," he replied, using FBI code for bank robber. "Sounds like a nasty one—won't be taken alive, all the usual bullshit."

Glancing around the room, I looked for Dick Cleary, who ran the office's bank robbery detail, while I mentally shuffled through a series of arguments about why he should give me a piece of this case. I didn't have anything major on my plate today—just a couple of 31s, as they were called in the Bureau, leads on Mann Act prostitution cases and God knows I'd had enough of those lately.

The truth was, though, that even if I'd had a full schedule, I would have nagged Cleary to deal me in anyway. At age twenty-nine, a few weeks short of my seventh anniversary with the FBI, I was one of the hardest chargers in the Columbus office. I didn't want to miss any action, ever, and I was still young and cocky enough to imagine that the war on crime couldn't be won without my help. Another agent, thinking he was out of my earshot, had recently observed that "Kerby thinks if he can just flap his arms fast enough, he'll be able to fly." If that was off-target, it wasn't by much.

I spotted Cleary across the room, huddled with several agents. But before I could even take a step in his direction, he motioned me toward him. Swiftly I went to his side.

"It looks like we've got a visiting bank robber," Cleary said, stuffing a yellow teletype into my hand. "A guy named Monk Huffman." As I scanned the messages from other offices, I noticed Huffman's real name was Edward, and I wondered where he ever picked up that nickname. About the only thing he had in common with real monks was that, like them, he had spent most of his life in spartan, cloistered places. In Huffman's case, however, we weren't talking about a monastery, but the Ohio prison system. For all but a few months of the past sixteen years, the thirty-four-year-old Huffman had been serving time, early on for larcenies and later for armed robberies.

Now there was an arrest warrant charging him with the robbery of a bank in New Lebanon, across the state, six months earlier. He was also a suspect in three bank jobs in Dayton and another one in Tampa, Florida. It seemed, however, that Huffman had tired of prison accommodations; one of the teletypes said he had told relatives he would die before going back to prison and should be considered A&D, armed and dangerous.

The teletypes from Tampa contained three different leads that needed to be checked out. Two were close friends of Huffman's in the Columbus area who probably knew where he was staying; the third was a man named Raymond Rollins, described as an acquaintance.

"I'll handle the first two," Cleary said, tapping his finger on the teletypes. "I want you to go with Scotty and stake out this guy Rollins's house. Decker will join you later, but he's got some other stuff to take care of first." Abruptly he turned and walked away, which did not surprise me. Cleary had a lot of sterling qualities—a Brown graduate, he was both physically and intellectually tough—but loquacity was not one of them. Some of the guys referred to him as The Man With No Lips.

Emmett Scott, my partner of the day, was already waiting at the door. There was a spring in my step as we walked downstairs to the building garage. It was the big case of the day, and I was in on it, even if it was only around the edges. Even a small corner of a bank robbery case was better than another day chasing hookers.

"I might as well drive," Scott offered as we entered the garage. "My Bucar's got a full tank." It was a canary yellow four-door Ford with black-wall tires that couldn't have screamed "cop" any louder if we'd painted the word on the doors, but the rest of the Bucars were equally obvious.

"Okay," I replied. "But let me get my shotgun out of the trunk of my car."

Scott waited patiently as I fumbled with my key ring, first to unlock the trunk, then to open the chain that had been installed for extra security. I mumbled curses as I always did when struggling with the crotchety lock on the chain. If this were an emergency, if Scott was a fugitive with a gun, instead of a fellow FBI agent, he would have been able to shoot me, empty my wallet, and lead the prayers at my funeral in the time it took to retrieve the shotgun. No matter. The rule was that the guns had to be kept locked up at all times, rather than to run the risk of embarrassment that would result if the weapon was stolen. Another policy devised by stupid old men in the FBI headquarters who never got any dirt under their fingernails.

With the shotgun safely stowed in Scott's back seat, we headed for the north side of Columbus. The house we were going to stake out was just off High Street, a long expanse of pockmarked bars and dingy pawnshops. The once-prim town houses running along the side streets were seedy and drab now, filled mostly with the down-on-their-luck flotsam and jetsam of urban life: transients, hookers, small-time drug traffickers.

Here and there you could see the fearful faces of elderly people peeking out from shuttered windows, the unlucky ones who didn't sell out and flee when the exodus to the suburbs began a dozen years ago. Now they were trapped, prisoners of a neighborhood that was sinking around them. The whole place reeked of despair and hopelessness.

We found the block where Rollins lived and made one slow pass. Nothing was stirring among the ragged brick town houses; I had the feeling that most of the people who lived here made their living at night. There was a parking lot directly across the street from the house, but we would have been too obvious there. We saw an open spot about three hundred feet down the street, and Scott pulled in.

"Nice neighborhood," Scott observed in his thick Virginia drawl. "I could probably pick up some freelance work here."

I laughed. Scott was a tech, an agent trained in picking locks and placing wiretaps.

"Don't worry, I don't think we'll be here long," I replied. "We'll enjoy the ambiance for a couple of hours, and then Cleary will call us and tell us he's got the guy."

Scott nodded. We both knew Cleary was the best all-around agent in the office, and his skill at dragging information out of a hostile source during interrogation was legendary. By the end of the day, Cleary would probably know every detail of Monk Huffman's life, right down to whether he slept on his back or his stomach.

We settled into the routine of surveillance. One of us peered down the street toward Rollins's house through binoculars, while the other kept his eyes moving all around the car. Periodically we switched roles. Meanwhile, we chatted casually about the Cincinnati Reds, our kids, and the latest stupid directive from headquarters. We ran the car's air-conditioning until we were afraid the engine would overheat, and then we put the windows down and sweated, bitching about how unseasonably hot it was for April. We were alert, but relaxed; we both figured we had a better chance of being struck by a comet than of bumping into Monk Huffman. Random surveillances just don't bear fruit very often.

In fact, if really pressed, I would have had to admit that the whole assignment was kind of slipshod. We had no plan, nothing worked out for contingencies. What if Rollins came out of the house, got in his car, and drove away? Would we follow him, or wait at the house to see if Huffman showed up? What if we followed him and he went into one of the scruffy little High Street bars? Should we follow him inside? And if we did, how would we pretend to be anything else but FBI agents? Our white shirts, dark pants, dark ties, and boot camp haircuts didn't allow for many plausible cover stories in a neighborhood like this one.

In the two years since Hoover's death in 1972, a few FBI policies had begun to change—most notably, we had a few woman agents now—but the Boy Scout dress and grooming codes were untouched. The rules didn't bother me as much as they did some of the other guys—my style was fairly conservative anyway—but there were times like this when the Bureau's fetish for conformity put us at a disadvantage in doing our jobs.

As my eyes swept up and down the street, I wondered how many people had already pegged us as cops. Two grown-up Ken dolls, sitting inside a stripped-down gas-guzzler car on a sweltering day, wearing white shirts and ties. *Oh, probably not too many*, I thought to myself. *Merely anyone over the age of four who's looked out a window and seen us.* The only thing we had going for us was that people in a neighborhood like this one are invariably alienated from it. Nobody was going to run over to Rollins's house and say, "Hey, did you know there are two FBI scumbags watching you from a car down the street?" This was strictly in-your-face territory.

As I write this, in 1997, I'm faintly amazed at how primitive the Bureau's methods were twenty years ago. We thought we were the best law-enforcement agency in the world, and maybe we were, but in retrospect it seems like a case of damning with faint praise.

To do this same surveillance today, we would send in a team of agents dressed for the street to blend in to the neighborhood. We would have consulted with the police department, including the sergeant in charge of that precinct, to see what anyone knew about Rollins. All the FBI vehicles involved (and they would be disguised, too) would have had radios tuned to the police frequency, so we could call for quick backup if needed. We would have a detailed set of contingency plans, including a SWAT team ready to move at the first sign of serious trouble. And we would have gotten the Ohio prison system to fax us some photos of Monk Huffman so we knew exactly who we were looking for.

But on that day in 1974, we didn't have any of those things. The Columbus police didn't know a thing about our operation, nor did we have any way to communicate with them; the radio in our car would summon only other FBI agents. With just twenty-two of us scattered across a city of 550,000, that meant the cavalry might be slow to arrive if we needed it.

And we had no photos of Huffman. The description we were working from—he was about five-foot-nine and medium build—would have been completely worthless if not for one detail: He was almost completely bald. In those days before heavy metal and punk rock led people down some strange fashion paths, we weren't likely to run across many bald thirty-four-year-olds.


It was my turn to use the binoculars. Taking a quick scan of the horizon before settling them on the town house, I noticed the Ohio National Bank's big boxy building. I chuckled softly. The place was like a magnet for robbers; I'd worked several holdups there myself. Maybe it was drawing Monk Huffman now, like a beacon in the dark.

Certainly there was something unnatural going on between Huffman and banks. Why else would he keep robbing them, even when he obviously wasn't very good at it? Nearly half his life had been spent in jail. Every time he got out, the cops picked him up a few months later and put him back in jail. I'd run across other Monk Huffmans, other perpetual losers at the game of crime. I didn't understand them. Could they be that stupid? Or did they have some unfathomable need to be caught? Certainly a guy like Huffman made you wonder. One of the teletypes that morning mentioned that Huffman's brother was a reporter for one of the Dayton papers. He had a reputation as an intelligent, thoughtful writer. Why did the two kids turn out so differently? As my seventh anniversary with the FBI approached, I didn't have a clue to any of the answers. Sometimes it seemed the more I learned about crime, the less I knew.

Scott stirred in his seat, breaking my reverie. "I thought I saw something up to the right," he murmured. Unimpressed, I kept scanning the house with the binoculars. "What the hell?" Scott said, his voice much sharper. "There's somebody coming out of that parking lot. Where'd he come from? No cars have pulled in there."

This time I swung the binoculars over to the right. A man was striding rapidly out of the lot toward Rollins's house. As he glanced furtively from side to side, the top of his head glistened in the sun like a large cue ball.

"Holy shit!" I gasped. "It looks like him." As I spoke, he looked straight at us, seeming to lock with my eyes right through the binoculars. In his gaze I saw awareness; he knew who we were. He sprang toward the house.

"He's made us!" I warned Scott, and turned to grab my shotgun from the back seat. As I racked a shell into the chamber, a tall man came walking out of the town house. From his height, I was certain this must be Rollins. He quickly climbed into a beat-up old Dodge and headed our way. I held the shotgun in my lap, ready to raise it and blast away if he tried anything, but the car continued on past us. From the way he stared at us as he passed, I was sure Rollins knew who we were, too, but that didn't matter; he wasn't our target, Huffman was.

"Get on the radio, get us some backup," Scott said tersely as he started the car, ready to roll if Huffman came back out of the house. Keeping one hand on the shotgun, I picked up the microphone of the car radio. "CI-75 to 392," I said, keeping my voice steady. Although I was calling the office, I knew every FBI car in Columbus would hear me. "The subject's here. He made us. We're going to have to take him."

Almost the instant the words were out of my mouth, Tom Decker, the other agent assigned to work with us, pulled up. With a gesture of his eyes and chin, he let us know that he'd heard my call and would follow our lead. Before we could speak to him, though, trouble appeared up the street. Rollins's car reappeared after circling the block. It rolled to a stop, the engine idling, in the middle of the street directly in front of the town house.

"Let's take him!" I urged Scott. He nodded. If Huffman got into that car, we would have to try to ram it, which is a lot more dangerous than it looks on television. And if that didn't work, the only alternative would be a high-speed chase through downtown Columbus in heavy mid-morning traffic, an invitation to catastrophe.

Scott popped the car into gear and we careened down the street like teenage hot-rodders. Brakes squealing, we pulled up nose-to-nose with the old Dodge, just a couple of feet away. As I jumped out of the car, shotgun pointed toward the Dodge, Huffman stepped out of the town house onto the brick porch. He took one hasty look at us and bolted back inside, the screen door banging explosively behind him.

But I couldn't follow him. Five feet in front of me, Rollins was reaching under the front seat of the Dodge. "Let's see your hands!" I barked. "Hands on the dash!" I had the shotgun trained on his face, safety off, my finger poised on the trigger. Rollins, his expression blank, kept groping under the seat. "Hands on the dash!" I shouted again, but he didn't stop. For the first time in my career outside the training range, I squeezed a trigger.

"Okay! Okay!" Rollins shouted, pulling his hands into the air. My finger, half a hair's breadth from detonating a shot that would have blown his head off, eased. He put his hands on the dash. For the first time, there was fear on his face.

Cars were fishtailing to a halt all around us as other agents arrived. Beside me I could hear Tom Forsha mumbling "Oh shit, oh shit." Glancing out of the corner of my eye, I looked to see if something was wrong, but Forsha just seemed to be delivering his general appraisal of the situation.

"Tom, take the shotgun," I asked him. When he had it aimed, I stepped forward and jerked Rollins out of the car, then slammed him down on the hood and slapped handcuffs around his wrists. "He's yours, Tom," I said, taking back my shotgun and stepping toward the house. I was expecting a barrage of gunfire from inside at any moment. Huffman had said he wasn't going back to prison, and here we were to take him. Something had to give.

From somewhere a bare-chested and confused-looking teenage boy had appeared near the front porch of the town house. "Give me that!" Tom Decker shouted, snatching the shotgun from my hand. He sprinted across toward the kid and protectively knocked him to the ground. "Stay down!" he ordered the boy, holding the shotgun's mouth against his back. I glanced at the kid in confusion—who was he and what did he have to do with all this?—but before I could make any sense of it, a rapid series of three explosions split the air. Both Decker and I hit the ground. I pointed my revolver as I searched the town house's windows and doors for the source of the shots.

"It's just Goodwin's car!" somebody yelled from the street. I turned my head, my pistol still trained on the house, and then let loose a huge sigh. Bud Goodwin, the supervisor in charge of the Columbus office, had just arrived, and his notoriously balky Bucar had signaled its excitement by backfiring three times. There was no gunfire—yet.

By now there were seven or eight agents gathered at the front of the town house. Two others had staked out the back door, which opened onto an alley. We huddled briefly behind a Bucar in the street, all of us keeping our eyes on the house.

"If there was any chance that this guy was going to surrender and come out on his own, it would have happened by now," I told Goodwin. "We're going to have to go in and get him."

"All right," he agreed. "Do we know who else might be inside?"

"No idea whatsoever," I replied.

"Hey, I've got a vest with me," somebody said. "Do you want it, Phil?" When I nodded, one of the other agents retrieved it from his car.

In those days, the Bureau had no comfortable lightweight vests like the ones now common in every police department. The vest I strapped on was a military model, with inch-thick ceramic plates sewn inside olive green canvas. When I took a few experimental steps, I felt like a knight lumbering around in a suit of armor.

"I don't know, Phil, I'm not too sure about this," Scott said, eying me gravely.

"What?" I asked, worriedly checking the straps on the vest. "What's wrong?"

"Your tie clashes," he replied. "I think you better get a green one in case somebody from headquarters stops by." Everybody laughed. No crisis is ever so serious that a good FBI agent loses his capacity for tasteless jokes.

The town house was two stories high with a basement half above-ground. To enter, we had to walk up a half-flight of stairs to a small wooden porch topped by a small mansard roof. The front door was open, but our view was obscured by a screen door. If Huffman was waiting inside, we would be easy targets as soon as we stepped into the doorway, silhouetted against the bright morning sun. The prudent approach would have been to keep the house surrounded while trying to talk to Huffman on the telephone or through a bullhorn, but that wasn't the way the Bureau did things in those days. We started up the stairs.

Goodwin, standing off to the left side of the porch, prepared to flip open the screen door. Decker, still armed with my shotgun, and I, revolver drawn, would be the first ones through the door. As it popped open, we lunged inside, Decker going left while I moved right. We found ourselves inside a large open room that contained nothing but a couple of small pieces of furniture—no hiding places. I could see through to the kitchen, where a terrified old man and woman huddled against the refrigerator. "He's not in here," the old man called in a tremulous voice. *Liar*, I thought. Where else could he be? Silently I approached the staircase to the second floor, Goodwin right behind me.

When we reached the landing, we could see down a long, bare hallway, sunlight flooding through a window at the end. There were two solid oak doors, both closed. As we walked toward them, everything else evaporated, like the wisps of a fading dream. There were no agents milling around downstairs, no J. Edgar Hoover, no FBI, no four-year-old son, no pregnant wife: just Bud, Phil, and the door, wrapped in a silent cocoon of concentration. Goodwin and I didn't speak, except through an eye contact and body language that seemed more eloquent to me than words ever had.

Goodwin squatted at the left side of the door and put his hand on the knob. At my nod, he twisted the knob and shoved the door open in a single fluid motion, while I lunged forward and swept the room with my revolver. The room was completely empty, not a stick of furniture inside. But on the opposite wall was a closet, the door closed. We crept toward it, listening for telltale squeaks inside. We couldn't hear a thing. Bud pulled the door open from the left while I covered it with my revolver. But it was as empty as the rest of the room.

We returned to the hallway, where we hesitated for a moment at the second door. Huffman had to be inside. Other agents had surely cleared the basement, a single large room, by now. There was no place else for him to hide. I stared at the last door, willing it to give up its secrets, to no avail. As Goodwin took up his position on the left once more, I raised my gun again and took a deep breath. When I nodded, he turned the knob and shoved . . . but nothing happened. The door wouldn't open.

I quickly took a couple of steps backward. Goodwin, seeing what I was going to do, trained his gun on the door. With two running steps, I smashed my right foot into the door and it slammed backward into the wall with a mighty crash. I swung my revolver up—but there was no one inside, just a couple of old twin beds. The only closet was already open.

"He's not up here," Goodwin shouted. All at once the rest of the world popped back into focus; I could hear the shuffle of feet and the muted babble of half a dozen conversations downstairs. As we walked back down the stairs, making no effort to be quiet this time, I permitted myself the luxury of a sigh. I could feel the sweat soaking through my shirt underneath the stifling ceramic vest.

"Well, he's not down here, either," Scott greeted us at the bottom of the stairs. "I'm beginning to think we had a collective hallucination. Where the hell could he have gone?" As we stood there trying to come up with an answer that didn't involve voodoo or flying saucers, an agent came through the back door, holding a ragged-looking man by the arm. "I've got a witness here who says he saw a bald man go running out into the alley and enter the basement of a house near the end of the block," he shouted.

"That's impossible," I retorted. "We had two agents on the back of the house. I heard them say so on the radio with my own ears." Scott nodded. "So did I," he agreed. We walked briskly through the kitchen, out the back door into the alley. The two agents were still standing there.

"There's a guy inside saying that a bald man ran out of this house and down the alley," I declared. "That's not true, is it?"

"Sure it is," one of the agents contradicted me. "He went into the next-to-last house at the end of the row down there."

"Well why the *hell* didn't you stop him?" I demanded. "What did you think we were doing here? Training exercises?" I thought of bursting through all those doors upstairs, and I felt like slugging him.

"Hey, how were we supposed to know it was the guy you wanted?" the other agent said defensively. "We didn't have a description. This isn't our case. We could have screwed the whole operation if that wasn't your guy."

I opened my mouth for a searing retort, but Scott shook his head. Instead of speaking, I took a deep breath, and started walking down the alley in the direction they had pointed. It seemed to me you didn't have to be Sherlock Holmes—or even Barney Fife—to realize that if you've surrounded a house with an armed and dangerous fugitive inside, and then a man comes running out, you grab him first and ask questions later. Sometimes I wondered if the Bureau had a secret affirmative-action program for idiots.

As Scott and I walked down the alley, we were joined by Goodwin, a veteran agent named Al Heffernan, and a gargantuan Columbus police sergeant carrying a shotgun who looked like the professional wrestler Haystack Calhoun. "We'll start from the base-

WITH HONOR AND PURPOSE

ment and work our way up," Goodwin told us. "Another team of agents will watch the front to make sure no one comes out."

The basement doorway lay at the bottom of a half-flight of stairs. As we walked down it, I had a sense of déjà vu: Yet another closed door concealing potentially bloody secrets. *How many of these are we going to have to open today?* I wondered. It was like being a contestant on a TV game show designed by a psychopath.

Heffernan was the first man through the basement door, and I was right behind him. The basement was a single rectangular room, long and narrow. Hardly any light filtered through the grimy windows, and we could barely see—although I was certain that if Huffman were down here, he would already have sent us a hot lead greeting. Scarcely visible in the murk was a cord dangling from the ceiling; when I yanked it, a single dim bulb blinked on.

In the faint, gloomy light, we could see broken furniture and boxes of old newspapers scattered here and there across the floor. None of it seemed big enough to hide Huffman, but we methodically paced the floor, checking each shadow. I was puzzled again. The only door inside the basement was boarded shut, covered with undisturbed dust and spiderwebs. It obviously hadn't been used in years. How could Huffman have gotten out of here? Had we been sent to the wrong house? Again I silently cursed the agents who had been stationed in the alley. It seemed they had screwed up twice.

As we poked through the piles of junk, the mountainous Columbus police sergeant stood near the entrance. He seemed to be staring at the wall. Curious, I walked toward him; as I got closer, I could see he was actually looking at a faded, threadbare Oriental carpet hung on the wall. The sergeant poked the barrel of his shotgun under a corner of the carpet. He lifted it to reveal a hole carved in the wall, perhaps four feet high and two and a half feet wide. As I peered into it I could see it was really a tunnel, about two feet long, that went clear through the wall and into the basement of the next town house.

The sergeant looked at me. It was obvious he could never squeeze through the hole. *Well, at least it's not another door,* I thought, flexing my shoulders in a vain attempt to make the vest more comfortable. Squatting, I folded my six-foot-three frame into a size that would fit in the tunnel and extended one leg inside. Then I froze. *I should at least turn that light bulb off before I do this*, I mused. *Huffman's already going to have a clear shot at me; I don't need to make it easier by giving him a backlit target.*

My thought was interrupted by the hard thump of a 12-gauge shotgun barrel against my back. "It's time, sonny," the sergeant directed me. I realized he was right—the stupidest thing I could do was to crouch there in the tunnel like a sitting duck. I turned and pushed myself through. At the same instant I stumbled out the other side, Heffernan burst through the old door, showering fragments of rotted wood everywhere. In the light spilling through the doorway, I saw another cord and jerked it, illuminating the second basement. For what seemed like the millionth time that day, I mentally heaved a sigh of relief: No sign of Huffman.

This basement, too, was strewn with junk. As the others fished through it, I inspected the back door. It was padlocked from the inside; no one had gone out that way. Nor was there anything on the walls in this room to conceal another tunnel—and in any event, this was the last house on the block, so there was no place to tunnel *to*. There was only one place Huffman could have gone: up a rickety flight of wooden stairs running along the wall up to the first floor. At the top was a closed door; a single beckoning ray of light slipped through the thin crack between the door and the floor.

Heffernan, Scott, and I gathered at the bottom of the stairway. About eight feet tall, it was narrow and steep, without a handrail. Heffernan placed a foot experimentally on the first step. I winced as it gave off a squeak that echoed through the dusky basement, but it didn't really matter. Huffman must have heard the door shatter when Heffernan kicked it in. There were no secrets between us now. We knew Huffman was upstairs, waiting for us; he knew we were downstairs, coming for him. This real life game of cops and robbers was coming to an end.

Heffernan took the lead. Scott and I were right behind him, with Scott on the side next to the wall, all of us with pistols in hand. The stairs shrieked like evil old women as we edged upward, following that hypnotic ray of light. I was more nervous than I'd been all day. *He's really got us where he wants us, bunched up on a narrow staircase with no place to hide*, I thought. *He's spent all morning setting us up for this.* But I walked ahead anyway. Who else could we call? The FBI was already here.

We paused at the top of the stairs, passing messages with our eyes. Heffernan, his gun in his right hand, leaned across the door to open it with his left. The beam of light coming through the crack played pitilessly on his face as he grasped the knob. Another pause, a split second that lasted hours, and he twisted it open.

"Don't do it, Monk!" Heffernan screamed, the sound like shattering glass. His head blocked my view, but as he stumbled backward, Huffman's face appeared, looming before us like an apparition. It was a hard, craggy face, showing the seams implanted by a couple of thousand nights in prison. His expression was empty, his eyes on the distance, a perfect mask of nothingness. In his hand was a .38 caliber revolver, pointed directly at us. And looking up its barrel I could see a void blacker than black, the dark side of the moon. In slow motion I watched the barrel rising, rising, past us, into his mouth.

And then Monk Huffman pulled the trigger.

A horrible red and gray slush splattered everywhere, and teeth scattered across the kitchen where he sat. It looked like someone had thrown a bucket of mushy leftovers against the wall. Huffman, seated in a chair, slumped over against the oven, blood geysering from his head with the rhythm of a hoodwinked heart that didn't yet know it was dead. Wordlessly we backed down the stairs. Monk Huffman had promised he wouldn't be taken alive, and he had kept his word.


The rest of the afternoon was a blur of paperwork and procedures, the mundane postscript to every FBI drama that somehow never gets into any of the movies. As we dictated statements about what we had seen, other agents wandered over to fill in pieces of the puzzle. Huffman's presence at the house wasn't as amazing as Scott and I thought, it turned out; though he hadn't told us, Cleary had a snitch who was pretty certain that Monk would turn up there.

And, in fact, he was there even before Scott and I were: Huffman apparently spent the night lying in a parked car, trying to decide if the coast was clear. That was why Scott and I hadn't seen Monk arrive. And the reason his pal Rollins was fumbling under the front seat while I aimed a shotgun at him was not, as I had supposed, that he was trying to draw a gun. He was trying to *disassemble* a pistol he had hidden under the seat. As a paroled felon, it was illegal for him to possess a firearm, but Rollins thought it wouldn't count if the gun were taken apart. Wrong again.

Debbie and I had a dinner date that night with our neighbors Rose and Dick Walker, and we kept it. My memories of the evening are a little vague, and I recently called Rose and Dick to ask what they could recall of it.

"Oh, yes, *we* remember it," Rose assured me. "Because it was so weird. You acted like nothing had happened at all. You just talked about names for the new baby and how you were going to rearrange the house to make room for it. It was like you'd seen a thousand men die right in front of you and it was nothing new."

Of course, I hadn't seen a thousand men die in front of me. I hadn't even seen one, nor have I since. And Monk Huffman's death is anything but a casual event in my life. Many times over the past twenty years I've wondered what he was thinking as he sat in that kitchen, listening as we came up those squeaky stairs.

What I like to think is that if a person has even a tiny glimmer of good in them, sooner or later it will come out. In Monk's case it was later, much later, as the length of his rap sheet attests. But maybe as he waited in the kitchen, that gun in his hand, he remembered something he'd been taught back in the hazy days of his childhood, before everything started to go wrong for him. That's just speculation on my part, of course, but what I do know is this: Several times that day Monk Huffman had a chance to shoot at easy targets, and he didn't.

What I also know, though, is that I saw him raise that gun barrel to his mouth. When the door opened, it was pointed at us.

# 8

## A DEATH
## IN THE
## WOODS

In television and the movies, FBI agents lead charmed lives. Efrem Zimbalist, Jr., always caught his man; the *X-Files* agents always catch their Martian. Jody Foster was still at the FBI Academy when she tracked down the serial killer in *Silence of the Lambs*, for Pete's sake.

Who's going to complain about a reputation for infallibility? Certainly not me. For one thing, it probably makes some criminals think twice about taking the Bureau on. And for another, it's not completely off-base. Not every case ends in spectacular success, of course, but we have a pretty good clearance rate. Break federal law in any serious way, and chances are you're going to get caught.

The flip side of that is that when the FBI screws up, it can have unspeakably terrible consequences. You don't hear about it much— partly, I'm happy to report, because it doesn't happen very much, and partly because like any bureaucracy, the Bureau is quite adept at burying its mistakes. But back in 1975, when I was in Columbus, I got a worm's-eye view of a case that ended in disaster. I still feel sick when I think about it.

"Phil," drawled Jerry Jones, "you know Newark pretty well, right?" I knew he was talking about the little town twenty miles east of Columbus, not the big city in New Jersey. I'd worked there on a couple of occasions, including the time Miller and I closed down the best little whorehouse in Ohio.

"I am possibly the single greatest expert on the town of Newark in the entire field of federal law enforcement," I admitted. "What do you want me to tell you?"

"That you're getting in the car," Jones said. "Detroit wants us to check out a lead there on a kidnapping. I'll tell you about it on the way." We grabbed Miller on the way out.

As we headed east on I-70 through the miserable December weather, Jones briefed Miller and me on the case. It had begun Friday, four days earlier, at a branch of the National Bank of Detroit. When James Crawford, the twenty-five-year-old assistant manager, arrived for work, two men carrying guns under their overcoats grabbed him in the parking lot. They forced him into a white Pontiac Trans Am.

In a series of calls to bank officials and Crawford's family (he still lived with his parents in the upscale Detroit suburb of Grosse Pointe), the kidnappers had demanded $250,000. The bank was willing to pay, but unfortunately, the guys who had snatched Crawford were not the Einsteins of the kidnapping world. They kept getting mixed up about their own instructions and missing ransom drops. Then, on Sunday, they broke contact altogether.

"So what makes the Detroit office think they're in Newark?" I asked.

"A snitch," Jones replied.

A pal of the kidnappers, who had listened to them plan the whole thing, had gotten nervous when he heard them saying they might have to "waste" Crawford. And he spilled everything to an FBI agent in Detroit, starting with the identities of the four kidnappers.

Three of them—Chester Wysocki, John Garside, and William (Skip) Nabozny—were career criminals from the Detroit area. All in their late thirties, they had rap sheets going back into the 1950s. The other one was Garside's twenty-four-year-old girlfriend, Sharron Scheurell, whose mother lived in Obetz, a Columbus suburb.

"Wysocki is still in Detroit," Jones said. "They've got him under surveillance. But Scheurell is staying in Obetz at her mother's house, and the other two have disappeared. The snitch thinks everybody's down here someplace, including the victim. We put a tap on the mother's phone last night, and the Detroit office sent us a bunch of leads this morning.''

According to Detroit, Garside had lived for a time with Scheurell in Newark. His best friend in the town was a guy we'll call Rocky who owned a small business. And—small world—our office had spent some time the year before looking into whether Rocky was dealing in interstate transportation of stolen property. Although he ran with a rough crowd, in the end we concluded his business was legitimate.

"So that's our lead," Jones said. "We want to see if Rocky's been in touch with these guys, if he might be helping them hide the hostage. And while we're at it, we're supposed to keep an eye out for two vehicles: The white Trans Am used in the kidnapping, and a green Ford station wagon that belongs to Garside. I've got the plate numbers here. You got any ideas, Phil?"

"There was a deputy at the sheriff's office who was pretty helpful during an auto theft case," I remembered. "Let's call him to meet us for coffee someplace. I don't think we can go by the sheriff's office. Otherwise we'll get all kinds of rumors started."

The deputy, when he met us at a coffee shop on the edge of town, was skeptical. "Rocky may skate along the edge of the law sometimes, but I don't see him getting involved in anything as hardcore as a kidnapping," he argued. But he did have a suggestion. "You know, there's a cottage out in the northeastern part of the county that my memory tells me is somehow connected to Rocky. It's pretty isolated out there—mostly woods, a few houses scattered around. I guess if I was going to hide a kidnap victim, it's the kind of place I might pick."

"Can you tell us how to get there?" we asked. The deputy pulled out a map and ran his finger along a blue line about six or seven miles from Newark. "This is called Eden Township Road 238, but don't expect to see any signs. It's just a little old dirt road," he advised. "And I'll tell you something else—you gotta be careful out

A Death in the Woods                                                    149 there. Folks move out to that part of the country because they want to be left alone, and anyone poking around gets noticed pretty quick. Even one pass by that house may be too many, and don't even think about two."

We thanked him as we left the coffee shop. Outside, on the snow-covered sidewalk, we tried to decide what to do.

"It sounds like bullshit to me, but I suppose we might as well check it out," Miller said.

"It's not like we have anything better to do," Jones agreed. "I just hope we don't get stuck in the middle of nowhere."

"Hey, don't you guys know enough to go inside out of the cold?" somebody shouted from a car. Looking up, we saw Joe Raspberry and Tom Gray, two agents from the satellite office in Zanesville, a few miles to the east. Newark was part of their normal turf.

"What are you guys working?" Jones asked.

"This Detroit kidnapping, same as you," Gray said. "You getting anywhere? We heard you on the radio."

"There's a house out in the woods northeast of here that we're going to check." Jones said. His eyes swept over the car the Zanesville agents were driving, a blue Chevy. We were in a typical Bureau dinosaur, a Ford only slightly smaller than the Titanic.

"Say, why don't you guys come out there with us?" Jones asked. "You can make the pass by the house—you look a little less obvious."

"Lead on," Gray shrugged.


"Here they come now," Miller said from the back seat. We were parked in a small strip shopping center several miles from the cottage, where we were waiting for Gray and Raspberry to come back from their pass. They'd been gone nearly an hour, and we were wondering if they'd gotten stuck in the mud. Now, though, we could see the blue Chevy rolling toward us. "But where's Gray?" Miller asked. It was a good question. Raspberry was alone inside the car as it pulled up alongside us.

WITH HONOR AND PURPOSE

Raspberry jumped out of the Chevy and slid into the back beside Miller. "You guys aren't going to believe this," he said calmly. "We found the house—and there's a white Trans Am parked in front."

The kidnap car! Raspberry was right—needle in a haystack leads like this one never turned out this way. We waited for a punch line. But there wasn't one.

"We didn't actually drive by the house, but we parked a mile away and got a pretty good look at it from the woods," Raspberry rushed on. "Then we talked to an old man who lives down the road. He said the place was empty until a couple of days ago, when two grizzled guys with long hair showed up. White, in their late thirties. It's gotta be Garside and Nabozny. And get this—they painted the windows of the cottage black. He's seen them taking target practice out in back, too."

"Did he see Crawford, the hostage?" I asked.

"No," admitted Raspberry. "But everything else fits. Gray stayed back there to keep an eye on the place. We need to call Columbus and get a SWAT team out here right now, along with some guys to handle surveillance."

Everyone nodded. When you find a needle in a haystack, you've got to grab it before you lose it again.

We hurried over to a pay phone on the wall outside one of the stores. Our car radios couldn't reach Columbus from there, and in any event, our radio frequencies weren't secure. Any reporter with a police scanner could have overheard us.

Raspberry made the call to Tom Mitchell, the Columbus office chief, who immediately put him on hold. Tom Kitchens, the SAC in Cincinnati, and the SAC in Detroit soon joined in. Raspberry quickly outlined the situation.

"We need some bodies for surveillance. And we need to get a SWAT team up here as quickly as possible," Raspberry concluded. He was silent a minute, listening to the bosses. "No," he finally answered. "We didn't see Crawford himself. But you know he's in there. Why else would the windows be painted black?" There was another pause. Then Raspberry exploded. "Boss, you've got to be kidding me!" he exclaimed. "Then what the heck was the point of coming up here?"

Among the rest of us, three jaws dropped in unison. Nobody questions an SAC. It's like questioning God. And Raspberry had just yelled at *two* of them.

He turned to us. "They say we have to go home," he barked, making no attempt to cover the telephone mouthpiece. "No SWAT team, no surveillance."

"I can't believe it," Miller sputtered.

"Give me that phone," Jones demanded. He took the receiver as Raspberry walked away stunned. Miller and I stood there, listening. I was certain there had been a misunderstanding. We had a twenty-five-year-old kid from the suburbs in the hands of a bunch of ruthless ex-cons. The SACs couldn't possibly have meant for us to turn around and leave without doing *anything*. Jones, I was sure, would get it straightened out. His no-bullshit, take-care-of-business attitude, coupled with his molasses drawl and a big-time temper, had won him the nickname Captain Jerry Lee Jones.

"Raspberry seems to think you just told us to pack up and leave," he began calmly. Pause. "Well, I don't agree with you. Crawford's either in there, or nearby. And once we've got those guys under arrest, they'll tell us fast if he's somewhere else." Pause. Jones's face began to redden. "What about surveillance, then?" he demanded. "We've got to at least eyeball the place. Otherwise, they might move, and then we've got to start all over again." Pause. Jones's face was puffing out like a cork about to blow. "Can't we even put cars out at the crossroads?" A final pause. "If they see us, then we'll take them," Jones snarled. His voice broke into a scream. "This is just *bullshit*, just goddamn *bullshit*!" He slammed the phone back into the hook so hard it sounded like a rifle shot.

"They said we should go home and get a good night's sleep," he growled, jerking open the car door. "Those stupid idiots."

———

It would be literally weeks before Jones could talk about the conversation without flying into a rage all over again. The SACs, it seemed, weren't convinced Crawford was inside the house. They saw real risks in the situation. What if, they asked, he's being held somewhere else, by a member of the gang we don't know about? What if they've set it up so Crawford gets killed unless they give a prearranged signal? That was why they didn't want to storm the house.

Those were serious arguments, as I would learn all too well a few years later when I ran a kidnapping investigation of my own. The business with the windows did argue strongly that Crawford was inside—why in the hell would they paint them, otherwise?—but there was no way to be sure. Maybe he had been in the house at one point and they had moved him. When someone's life rests in your hands, those kinds of uncertainties weigh heavily.

When it came to surveillance, the SACs repeated pretty much what the Newark cop had said: It's a remote rural area, surveillance is going to stand out, they'll make you, and then the whole case is blown. That was a good argument, too. J. Edgar Hoover had been dead three years, but the FBI was still stubbornly clinging to some of his most outmoded theories. We still didn't have any real undercover capacity: We were a bunch of white guys with short hair wearing ties, driving cars with big antennas. And the words "surveillance aircraft" had never passed an agent's lips.

But as difficult as it might have been, it still bothers me that the SACs called off the surveillance. We could have worked with the neighbors, we could have borrowed a private vehicle that was less obvious, we could have dressed somebody in overalls and a John Deere hat. It would have been tricky, sure, but the only alternative was leaving James Crawford to the mercy of his kidnappers. And that was no alternative at all.

As we started the drive back to Columbus, dusk was falling. The wild, scraggly terrain looked ominous in the shadows. I wondered what might happen in the dark.

———

I obeyed orders: I went home and got some sleep. But the case continued to roll along.

The tap on the phone at Sharron Scheurell's mother's house picked up a call from Garside, someplace in Michigan. "I've been made," he told Scheurell. "Tell Skip to go clean up the place."

The Bureau brass promptly ordered agents to watch the mother's house. Bob Federspiel got the assignment. Around 3 A.M., he saw a car leave the residence. Staying at a safe distance, with his lights out, Federspiel followed until the car pulled into a gas station a couple of miles from the cottage. Fed waited a minute, then turned on his lights and turned into the station himself.

There were three people in the car. The two ex-cons, Garside and Nabozny, were easy to recognize. When he got closer, Federspiel saw the third person was a skinny young woman—Sharron Scheurell. As he pretended to look at a map, Federspiel's eyes scanned the car carefully. But there was no sign of James Crawford, the hostage.

Moments later, the car pulled out again. Federspiel watched as it headed north through a crossroads. That was the route to the cottage, he knew. Instead of following and running the risk of being spotted on the remote road, he called the Columbus office. The brass finally relented. A surveillance team was ordered to take up posts around the cottage. It was 4 A.M. We had been pulled off nine hours earlier.


When I got up at 5 A.M., I called Bob Gillespie. He'd recently been assigned a station wagon as a Bucar, and I figured that would be a much better surveillance vehicle. I didn't know anything about what had happened during the night, but I was sure that sometime today the SACs would change their minds and let us get closer to the cottage. And I wanted to help.

"Gilly, why don't you swing by here and pick me up?" I suggested. "We'll go up to that Union 76 truck stop on I-70 south of Newark and have breakfast. By the time we're finished, maybe they'll have a surveillance assignment for us."

"Sure," he said. "But don't count on those shitheads changing their minds." Word had spread throughout the office about what had happened the previous afternoon, and there was mutiny in the air.

It was a little after 7 A.M. when we veered off the interstate toward the truck stop. I was looking forward to my first cup of coffee. But as we swung past the gas pumps toward the cafe, a car caught Gilly's eye.

"Jesus, Phil, it's them!" he exclaimed. "That muddy old green Ford station wagon over there. That's the other car they told us about in the briefing."

"No way," I declared. "No way. Life isn't that easy." I pulled a small note from my pocket. "I've got the tag number here," I said. "Move up closer, and let's check the plates."

The numbers matched. As we circled past the Ford, I glanced inside for a closer look. Two long-haired men were sitting in the front, a lone woman in the back. One of the men cranked the engine, and the station wagon pulled onto the interstate, heading east toward Columbus. The adrenaline surging through my body turned sour. They were leaving, closing up shop. And Crawford wasn't in the car.

"Maybe they've laid him down in the back," said Gillespie, reading my mind. Without another word, he wheeled up the ramp onto the freeway. Staying a quarter of a mile back, keeping a car or two between us at all times, we followed the Ford.

Because it was so early, it was several minutes before I was able to raise any other agents on the radio. But one by one, they checked in. "Gilly and I are near the Columbus city limits, headed east on I-70," I said. "We've got that green Ford station wagon everyone's been looking for in sight, with three subjects inside. But traffic is getting heavy—we need some help."

"On the way," came the reply.

Within minutes, five other cars had joined the chase—which wasn't really a chase, since the kidnappers had no idea we were following them. Gillespie and I lagged back a mile or two, and I directed the other cars.

"CI-40, take the eye," I said. For the next few minutes, as the other cars shuffled their positions, agent 40's responsibility would be to keep the Ford in sight at all times. "CI-7, drop the eye and fall back a mile. CI-30, pass the package and go ahead. CI-12, start edging up." Constantly moving the vehicles around and switching the eye among them minimized the chances that anyone in the Ford would notice a particular vehicle following them.

We traveled through Columbus and continued west toward Dayton and, for all I knew, Indianapolis. The SACs in Detroit and Cincinnati were on the phone with U.S. attorneys in both cities, trying to decide whether to force the Ford off the road and make arrests, or keep following to see what the kidnappers were up to. Almost an hour passed before Tom Decker, who had the eye, reported that the Ford was stopping at a gas station.

"Okay, follow it in, then let me know when it's moving again," I told him. "There's a turnout on the highway just ahead—Gilly and I will wait there." The other agents knew what to do: stay in the area, blend in, and wait for new instructions. I switched radio channels to let the Columbus office know what we were doing.

Gillespie eased the car over into the turnout, and we stopped.

"Wish I had some coffee," I said, stretching my legs.

"Wish the SACs would have let us arrest these guys yesterday," Gillespie responded.

"Shitheads."

"The SACs? Or the kidnappers?"

"Both."

"Wish I had some coffee."

For fifteen minutes we made small talk and cursed our superiors. At last, Gillespie asked: "What the hell are those people in the Ford doing?"

I picked up the microphone to call Decker. "CI-12, what's the situation?" The only reply was a soft hum of static. "CI-12," I repeated. Still nothing. I glanced at the radio, wondering if it had broken. "Oh, shit," I blurted. After talking to Columbus, I hadn't switched back to the surveillance channel. Twisting the dial, I quickly picked up the chatter of surveillance being called by another agent.

"We've probably lost ten miles, at least," I told Gillespie.

"Bet you've never seen a station wagon that could go this fast," he said, flooring the gas.

He was right. We rocketed west at 110 miles an hour, flashing past other traffic like something out of *Star Trek*. Between the roar of the engine and the crackle of the radio, I'm not sure how long the siren had been wailing before I looked back and saw an Ohio state police cruiser behind us, flashing its light.

"Jesus, Gilly, did you know there's a cop following us?" I asked.

"Yeah, he wants to know if I can do 115," he said, pushing the accelerator a little further. It took me a couple of minutes to convince him to stop. I flashed my credentials at the cop, told him we were in hot pursuit of a kidnapper, and we roared off again, leaving behind an officer with a face redder than Captain Jones's.

Five or six miles up the road, we saw traffic bottlenecking. "Better slow down, it looks like an accident," I warned Gillespie. And indeed it was—the green Ford station wagon was sitting in the low highway median, pitched at a precarious angle. As we jumped from our car, we saw a couple of agents leading Garside and Nabozny away in handcuffs.

"What happened?" I asked Decker, standing nearby.

"We got an order from headquarters to arrest them, so we bracketed them with cars and then forced them off the road," he said. "It was kind of messy—their car almost rolled over."

"Did they put up a fight?" I asked. Decker laughed. "Pretty hard to do that with your pants down," he said. "Garside had his pants open. I couldn't even guess what was going on."

I took a minute to digest that, then asked: "What about Crawford?"

"No sign of him," Decker said, sobered. "We're taking everybody back to the U.S. attorney's office in Columbus. Maybe we can get something out of them on the way. I'm going to ride with Garside."

He climbed into the back seat of a Bucar where one of the kidnappers was sitting. As Gillespie and I followed it back to Columbus, I tried to imagine the conversation. I knew exactly what Decker was doing. It was also going on in two other cars, with different agents and the other kidnappers. I call it "take a number, any number." It was sort of like a song that was popular at the time, *50 Ways To Leave Your Lover*. There might be fifty ways to get a suspect to talk, and your job is to probe around and find the right one.

I might have tried this one: You're in a big jam, fellow. But if you help us find Crawford, we can try to get the judge to cut you some slack. Or a similar one: I can be your worst enemy or your best friend. I'd rather be your best friend, rather be able to tell the judge you came clean early.

Sometimes I come on like a social worker: I can tell you're not a bad guy. I think you're a victim of circumstance. But you have to tell me how that happened, so I can explain it to everybody else.

When women are involved, that opens a whole new set of possibilities: Your girlfriend is up to her butt in this thing. Be enough of a man to save her. Or, the opposite: See your girlfriend over there? See her lips moving? What do you think she's saying? She's sticking it up your ass, pal. For the woman herself: Have you got kids? Want to see them again? What do you think the Department of Social Services will do with them if you're in the slammer?

Whatever Decker tried, it was only partly successful. When we arrived in Columbus, he pulled me aside. "That bastard says Crawford has been cut, and he's dying," Decker said. "But he won't tell me any more." My stomach heaved. Was it true? Had they stabbed the kid after we pulled off our surveillance the night before?

I followed Decker as he marched the handcuffed Garside into an empty cubicle in the U.S. attorney's offices. Sometimes just seeing a new face makes them talk.

"What do you mean, Crawford's cut?" I asked. "How bad is he hurt?"

"It means he's been cut, man," Garside replied without a trace of emotion. "Cut pretty bad, and he's going to die unless he gets help."

"Then tell me he where is," I said urgently. "We'll help him. We'll save him. We'll save you from a murder rap."

Garside's face turned smug. "Sure, I'll tell you—for complete immunity," he offered.

"You've been around, you know we can't do that," I said. "Ask for something that's possible."

"Take it or leave it," he said flatly.

Knowing it was useless, I stepped into the next office, where William Milligan, the U.S. attorney, was conferring with some other agents. "Garside says Crawford's been stabbed, and he'll lead us to the kid in return for immunity," I told him.

"No way," Milligan snorted. "I'm not granting immunity when I don't know what happened. It could turn out we're giving him a get-out-of-jail-free card on a murder rap."

I returned to the cubicle. "The U.S. attorney says no dice," I said. "But for the love of God, we're talking about a man's life! Just tell me where he is so we can help him."

"Fuck you," Garside sneered.

In a different room, agent Terry Ware was having better luck picking the numbers with Sharron Scheurell. She agreed to take him to the place where Crawford had been left. They took a series of winding roads to the edge of a forest, a mile or two from the cottage. But by the time they arrived, it was dusk. Ware, Federspiel and a couple of other agents walked a few dozen feet into the murky woods, but they were tripping and stumbling everywhere. The search would have to wait until daylight.

Federspiel, Decker, Jones, and I went back to the woods the next morning. Our assignment was to make a quick survey, figure out how many agents would be required for a full-scale search.

"Oh, man," Decker grunted, gazing at the tangle of roots and underbrush just inside the tree line. "Why don't we just call the 82nd Airborne and be done with it?"

"This looks like the land time forgot," I agreed. But Federspiel waved his hand dismissively. "You guys should have seen it in the dark," he said. "This is gonna be a piece of cake compared to last night."

We spread out and forged into the woods, which sloped gently downhill. It was easier going than it looked, and we made progress quickly—until Federspiel stopped us with a shout. "Come look at this!" he called.

There was a small depression in the ground, as though someone had lain down there. In the middle of it was a military-style khaki jacket, puddled with blood. Leading away from it, deeper into the woods, was a thin trail of blood drops.

Moving slowly but deliberately, so we wouldn't miss anything, we followed the trail. About fifty yards away, we suddenly emerged from the woods to find ourselves at a broken-down old wire fence. On the other side was a deep ditch, where we saw more blood.

A few yards away, the trail of blood started anew. This time it led up a winding dirt road, which continued up toward a white, two-story farmhouse about a quarter of a mile away. But we couldn't find a trace of blood either up or down the road. After searching in both directions for several minutes, we gathered by a large log a few hundred yards below the farm house.

"They stab Crawford and he falls down," Federspiel said, thinking out loud. "They think he's dead, and they leave. But after they've gone, he gets up. He pulls off his coat and staggers through the woods. Trips over the fence, lies in the ditch for a minute and then gets up again. He sees the lights of that farmhouse, starts dragging himself up the road. And then—and then—what? Why does the blood stop?"

"You think he could have turned back the same way he came?" I mused. "You think we could have missed him in the woods back there?"

"It doesn't make any sense," Federspiel said. "But who knows how clear his mind was after losing so much blood? I guess he could be lying back in that brush."

"You think we should go back and look some more? Or get back to a phone and start organizing the full search?" The chances that Crawford was still alive were about a zillion to one. Even so, it made me uneasy to think of leaving, delaying another hour or two.

"Never mind," said Decker quietly. "He's here." He gestured at a log, and we moved a few steps toward it. I could see the tips of two feet propped on the other side.

Later the newspapers would carry what must have been James Crawford's college graduation picture: a handsome young man with a fashionable wave of hair dipped over his forehead, a slight smile playing on his lips as he looked into his future. That photo didn't have the slightest resemblance to the contorted face I saw when I stepped around the log, twisted into the dirt. It looked like someone had used Crawford as a human pin cushion. A sheet of black, caked blood framed his head.

"He wandered off the road," Federspiel said, his voice so low I could barely hear it. "tripped over this log, and bled to death a few hundred yards from help."

I looked away from the pale, wasted body. Across the road was a towering oak tree, its thick branches raised to the sky in prayer. I wondered if they were strong enough to hang a man on. If Garside and Nabozny had been there, I surely would have tried.

The coroner counted twenty-two stab wounds in James Crawford's body: ten in the back, seven in the chest, four in the neck, and one in the left temple. That didn't count the slash marks on four fingers where he had apparently grabbed at the knife that killed him. His skull was fractured, too. Testing what little blood was left in his body, the coroner discovered he had been heavily drugged at the time of his death.

That time was about 7 P.M. on Tuesday, less than two hours after the FBI brass told us to go home and get a good night's sleep. If we had stayed, if we had kept the house under surveillance, we would have seen Sharron Scheurell arrive at the cottage to pass along Garside's order to "clean up the place." We would have seen Scheurell and Nabozny emerge from the house with Crawford, stumbling along in a forced opiate haze. We would have seen the three of them drive off toward the woods, and we would have seen Scheurell and Nabozny come back alone.

And James Crawford might have lived.

But though we bitched endlessly about it among ourselves, none of us ever confronted the SACs over the order to go home that night. It still seemed like a minor miracle to most of us that Raspberry and Jones hadn't been struck by lightning that afternoon at the pay phone. We weren't willing to tempt fate twice. Everyone kept quiet, and although a few stories in the Detroit papers hinted that something had gone wrong, the story of how a couple of well-intentioned, but cautious FBI bureaucrats left Crawford and he died that night never came out.

Another ugly story, however, did. Garside's first phone call after he was arrested was not to a lawyer but to an agent in the FBI's Detroit office. It seemed Garside had been a paid Bureau informant for three years. Agents in Detroit actually let him practice target-shooting on a Bureau range. FBI ammo was found in his car. In fact, he'd even double-dated with an agent.

While that certainly demonstrated blatant stupidity in Detroit, it didn't really have anything to do with the Crawford kidnapping. Not that his defense attorney didn't try to prove otherwise. The whole defense strategy was to show that Garside was working for us inside the kidnap ring, trying to bring that terrible Nabozny to justice. It didn't work. Garside was convicted of murder and sentenced to death, just as Nabozny was. A couple of years later, the U.S. Supreme Court struck down Ohio's death penalty, and their sentences were reduced to life. Chester Wysocki, the kidnapper who never left Detroit, got a fifteen-year sentence after agreeing to testify against the others. Sharron Scheurell (who always denied that she was present when Crawford was stabbed) pled guilty to aiding and abetting kidnapping and was sentenced to twenty years.

The epitaph to the case was written long before the final trial was over. It came as we clustered around a phone booth in Newark, where Jerry Jones was reporting the discovery of Crawford's body to Tom Kitchens, the SAC in Cincinnati. The autopsy would be done there, Kitchens said, and he wanted Jones to accompany the body. Jones had just completed a training course on blood spatters, dental records, and other medical forensics, and Kitchens thought it might come in handy during the autopsy.

"Right," Jones agreed. He hung the phone up and turned to Tom Decker. "The SAC says you're the senior agent on the scene, and he wants you to go to Cincinnati with the body," Jones lied. Decker went home to pack a bag, grumbling every step of the way. It seemed nobody wanted to go to James Crawford's autopsy. We already had his blood on our hands.

# 9

# TALES OF WELLS FARGO, 1970s STYLE

"You know, I believe they lied to us back at the FBI Academy," Jerry Jones drawled, popping the handcuffs shut with a soft click. Flint Gabelman and I, holstering our guns, eyed him quizzically. Even the bank robber stopped squirming in his chair and chafing against the cuffs long enough to shoot Jones a puzzled look.

"Well, *look* at this place," Jones exclaimed, waving his arms in a half-circle at the split-level town house, a sunswept array of blond beams and high ceilings, so new the wood still seemed to glow. "Does it look to you like this punk bought it with what he saved working nights at McDonald's? I'm telling you, when Hoover said crime doesn't pay, he was lying to us."

"Well, they've changed the lecture since you went through the academy," I retorted. "When I was at the academy, what they said was, crime doesn't pay *well*. And it's true. Look, the guy can't even afford furniture." The robber snorted, perhaps despite himself. He'd just gotten the keys to the town house that morning, his first toy purchased with the proceeds of several stickups over the past couple of months. We'd busted him before he'd had time to buy anything but the dining room set.

Gabelman smiled patiently. "I love it when we talk about criminology," he observed. "But I think we ought to check the rest of the house first." *That's Flint*, I thought. *This guy is so by-the-book on arrests that he probably checks his mattress every night before he goes to sleep to make sure nobody tore the tag off that day.* But Gabelman was right; we had arrested the robber right at the front door when he answered the bell. The rest of the house did need to be checked, if only to see if he had stashed any of the money from the robberies upstairs.

"Flint and I will take a look upstairs," I said apologetically. "Why don't you stay down here with Robin Hood?" Jones nodded as Gabelman and I drew our revolvers and started up the stairs.

The doors to the two upstairs bedrooms were standing open, as though the house had gotten some kind of "hands up!" command. They were as empty as the downstairs. I turned to go.

"Hold on," Gabelman interjected. "There's a closet over there." He pointed to the far wall of the second bedroom.

"Right," I agreed. I walked across the room and extended my hand toward the doorknob.

"Wait a second!" Gabelman interrupted in a mild voice. "Careful!" I sighed, waiting to open the closet door until Gabelman could train his revolver on it. Just the way they taught you at the academy. *How in hell did this guy ever do his job in Vietnam?* I wondered.

Though it was hard to reconcile with either his amiable, next-door-neighbor smile or his love affair with proper arrest procedures, Gabelman had been a sniper in Vietnam, creeping into enemy-controlled villages to systematically hunt down and kill enemy soldiers. It didn't seem like the right job for a guy who stuck to the rules. But Gabelman was good at it. One night Debbie and I were at Gabelman's house for dinner when he offered to show some slides. In the middle of the distant, blurry photos of jungle, there was a shot of Flint's squad waving their rifles triumphantly overhead. At their feet was a mound of about a dozen dead Viet Cong or North Vietnamese regulars.

When Gabelman nodded, I yanked open the door with a casual tug of my elbow. The face that suddenly loomed in front of me was a light beige brown, topped with a mighty Afro hairdo, but it was the eyes that riveted me. The black pupils, tiny as pinpricks, spinning like the wheels of a slot machine, cornered and desperate. I didn't dare look away from them, even as I felt the rifle barrel pointed at the underside of my chin inching upward, toward my face.

We stood there together, motionless: a wax museum tableau, Great Moments in Law Enforcement History, part five, what to do when a junkie bank robber shoves a rifle up your nose. No one made a sound. I couldn't think, couldn't do anything but look into those crazed eyes. After a time that might have been ten seconds and might have been ten hours, I forced myself to blink. Then, slowly and deliberately, I turned my head, spinning my face on the axis of the gun barrel, until I could see Gabelman.

The next-door-neighbor smile was gone. In its place was a tight, expressionless line. A cold, gray reptilian hood had dropped over the friendly eyes as they sighted down the .357 magnum revolver trained on the forehead of the man in the closet.

I wondered how many men in Vietnam had seen that face, and how many had lived to tell about it. *Flint's taking care of business*, I thought, and felt the muscles in my neck start to loosen and relax.


In the summer of 1934, bank robbery was getting to be the national sport. John Dillinger, Baby Face Nelson, Creepy Karpis, Ma Barker, Machine Gun Kelly, and Pretty Boy Floyd were emptying vaults of cash faster than the U.S. mints printed it—and becoming heroes in the process, at least in some parts of the tabloid press. Congress responded by giving the FBI jurisdiction over any robbery of a bank that was part of the Federal Reserve system. (It also authorized agents to carry guns for the first time.) For the next fifty years, until we began going after narcotraffickers in a major way, bank robbery was the King of Crimes around the FBI. Nobody clanked his balls louder than an agent who had just busted a bank robber.

The funny thing is that robbers have kept at it even though advances in technology have made it practically impossible to get away with. Many banks screen their tellers with bullet-proof glass, which means that anyone who demands money can simply be told to stuff their gun up their ass. Then there's the silent alarm, which automatically alerts police when money is removed from the teller's drawer.

If a robber does manage to get out of the bank with some money, we usually have photos to identify him, courtesy of video surveillance cameras. The loot will almost certainly contain a stack of bait money—bills whose serial numbers will be registered in NCIC, the computerized data base that cops use when they stop cars.

And often, a robber who tries to spend any of his spoils will discover the bills have turned bright red, a tipoff to all concerned that the money is stolen. Bait money often contains a dye pack that explodes a few minutes after it's pulled from a cash drawer. Practically every FBI agent has at least one story of a robber who hadn't done his homework and almost lost his balls after stuffing loot into a pocket or down the front of his pants.

Even clever robbers don't seem to make allowances for the dye pack. The Bureau handled one case where a black robber hit a savings and loan in a lily-white neighborhood. He sprinted out of the bank, around a corner, and jumped into the trunk of the getaway car—which was driven by his white partner. It was a good scheme that should have allowed the car to get out of the area unnoticed by police. Except the dye pack exploded in the trunk, and the black robber turned red.

Somehow, though, I suspect robbers will keep hitting banks. They still try it about ten thousand times each year in the United States, despite the long odds against success and the relatively low payoffs. That doesn't even count bank larcenies, which is when a thief takes money from a bank through scheme or artifice rather than force. These days these larcenies mostly involve theft of automatic teller codes, but years ago there was a famous case in Detroit where someone was dangling a fishhook into night-deposit slots and reeling in loads of cash. One night the Detroit office sent a team of agents to lie in wait at a bank in a small shopping center that had been fished almost dry. Sure enough, near midnight, they saw a man pass by, staring intently at the deposit slot. A few minutes later, he came back. When he walked up to the slot, the agents jumped from their cars, yelling "Freeze!" The man jerked a gun from his pocket and sent several slugs whistling past their heads. They shot back, hitting him, but instead of falling down, he took off running—out of the strip shopping center where the bank was located into the adjoining residential neighborhood. He ran into a backyard, crashing through a sliding-glass door. The agents followed a trail of blood and broken glass into the bathroom, where the man was lying facedown, coughing up blood. They kicked his gun away and rolled him over, flashing their badges. "FBI, don't move!" warned an agent. "FBI?" the man croaked. "Oh, thank God you're here! I'm with Chicken Delight." He'd just closed up his restaurant for the night and wanted to put the receipts in the bank. But he'd been robbed several times, so he was in the habit of walking past the bank once and checking it out before approaching the night-deposit slot. Time-release locks have made it nearly impossible for robbers to get into vaults, where the big money is, so usually they just get the contents of a couple of tellers' cash drawers. Average take: around $4,000, not much when the risks of imprisonment for twenty-five years are so great. Oh, yeah, and death—about thirty people get killed each year during bank robberies, and one hundred thirty or so wounded. It's still one of the most dangerous crimes for the street cops who reach the scene first. I once worked a robbery at Ohio National Bank, near the Ohio State campus in Columbus, an old-fashioned place with big yellow venetian blinds all across the front windows. The first patrolman to respond to the alarm couldn't see anything inside, so he walked in the front door just as two robbers with sawed-off shotguns were coming out. As the patrolman spun sideways, one of the robbers fired from less than two feet away. We counted pellet holes in his necktie later, but miraculously, there wasn't a mark on his body.

I must have handled half a dozen cases at that bank; it got hit all the time. In fact, it seemed like *every* bank in Columbus got hit all the time. We had so many stickups that three agents were assigned to work almost nothing but bank robberies. In 1973, as the Afro Set cases wound down, I joined Dick Cleary, Paul Miller, and Jerry Jones as the fourth.

It was, in many ways, a peculiar grouping of agents. Cleary was an Ivy League poster boy: Brown grad, great athlete, naval officer. The cerebral Miller, still complaining you couldn't find a decent hoagie in Columbus. Me, doubting the existence of civilization outside the Midwest. And Jones, a truly volcanic southerner. When his temper went off, it scorched everything for miles around—sometimes including himself.

Jones was a former Air Force missile commander. I liked to needle him by telling him he'd sat down in those silos too long and scrambled his brains, but actually I really liked him—except during our weekly nickel-and-dime poker games. It was dealer's choice, and when the deck reached Jones, you could forget five-card draw or seven-card stud. "It's time for Jaw-ja poker, boys," he would drawl, "queens bleeding, pigs in a stockade, and hooks right." None of us ever had any idea what he was talking about, which may explain why he always won.

Somehow all our disparate styles came together in a tight fit. Everybody contributed something: Cleary's splendid capacity for planning and coordination, Miller's ability to assemble the jigsaw puzzle of clues that an investigation produces, Jones's talent for just plain making things happen. I turned out to have a flair for coaxing confessions out of bank robbers. It wasn't even really conscious on my part. I just enjoyed talking to the guys. They usually told interesting stories, and at the end of the conversation, I sometimes felt like saying, look, let's forget about all this, you just go home and behave yourself.

Sometimes, in fact, working bank robberies could be quite funny. We once busted an old-time robber we'll call Lucky Thompson for a bank job. At the jail, filling out the booking forms, we asked him our routine question about distinctive tattoos or scars that can be used for identification.

"Yeah, I got a tattoo," he affirmed.

"What part of your body?" I asked.

"That's a little difficult to say," he replied, frowning. "It's— well . . ."

"Why don't you just show it to me?" I suggested.

Obligingly, Lucky pulled down his pants. A large blue serpent's head was engraved on his penis. Its body curled back up under his clothing.

"Where does it end?" I asked, mildly awed. Lucky took off his shirt. The tattooed snake coiled around his body several times. Then he turned around and tapped his butt. The snake's tail disappeared up his anus.

"She's somethin', ain't she?" Lucky asked proudly. On that, we could all agree. The tattoo was certainly something.

Another time several of us went to an apartment where we thought a couple of fugitive robbers might be holed up. They were gone, but there was plenty of evidence they had been staying there—and enough to implicate the woman who lived there as an accessory. The first agents in the door arrested her as she got out of bed, cuffed her hands behind her back, and brought her downstairs—completely naked.

"Hey, Mabel," I said in surprise. "How are you? Haven't seen you in a while." I knew her—she worked in a government office by day, but at night often partied with bank robbers. Because she seemed straight, I'd talked to her a couple of times on other cases. She wasn't very cooperative, but she was intelligent and well-spoken. With some deft handling here, I thought, we could get her to give up the robbers.

"Kerby, I'm standing in the foyer, naked as a jaybird, in handcuffs, and you ask how I am," she scoffed. "Is that a dumb question, or what?"

"Look guys," I said to the other agents, making a big show of being the nice-guy cop, "I know Mabel. Somebody go get her some clothes. And let's take the cuffs off and put them back on with her hands in front, so it's more comfortable."

"I really appreciate that, Kerby," she said gratefully.

"Kerb, don't undo the cuffs," interrupted Tom Decker. "Throw a sheet over her, throw her in the car, and let's get out of here. She's trouble."

Decker, a veteran of the Hoover FBI, sometimes taught firearms and defensive tactics to other agents. Sometimes, I thought, he took his own training lectures a little too much to heart. I put an arm around his shoulders and stepped away from the woman. "C'mon, Deck, I know her," I murmured. "I think we can roll her over. And, anyway, look at her. She's not exactly a threat." Hazel was perhaps five-foot-six and 130 pounds, and there was certainly no place she could be hiding a gun.

"Don't undo the cuffs," Decker repeated. "She's trouble."

I shook my head and walked back behind Mabel. I slipped the key into the handcuffs and popped them open so she could move her hands around in front of her. Instead, she threw a whistling punch at Decker's head.

"Grab her!" he shouted, sidestepping the blow.

I managed to snatch one of her arms, but she pulled her right leg back and delivered a pile driver kick to Decker's nuts. As he collapsed in a heap, I spun her around. There was a nutty gleam in her eyes and a thin white foam at the corner of her mouth. As she lunged at me, another agent knocked her to the ground with a flying tackle. As the two of us grappled with her, a third agent joined the pile. But—it was incredible—we were *losing*. She was bucking up and down like a herd of wild broncos, snot and spittle flying everywhere, and I could feel my grip slipping.

Decker crawled over, grabbed her bushy Afro-style hair, and started banging her head on the hardwood floor. But every blow just made her buck harder. Finally I seized her other arm and managed to snap the handcuffs closed again.

Mabel was still throwing kicks in every direction, and since none of us wanted our nuts to join Decker's in testicle heaven, we backed away. Decker dragged her over to the car by her hair and somehow managed to heave her into the back. When we got to the U.S. marshal's lockup, it took both of us to move her inside, and after that it was hours before anyone could even get near her. Decker looked like he wanted to kick *me* in the nuts, but instead he went home and prayed for a prompt death.

I never could figure out what set Mabel off. I guess if we still had

*The Book of Losers*, I would have gotten my own entry: *Never take the handcuffs off a lunatic secretary*. Decker did eventually resume speaking to me.

Decker probably doesn't remember that case with quite the detached sense of amusement that I do. But I have my own scary memories of bank robbers. Four times during my FBI career, I brushed shoulders with death. And every time, it involved a bank robber in Columbus. The first was the day in April 1974 when we chased Monk Huffman. The second, just a few months later, involved an elusive robber named Harvey Clay Griffith.

There was something a little squirrelly about the Griffith case right from the start. The robbery alarm came in from Upper Arlington, an upscale neighborhood in northwest Columbus where stickups were considered not only illegal, but in poor taste: They just weren't done. During my entire eight years in Columbus, this was the only time I responded to a call in Upper Arlington.

Cleary was already at the bank when I got there, organizing a canvass of the neighborhood to see if anyone had seen which way the robbers went or what car they had switched into. "Take the tellers," he instructed me.

One by one, I talked to the bank's half-dozen tellers. They weren't much help: two robbers, white, armed with rifles and handguns. Only one teller had seen the getaway car, a large luxury car. I wasn't surprised; nobody likes to make eye contact with an armed bank robber who's shouting threats. It's too much like a challenge.

Just as I finished the interviews, we got a call from one of the agents checking the neighborhood. A Cadillac had been found a few blocks away. Did I have a witness who could identify the car? Could I bring her over to take a look?

I went back to the teller who had seen the getaway, a plump, pretty blonde of about thirty-five or so. "I think we've found the Cadillac," I told her. "Let's go see if it's the right one."

"No," she replied.

It took a minute for the word to work its way through my brain. No? *No?* "Look, we've got to do this right away, before they get too far out of the area," I said urgently. "Your boss won't mind."

"I don't care what my boss says," she snapped. "I just had a man threaten me with a gun and I feel like throwing up and I'm not going anywhere."

I was used to the fear tellers experience at robbery scenes—people who've been looking down the business end of a gun rarely feel like talking about it—but this was the first time I'd ever had one flat-out refuse to cooperate. It upset me. If we didn't catch these guys, they'd just rob another bank (like the old potato chip commercial, nobody can do just one), and the next time somebody might get killed. I picked up a telephone from a nearby desk and dialed the number of an assistant U.S. attorney.

"I've got a bank teller here who admits she saw the getaway car," I said, speaking loud enough for her to hear, "but she refuses to identify it. Can I arrest her?"

"No," he said.

"Okay, lady, we're going to get in my car," I bluffed her. "It's up to you: We can go look at the Cadillac, or we can go downtown and I'll book you for obstruction of justice. I hope you've got somebody with good credit to make your bail, because I have a feeling you'll be unemployed when the bank finds out what happened."

My threat to arrest her wasn't serious. Her threat to vomit, on the other hand, looked all too real. Her face went a queasy pale, and she had to sit down for a minute. But in the end, we went to see the Cadillac. She identified it, but we couldn't find anyone who had seen the switch. Hot pursuit was over; now we switched to detective work.

Cleary generated the first break on the case. After sifting through records for a while, he tied the abandoned Cadillac to somebody named Harvey Clay Griffith. And Griffith was a guy who liked to rob banks. We already had a warrant on him out of Michigan. Now all we had to do was find him.

That sounds easier than it really is. Most of Columbus's bank robbers were junkies—I have no idea if that holds true in the rest of the country, but I rarely talked to a robber in Columbus who didn't sport an arm full of needle tracks—and they lived in that aimless, transient world of the drug addict: Sleeping on somebody's couch or spare bed, moving along every week or two, spinning around from here to there like a slow-motion pinball.

Griffith, our snitch said, mostly stayed in the Bottoms, a seedy section on the west side of town that was the polar opposite of Upper Arlington, where he had robbed the bank. Cleary tracked him for weeks through the bars and flophouses over there, sometimes with my help. Not everyone in the Bottoms was a crook, but most of them had taken some pretty hard body blows from life. They didn't have much use for cops, and they didn't see what concern it was of theirs that somebody had knocked over a bank in a country-club neighborhood that might as well have been on the other side of the moon as far as they were concerned.

Cleary, though, was surprisingly adept at getting past that. Every time somebody told us *never heard of him* or *I don't know a thing about that*, Cleary would nod politely, snap his notebook shut, and go on his way—but he'd be back the next day, asking the same question a different way. And he kept on doing it until he got an answer.

Sometimes the stifling, dingy apartments of the Bottoms turned us into social workers against our will. One day we visited a trash-strewn flat right out of *Tobacco Road*, complete with a grotesquely obese girl of nineteen and her squalling daughter. It was a toss-up as to which was filthier, the mother's stained T-shirt or the daughter's grimy face.

Cleary kept trying to ask the mother about Griffith, but my eyes kept turning to the little girl, a toddler of two or so. Under the dirt, her face was a firetruck red. Reaching over, I touched my palm to her forehead. It was like dipping my hand into a barbecue pit. "For

Christ's sake, Dick, feel this kid's temperature," I interrupted. Giving me a puzzled look, he pressed the back of his hand against her face and then quickly jerked it away.

"This child is burning up with fever," he said sternly to the mother. "Have you taken her to a doctor?"

"I ain't takin' her to no doctor," she answered in her West Virginia mountain twang. "I ain't got no money for that."

"Go to the emergency room," I suggested. "They'll treat her whether you can pay or not. And she's certainly sick enough."

The mother looked uncertain, like we were playing a trick. "My husband don't like me runnin' around during the day," she finally said. "He'll be home by and by. If he wants to take her, he can."

Cleary and I glanced at each other. Without a word passing between us, I knew he was about to expand FBI jurisdiction. "Ma'am, I'm afraid I'm going to have to arrest you under the Federal Emergency Medical Act for failure to provide proper medical care," he said, pulling his handcuffs from his pocket.

"Arrest me?" gasped the mother. "Oh Lord, oh shit, arrest me? I ain't got no money for no lawyer or no bail."

"Well," Cleary said, stroking his chin thoughtfully, "we *might* be able to let it slide. But only if you follow us to the hospital in your car. Once we see the child's got a doctor, maybe we'll let you off with a warning."

"Arrest me, oh Lord, oh shit," the mother said, lumbering to her feet. "Oh Lord, oh shit."


Our second bogus arrest threat of the investigation may have saved that little girl's life, but it didn't get us any closer to Griffith. Cleary had learned a lot about him but we never got a lead that was even medium-warm as to his whereabouts. Everyplace we looked, he was long gone.

One night a few weeks later, I planned to play softball and go to a cookout. Instead I got an urgent call to meet Cleary and Jerry Jones at the Ohio State University Hospital. "Griffith's here," Cleary told me as he grabbed me in the lobby and steered me down a hallway.

"What do you mean?" I asked. "He's a patient?"

"No, his *wife* is," Cleary explained. "A snitch told me a couple of days ago she was here in a gynecological ward. I left one of his mugshots with the ward nurses. They called me a few minutes ago. He's in there now, visiting her."

We had reached the ward nursing station, where Jones was huddled with a nurse. "It's him, I'm sure of it," she said, tapping her finger on the booking photo of a pudgy young man.

"What can you tell us about the layout of the room?" Cleary asked.

"That's the door," the nurse said, pointing across the hall. "Inside, the room goes to the right. There are two beds on the same wall as the door, two more on the opposite wall. Mrs. Griffith's bed is in the far-right corner, and that's where he's sitting, talking to her."

"I'm ready to go," I announced, pulling my gun from my holster. "Put that away," Cleary said immediately. "We can't walk into a ward full of sick women waving our guns."

I stared at him for a moment, speechless. Griffith had been shot at by Detroit cops just a few weeks earlier during an armed bank robbery and only escaped by running through a plate glass window. I couldn't believe Cleary wanted to walk in empty-handed. That Ivy League gentleman shit only carries you so far.

"Dick, he's going to kill us," I finally stammered. "Sure as shit, he's going to kill us."

"You've got to consider the situation." Cleary replied. "Those women aren't well, and if we go in there with guns drawn, it's going to scare them to death."

"It's going to scare them a lot more if we all get our brains blown out in front of them," Jones interjected, following my lead. "You may be worrying about how they'll react to seeing a gun, but I guarantee you that asshole in there"—he gestured toward the room—"isn't going to think two seconds about it. He'll just shoot."

The three of us fell silent. "Okay," agreed Cleary after a long pause. "Let's do it."

Moments later, we burst into the room. Griffith was at the far end of the ward, perhaps fifteen feet away, dressed completely in blue denim: jacket, jeans, and crushed hat. He dropped from his chair and crouched behind the high hospital bed where his wife was lying. A .357 revolver magically appeared in his hand. The women were probably squealing and crying, but I didn't hear a thing, didn't notice them. I had tunnel vision for that gun.

"FBI!" Cleary yelled. "Put it away! Put it down or we'll kill you!" In truth, he should have fired—we *all* should have fired the instant Griffith drew. But it's hard for decent people—even decent people trained in the knowledge that it may be necessary to kill in self-defense—to root out that instinct for civilization; it extends right down to your trigger finger. That's why we're on this side of the badge, and the Harvey Clay Griffiths of the world are on the other.

We hesitated because we're not killers. Griffith hesitated too—but only, I'm convinced, because the odds were 3 to 1 against him. His split second lasted longer than ours. Jones and Cleary, who were closer, lunged around the bed and pinned him to the wall, pushing his gun away.

As they struggled with him, I caught something out of the corner of my right eye. Lo and behold, here was *another* young man, dressed in the identical blue denim outfit. As far as I was concerned, sharing Harvey Clay Griffith's fashion sense was a felony. I rammed him into the wall and spun him around, clapping the cuffs around his wrists before he had a chance to resist. Quickly I patted him down and didn't find anything. I turned back to see if Jones and Cleary needed help, but they had Griffith cuffed and under control.

"Don't you think you want to search again?" Griffith's partner said in a mockingly polite tone.

"Why, did you like it?" I sneered, but I started checking his pockets again. Oops. A P-38 automatic, wedged between his pants and the small of his back. Oops. A double-barrel over-and-under .357 Derringer in the back pocket of his jeans. As we marched out of the ward,

WITH HONOR AND PURPOSE

I debated whether to smack him for being a wise guy or thank him for the help.

Three years later, in 1977, Miller and I were on our way to a routine interview in west Columbus when we heard a robbery call. "To all units," the radio squawked, "we have a 10-77 at Dollar Savings on Nelson Road." Miller, without speaking, wheeled the car around and headed for the bank. Seconds later, the dispatcher was back on the air. "Suspect is a black male in his early twenties, tall Afro hairdo, very light-complected, about six-foot-five and two hundred pounds."

"That's gotta be Jimmy Shipman," I told Miller. By now, we'd been working banks so long that we knew a lot of the robbers in Columbus. We could identify many of them instantly from even a partial description. One time I heard the dispatcher summoning agents to the scene of a bank robbery where a gunfight between police and robbers had just ended. Based on the dispatcher's description, I was pretty certain I knew who the robber was. When the cops swung by his house, his car was sitting in the driveway, engine still warm, a bullet hole in the side.

"Nobody else is that tall," Miller agreed. "But isn't Shipman still in the joint?" That was a very good question. We had put Jimmy Shipman in federal prison twice for the same robbery—one of the weirder cases I ever handled—and he couldn't possibly have finished his sentence. Of course, it was possible he had escaped.

I raised the office on the radio. "Can you check with the Bureau of Prisons and make sure Jimmy Shipman is still in the joint?" I asked. Five minutes later, as we were pulling up at Dollar Savings, a clerk called back. "Bureau of Prisons advises that Shipman remains in federal custody," he said.

"Well, scratch him off the list of usual suspects," I said to Miller. "We must have a rookie robber here, somebody we don't know." But try as we might, we couldn't find a trace of the Dollar Savings robber. Maybe he'd just been passing through.

I said we put Shipman away twice for the same robbery, which may strike you as not only strange but even unconstitutional. Here's something stranger still: It was a robbery he didn't even do. I told you it was a weird case.

It started in late 1975, when I got a call from the Columbus Police Department. The cops had a guy named Jimmy Shipman in custody on state robbery charges. But Shipman was willing to save everybody some trouble and confess to a bank robbery I was working if he could serve his time in the federal prison system, a much less unpleasant place than the Ohio system. Would I come take the confession?

This phone call would have been unthinkable just a few years before, when I was starting out in the FBI. In those days, the Bureau and local police usually treated one another like rivals instead of allies in the fight against crime.

Never was that more apparent than when working bank robberies, as I observed the very first time I went out on a bank job. It was a little bank located in a mobile home in Troy, New York, and I was so excited at hearing the call over the radio that I went roaring away from a gas station without paying. When I got there, the FBI was at one end of the trailer and the state police at the other. Each side was interviewing the same witnesses. And in the half hour I was there, I didn't hear a single word exchanged between cops and agents. Under those circumstances, it was a wonder any cases ever got made.

After that, I always swore that when I was senior enough to start calling my own shots, I was going to work with police instead of compete against them. And in Columbus I did just that. It helped that there were more damn bank robberies than either of us could handle by ourselves. We routinely traded prosecutions with the Columbus cops, depending on who could make the robber serve more time on a conviction.

So I was happy to go take Jimmy Shipman's confession and afterward arrest him on federal charges. He admitted to robbing Railroad Savings and Loan in Columbus and was quickly packed off to the federal slam in Ashland, Kentucky. Just like *Dragnet*, right?

Except that eight months later, we busted another gang of bank robbers—and *they* confessed to the Railroad Savings and Loan robbery. What's more, they never even heard of Jimmy Shipman. Trying to sort this all out, I went down to Kentucky to talk to Shipman in his prison cell.

"It's easy," he explained. "I didn't do the Railroad Savings job. But I didn't want to do time in the state joint on the robbery they busted me for, so I copped to Railroad. And you know something? Now that you know I didn't do it, you got to let me out. Ain't no judge gonna hold me for a robbery the FBI says I didn't commit."

"Suppose you did get out," I said. "The Columbus cops will be right there to arrest you on the same charges they arrested you for in the first place."

Smiling broadly, Jimmy shook his head from side to side. "Dismissed with prejudice, man, as part of the deal. I'm out of here. Vacation time."

I thought it over for a moment. "Maybe you're right," I told him. "But you're going to have to wrangle it all out with the lawyers. Meanwhile, would you give me a written statement about Railroad Savings? I have to show something to my boss and the U.S. attorney to explain what you did."

"Gladly, my man," Jimmy said. A couple hours later, I left the prison with the signed statement. And I drove straight back to the U.S. attorney's office in Columbus. We filed charges against him under Title 18, U.S. Code, Section 1001, Furnishing False Information to a Federal Agent, punishable by ten years in prison. The trial was like shooting fish in a barrel. Jimmy's vacation would be delayed a few years.

About three weeks after the Dollar Savings robbery, I paid a visit to a woman I was trying to turn snitch. She wasn't a criminal herself, but she loved to party with bank robbers, and she was potentially a gold mine of information. She hadn't been very helpful on my first visit, but I had a good feeling about her. Another conversation or two, and we might get her to flip.

She lived in an old Victorian home that had been split into several apartments. Hers was on the third floor, a neat, trim little place. She swung the door wide open when I knocked, and over her shoulder I could see Jimmy Shipman, big as life, sprawled on her couch. His eyes hardened as he saw me. *This could get a little sticky*, I thought.

"Hi, I was in your neighborhood and thought you might have a few minutes to chat," I said to the woman. "But I see you have company, so maybe it's not a good time." Then I raised my hand in greeting to Jimmy. "Hey, Jimmy, how you been doing?" I asked, although my brain was beaming quite a different question: *How come you're here and not in the federal pen where you belong?*

"I'm okay," he grunted, eying me carefully. I was sure he believed I had come to the apartment looking for him. There was a calculating look in his eyes, as though he were trying to guess how many other agents might be downstairs, should he try to take me or try to run.

"Well, I'm sure I'll be seeing you around," I said. I turned and walked back down the stairs. Outside I used the car radio to call for backup. I wanted to bring him in for questioning, but for all I knew, Jimmy had an army standing by in the back room. Miller arrived ten minutes later, and we went upstairs, but Jimmy had slipped out a back way.

When I got back to the office, I called the Bureau of Prisons myself. The first couple of clerks I talked to assured me once again that Jimmy Shipman was still in custody. I suggested, loudly and colorfully, that he was not. Finally I got someone on the line who knew what he was talking about.

"What we have here is a semantic mix-up," the man said. "Shipman *is* in federal custody—but we've put him in a halfway house there in Columbus."

"What's a halfway house?" I asked. In those days, it was a new program, to me—I'd never heard of it.

"It's a program for well-behaved inmates in the final phase of their sentence," he explained. "We move them into a supervised group house, and they get used to living in society again. They're allowed to go out on their own to look for jobs during the day, but they have to be back at the house by dark. In a technical sense, someone assigned to a halfway house is still a prison inmate, and that's why you were misled when you called before."

"Thanks," I said and hung up, sparing him my opinion of the halfway house program. Jimmy Shipman had been looking for jobs during the day all right—bank jobs. I bet he wasn't the only one using that halfway house as a federally subsidized hideout while he pulled stickups or mugged old ladies.


Just in case Jimmy was a complete moron, I checked with the halfway house. As even Inspector Clouseau could have predicted, he had walked away without so much as a thank you to the nice people who fed and clothed him while he was breaking back into the workforce. On the other hand, we could stop worrying about some new six-foot-five bank robber in town—when I took Jimmy's picture over to Dollar Savings, the tellers all identified him in half a heartbeat.

For weeks I beat the pavement looking for him without a bit of luck. The only tip I picked up was that he had a girlfriend serving time in the state women's prison in Marysville. It didn't seem like much of a lead, but one morning when I found my calendar open, Miller and I drove over to talk to her. I never did meet with the woman. But I did talk with a prison official who knew her pretty well, who gave me a great tip: Jimmy was seeing a woman in Columbus whom we'll call Lorraine, and somehow the prison girlfriend had found out about it. She was in a spitting rage, firing off letters to Lorraine every day, warning her to stay away from Jimmy or be prepared to lose several very personal parts of her anatomy when the prison girlfriend finished her sentence. Love is a many-splendored thing, they say, and I certainly thought so that day. It didn't take me long at all to find Lorraine: Her address was on every piece of hate mail going out of the prison. For the first time, we had a solid lead on Jimmy's whereabouts.

Lorraine's address was in a neat but shabby housing project, a two-story building with four apartments on each floor. We went over there the next morning at 7 A.M., figuring we'd catch Jimmy before he went off to make his daily mischief.

"What do you think?" I asked Miller as we sat in the car, taking a look at the building from about fifty feet away.

"I think it looks like the kind of place that nobody lives in five seconds longer than they have to," he answered. "I wonder if Lorraine has already moved. If *my* boyfriend were a rich bank robber, *I* sure as hell wouldn't live there. Before we go too far with this, let's check the building mailbox, see if her name is on it."

"Okay," I agreed. "Her apartment is supposed to be in the front of the building. Why don't we approach from the back? That way, if Jimmy's there, he won't be able to see us."

"Let me do it," Miller said. "You park out here and keep an eye on the front of the place, in case they leave." That made sense, and Miller got out of the car and disappeared behind the building. I leaned on the hood of the car and enjoyed the cool morning air, which all too soon would turn into the soup of a Columbus summer. I wasn't the only one. Down the sidewalk, about seventy-five feet away, I could see a couple on a leisurely sunrise stroll.

But not just *any* couple. It was Jimmy and Lorraine, coming home from somewhere. A .357 revolver was tucked in his pants. Almost the instant that information registered on my brain, Miller emerged from the back of the building. "Get back, Paul!" I shouted. "He's out here with a gun!"

As I shouted, Jimmy whipped the pistol out of his pants. Less than thirty feet away, he had an easy shot at me. I dived to the other side of my car, drawing my own gun as I moved. When I bobbed my head back over the fender, Jimmy had his elbow around Lorraine's neck and had pulled her in front of him, a human shield. The barrel of his pistol was jammed against the side of her head. Without saying a word, he backed toward the apartment door and ducked inside, dragging Lorraine every step of the way.

"Stay where you are, Paul!" I yelled. "He's inside, but the apartment has a big picture window. He could open fire at any second!"

Crouching down on the floor of the front seat of the Bucar, I clutched the radio microphone. "We've got a hostage situation here," I told the office. "The subject is armed and barricaded inside an apartment."

Help arrived within minutes: ten FBI agents, the Columbus police SWAT team, even a helicopter. As the cops emptied out the surrounding apartments and deployed what looked like enough artillery to conquer a small country, I started breathing easier. But Jimmy Shipman was still in there, with a gun and a hostage. And I wasn't sure what it would take to bring him out. The police were phoning Lorraine's apartment, trying to start a dialogue, but nobody answered.

Somebody pulled out a bullhorn, and I started talking to Jimmy over it. "Come on out, Jimmy," I said, just like one of those old movie G-men. "We won't hurt you. Just put your hands up and come on out." But the only answer was the eerie electronic echo of my own voice, bouncing back to me.

It was an hour and a half later when Jimmy surprised us by answering the phone. "I'm ready to come out, man," he said. "But don't be shootin' me when I come outside."

"Open the door and stick your arms out first," the agent on the telephone instructed him. "One agent will approach and snap handcuffs on you. Then you can come out."

"Okay," Jimmy agreed. "But make sure the guy you send to the door is Kerby." The line went dead, and less than a minute later the front door opened. A long pair of weirdly disembodied arms slowly extended outward into the building's hallway.

Pistol in one hand, cuffs in the other, I entered the hallway and walked briskly toward the door. Jimmy would have to be crazy to try something—he knew there were twenty or so guns trained on him—

but we couldn't really be sure that there wasn't someone else in the apartment, a wild card we hadn't accounted for.

I popped on one cuff, then the other. Without warning, I abruptly jerked him into the hall. Agents poured into the apartment as the SWAT team took up positions around the building's perimeter. "Find his gun," I called out as I led Jimmy away. "It's not on him."

But it wasn't inside the apartment, either, as other agents reminded me all afternoon. "Say, Phil, are you sure he wasn't just pointing his finger at you?" jibed one. "Man, next time you're lonely, just invite us for coffee," said another. "You don't have to make up a story about a gun."

"There *was* a gun," I told Miller, my voice rising in frustration. "Didn't you see it?"

"You told me not to come around the corner, remember?" he answered apologetically. "I didn't see anything." But as he turned away, I thought I saw the beginning of a smirk. I suspected he was enjoying the way everybody was needling me. How cruel and unprofessional! Just because I once conspired with Decker to trick Miller into dropping his pants for a fake hernia exam in a restaurant bathroom. Was it my fault a half-dozen agents trooped in to make fun of him? Some people have no sense of humor.


"Good morning, Lorraine," I said to the surprised woman at the door. "I'm sure you remember me from yesterday. This is Agent Mike DeGuire, who's working with me today. We want to search the apartment again." I was determined to find that gun. It wasn't all that important from an evidence standpoint—we had enough eyewitness testimony on the Dollar Savings robbery to put Jimmy Shipman in jail until the next time it snowed in the Sahara—but damned if I was going to become a Bureau legend, Phil Kerby and the Invisible Pistol.

Lorraine was silent for a minute, sizing the situation up. She could tell us to go screw ourselves, and that's pretty much what we would have to do. A judge would be unlikely to give me a search warrant. He'd say: "You guys already tossed the place for two hours yesterday. How can you be sure it's there? And even if it *was* there yesterday, what makes you so sure it's *still* there today?" I wouldn't have very good answers for either of those questions.

On the other hand, Lorraine knew she was skating on the ragged edge with us. If we decided to get serious, we could probably scrape together a case against her for harboring an escaped felon and accessory to God-knows-what.

She decided we could be friends. "Sure, come on in," she said with a waste-your-time-if-you-want-to flip of her wrist.

We stepped inside, and I pointed to the kitchen. "Mike, you start in there," I told him. "I'll take the bedroom."

DeGuire was a quiet, studious guy with a sharp mind—his hobby was solving differential equations—that had carried him up through the ranks of Bureau clerks and made him a full agent. Behind his bookworm exterior (he even wore horn-rim glasses), he was pretty interesting. One of his assignments as a clerk was in Mexico City, where we had an office in the U.S. embassy. DeGuire told me that the week before the Kennedy assassination in 1963, the Soviet embassy in Mexico City was sending out a phenomenal amount of radio traffic. Then, the day before President Kennedy was shot, it dropped to virtually nothing. Coupling that with Lee Harvey Oswald's visit to that embassy two months before the assassination, DeGuire was always very suspicious about the role the Soviets might have played.

As a first-office agent, DeGuire wasn't often assigned to the glamour cases. I thought crossing his excitement at working a bank robbery and his patient approach to work would probably result in a good, thorough search. And that was what we needed. For that gun to have eluded the first search, it had to be well-hidden. Or else I was just plain crazy.

Doggedly we set to work. It was mind-numbing stuff. Every drawer had to be pulled out, every stack of clothing had to be rifled, every shoe had to be probed. Any nook or cranny big enough to hold a pistol had to be explored, and nothing was too improbable or too ridiculous to consider. I once worked with an agent who solved a case when, on some blessedly deranged impulse, he poured out the entire contents of a twenty-pound sack of cat food. Sure enough, a gun came tumbling out with the Cat Chow.

We had been there two sweaty hours when DeGuire called out some of the sweetest words I have ever heard: "I found it!" I was out in that kitchen like a flash. "Look at this," he gestured under the sink. The fiberboard back of the cabinet looked like it was flush with the drainpipe. But when DeGuire pressed it at a certain spot near the bottom, it popped back to open a space about two inches wide. When he pulled back his fingers, the board snapped back into the flush position. He opened it again, and we could clearly see the gun lying down at the bottom.

"Don't that beat all!" exclaimed Lorraine, standing behind us. When I turned, she had a look on her face that reminded me of Claude Raines in *Casablanca:* I am shocked, *shocked* to discover gambling in this club! I burst out laughing, partly at her ridiculous laugh and partly because I was so damn happy to have been proven nonhallucinatory. DeGuire had a big dumb grin on his face that, as far as I was concerned, he'd earned about a hundred times over.

"Don't get your fingers on the gun when you pick it up," I warned him, still smiling. "Remember, it's evidence." DeGuire carefully snagged the pistol with a pen and slipped it into a plastic bag. I took it back to the office and left it on my desk while I went to the bathroom.

When I came back less than two minutes later, an agent had taken the gun out of the bag and was dry-firing it out the window. "Instead of ruining evidence," I snarled, snatching it away, "you should be writing an explanation of why you guys can't find your own butts in a dark room with two hands." As he slunk away, I began planning the weeks of torment I would inflict on Miller for doubting me.

It turned out that gun had a rather lurid history. It had been stolen in a robbery at a furniture store where the elderly owner had been shot in the head. We were never able to prove Jimmy Shipman did it. But we suspected there must have been some reason he spent so much time and trouble hiding that gun from us.

Although I was delighted with the way the Jimmy Shipman story ended, I can never think of it without a twinge of sadness. A few weeks later, Mike DeGuire, trying to shed his semi-nerd image, came out to the YMCA to play basketball with us. We played a pretty fierce full-court game—several of us were college jocks—and the pace was ferocious. After about forty-five minutes, DeGuire wandered over to the side of the court and sat down.

"Hey, you gotta play defense, too," Federspiel joked.

"I don't feel too good," DeGuire confessed.

"Yeah, right, I suppose it's a heart attack," Decker taunted. He trotted over and pretended to hook up an IV tube to DeGuire's arm. DeGuire didn't say anything, just got red in the face and slumped back in his chair. "Hey!" Decker yelled. "He *is* having a heart attack!"

We rushed him over to Grant Hospital, a few blocks away, where he had open-heart surgery. He was in intensive care for a week, touch and go, but finally he came out of it okay, and in our customary take-no-prisoners style, there were a lot of jokes about how some guys would do practically anything to get sympathy. But in 1995, assigned to an FBI office in Florida, Mike DeGuire collapsed again, and this time there was nothing the doctors could do. He was forty-nine years old.


"You don't happen to know the dude in the white fur coat, do you?" I asked as Angela poured me another cup of coffee. Angela (that's not her real name, by the way) was a very pretty black woman, with delectably creamy skin. When she was a thief, which wasn't too long ago, she was top of the line. Angela was one of the few women I ever met who was smart enough to get out of crime before her life went completely haywire. She had saved her money, too, instead of putting it up her nose, as her chic wardrobe and elegant apartment attested.

She did, however, cling to one remnant of her old life: an affinity for bank robbers. She liked to go out with them, party with them, sleep with them. And, when I stopped by, she would talk about them. Today I was asking about a group that had been hitting banks with monotonous regularity over the past few months. Their trademark:

One of them wore a full-length fur coat, so long it brushed the tops of his toes. It was perfect cover for the sawed-off shotgun he carried on a sling under his arm.

"Oh, yeah, Kenny Naphier," Angela agreed. "He loves that coat, thinks it makes him look like a movie star. Sure, I've partied with him. Big-time bank robber. Works with three other guys. But you want to be careful—they don't fuck around. They'd just as soon shoot you as say hello."

"Who are the others?"

"Let's see, there's Spoon Thompson, pretty heavy doper. And Lonnie Gates. And the fourth one, I don't really know. I'm not sure if he even robs banks or just likes to hang with them. They call him the Red Rooster."

"Why's that?"

"Beats me. I told you, I don't really know the fourth guy. But I think I have an address for him; I was supposed to meet Kenny over there one day." Fishing around in her purse, she found a small piece of paper and pushed it across the table for me to see. It was out in the east side housing projects.

Miller and I planned to go out there the next day, but all our plans got knocked askew by another robbery at the Ohio National Bank, which got hit so often that I sometimes thought they should just have the tellers stand out on the sidewalk and hand out bags of money.

We had barely arrived at the bank when a couple of cops came in and told us they'd found a car parked two blocks away, an old Cadillac with tail fins. Obviously it's a switch car; you don't rob a bank in your own car and then park a stone's throw away. The only thing to do was to go door-to-door among the student apartments that lined the street and hope to find a witness who had seen the switch. Miller took one side of the street, I took the other.

There was no answer at the first three doors where I knocked. At the fourth, a girl of about twenty answered. She was wearing a robe, and her hair was wrapped in a towel. Right out of the shower, and knockout gorgeous: She looked like the actress Halle Barry, who wouldn't come along for another fifteen years or so.

"Phil Kerby, FBI," I said. "We're interested in that Cadillac over there. Did you see anyone get in or out of it this morning?"

She gave me a smile, bright white teeth against coffee-colored skin. "I just got up a few minutes ago and got into the shower," she said. "I haven't even turned on the TV yet. So I'm afraid I'm no help."

"Thanks, sorry to bother you." I finished the block and didn't find out a damn thing. Neither did Miller. But I didn't care. Man, I'd knock on every door in Columbus if I could see a girl like that once a block.

It was a couple of days before I got to the east side projects, and no one was home at the address we had for the Red Rooster. I waited a few days, tried again. Still no luck. The third time, with an agent named Jimmy Rogers accompanying me, the door swings open. Jeans and a halter instead of towel and robe, but that same dazzling smile, bright white teeth against coffee-colored skin—which disappeared instantly when she saw me. I pushed past her into the apartment without an invitation, a perplexed Rogers following in our wake.

"Lady, you have a serious problem," I warned her. "Two times in two weeks I'm looking for bank robbers and you answer the door. I don't believe in coincidences or Santa Claus."

"But I don't know—"

"You're gonna get in a lot of trouble if you try to bullshit me," I interrupted. "So don't start."

She sighed and motioned for us to sit down. "What do you want from me?" she asked wearily.

"The truth, starting with the other day over near Ohio National Bank. You know who robbed it, don't you?"

She nodded. "Yeah, they were there. I was trying my best to get you to go away, because they were going to kill you if you came in. They were hidden in the hallway, guns out, and they said if you came in, you were dead meat. So I was trying hard not to act suspicious. What did you think?"

"Not bad," I admitted grudgingly.

I thought for a moment the girl—we'll call her Julie—was about to tell me Lonnie Gates, Kenny Naphier, and Spoon Thompson were behind this robbery, too, but that wasn't true. She identified the robbers as two other men, friends of hers. She knew the other guys, though—and knew the Red Rooster, too. He sometimes dated her sister, she said. He'd been around the apartment here a lot, but not recently.

Toward the end of the interview, when we were talking about the Red Rooster, Julie's mother came into the living room to listen. She nodded her head vigorously up and down every time Julie finished a sentence, murmuring, "That's right! That's right!" I never saw anyone so dying to be included in a conversation.

"Do you know the Red Rooster, too, ma'am?" I asked, faking a sociability I didn't really feel.

" 'Deed I do," she confirmed. "He used to G Julie's sister."

*G* was housing-project slang for sexual intercourse. I tried to steer the conversation onto safer ground. "Why does everyone call him Red Rooster?" I asked.

"I reckon I started that," she said. "He used to come over and go out on the back porch with my daughter. One day I went out there to sweep the porch and they were there G-ing on the floor. And when he rolled off her, he had red hair all over his thing."

"Thing?" asked Rogers, who still had not grasped that we were not on the *Ozzie and Harriet* set.

"Dick," the old lady explained kindly. "He had red hair on his dick. So we started calling him Red Rooster."


It took some time, but the leads from Julie and her family put us close on the heels of Naphier, Gates, and Thompson. (The Red Rooster, however, had flown the coop. He didn't seem to be in Columbus anymore, and we never did determine that he was one of the bank robbers.) Eventually, Jerry Jones, Flint Gabelman, and I got a tip that Lonnie Gates had rented a fancy new town house. We went over to arrest him, and we got a bonus: Spoon Thompson hiding in an upstairs closet, waiting to stick a gun up my nose.

Spoon, though, must have seen the same thing in Flint's eyes that I did. He let the rifle fall to the floor. We arrested him, and a few days later, we got Naphier, too. And afterward, I never again attached swastika armbands to the full-length leather coat that Gabelman sometimes wore that made him look like an SS colonel chasing Humphrey Bogart. The fun had gone out of it.

The fun had gone out of Columbus, too. That Wild West shoot-'em-up stuff always looked exciting when Dale Robertson did it on TV. But four close calls was enough for me. I started to look for a quieter assignment.

# 1 0

## UNDER
## THE
## HOOVERDOME

I glanced nervously up and down the sidewalk. Meeting William Saxbe, the attorney general of the United States— the head of the Justice Department, the boss of all bosses—would have made me fidgety under the best of circumstances. But being assigned to guard him! As we waited for his car outside Columbus International Airport, I was acutely aware that I didn't know the first thing about being a bodyguard. What should I be watching for? If some nut popped out of a crowd with a gun, was I supposed to jump forward and grab him, or fall back to protect the attorney general? *The Book of Losers* had disappeared since J. Edgar Hoover's death, but if the attorney general got shot while I was guarding him, they'd probably bring it back with my picture on the cover.

Three Bucars were parked in front of us. Saxbe and his wife, Dolly, got into the first one, and his small entourage of flunkies surged toward the others. One of them, a brisk little man with the words *officious Washington prick* stamped all over him, pointed to a large leather suitcase. "Get my bag," he said to the agent next to him. I shuddered, certain what was coming.

The agent, Anson Hopper, leaned over until his face was about two inches away from the aide's. "How would you like to kiss my ass?" he roared. "What do I look like, your houseboy?"

Hopper spun on his heels and walked away. The aide stood there, paralyzed and maybe even lobotomized. I glanced over at Saxbe's car and waited for the explosion.

A favorite lunchtime game among agents is: If I Ran the FBI. If I ran the FBI, I'd have more agents work drug cases. If I ran the FBI, I'd put more money into training. But the all-time winner was a guy I had lunch with years ago, who said: "If I ran the FBI, the first thing I'd do would be to go straight to personnel, pull all the files, and start going through them. And every time I found someone who had ever been assigned to headquarters, I'd fire him on the spot."

That's one way to gauge the way the average FBI agent feels about headquarters. Another is to consider some of the nicknames we have for the place. One of the more polite is The Seat of All Knowledge. One of the more common is The Crotch. In Detroit, a very talented but also very disgruntled agent named Paul Lindsay began referring to the place as the Hooverdome, which also acquired a certain covert popularity.

In the old days agents—honest-to-God agents interested in law enforcement—almost never wanted to go near Washington. They saw it as a giant, voracious maw that sucked in endless amounts of paper and spit back stupid rules. Only the Hooverdome, we knew, could have devised anything as useless as the FBI Daily Report, which you had to fill out each afternoon, showing how you spent all your time that day in fifteen-minute blocks.

Not even the people who wrote these rules could understand them. For example, every time you investigated a bombing, you had to fill out a special form. One of the questions: What quarter was the moon in at the time of the explosion? For years, I obediently hunted down the answer every time I worked a bombing. Then, during a seminar on bomb investigations at the academy, I asked the instructor why the phase of the moon was so important.

"You know, I've always wondered that myself," he confessed.

But the FBI bureaucrats who were so good at devising those forms and creating new rules (desperate, pitiless woe unto the agent who missed the five-thousand-mile oil change on his Bucar) often seemed to lack even the simplest common sense when it came to the real world of law enforcement.

In 1971, burglars broke into the FBI resident agency in Media, Pennsylvania, and carted away hundreds of documents. For weeks the burglars—who were apparently New Left activists, although the break-in was never solved—leaked the stolen documents to the media. Some were embarrassing (a memo banning the employment of people with "pear-shaped heads" as clerks) and some were *really* embarrassing (reports describing the COINTEL programs, the Bureau's spying and dirty-tricks campaigns against leftist groups).

It soon turned out that hardly any of the FBI's 450 or so offices—including the one in Media—had burglar alarms. In some, the building cleaning crews could come and go at will after hours. For the next couple of months, $40,000-a-year agents had to be paid overtime to work as security guards, watching the offices overnight while alarms were installed.

When the Hooverdome took an interest in investigations, things could get absolutely surreal. A couple of years earlier, the late Vice President Spiro Agnew had visited Columbus to give a speech at the Ohio State Fairgrounds. As usual, there were demonstrators all over the place. As Agnew arrived to give his speech, someone threw a rock that shattered a back window in his car.

Within minutes, the teletype lines from Washington were smoking. Headquarters wanted a full-scale investigation, and I was the lucky guy designated to run it. I had *two* teams of agents out for two days interviewing hippies and anti-war activists, who alternately wouldn't tell us anything or sent us chasing after drug-induced hallucinations. Every ridiculous report generated a new teletype from headquarters. I began to feel like I was running a second Warren Commission, checking out every story about a puff of smoke on the grassy knoll.

In my airtels to headquarters, I codenamed the case AGROCK. Nobody in Washington blinked. Then someone got the idea that the FBI lab should be called in. Agnew's car had been shipped to Japan, where he was visiting, and the Bureau had it shipped home immediately so the lab could check out the broken window. After an exhaustive examination, the lab reached a conclusion: It had been hit from outside with a rock.

In my five years in the FBI, I had managed to avoid Washington almost completely. The single exception came during the big May Day demonstrations in 1971, when the anti-war movement had pledged to shut down the capital. Headquarters asked every division to send two agents for special duty during the demonstrations. Bob Federspiel and I were the nominees from Columbus. I wish I could say we were chosen because of our Sherlock Holmes–like powers of detection, but it had more to do with the requirement stipulated by headquarters that the agents had to be at least six feet tall.

Nothing about the trip made me feel any differently about Washington. On the morning of the demonstration, Federspiel and I stopped outside headquarters to relay a message. An FBI supervisor standing on the sidewalk, who didn't know we were agents, glared at Federspiel. "You asshole, why don't you get a haircut?" he bellowed. Federspiel and I gazed at each other in amazement. The only part of his hair that was even *slightly* long were his sideburns, which extended barely an inch below his ears. Anyone in America would have taken one look at him and recognized him as a cop—anyone except the hopelessly-out-of-it bosses at the Hooverdome.*

I swore I would take an assignment to the fabled Butte, Montana, office—long considered the Siberia of the FBI—before I'd set foot in

---

*The Mayday demonstration itself was a complete bust. Washington police made thousands of preemptive arrests, turning RFK Stadium into a giant holding cell, and the whole thing was over before noon. Federspiel and I went for lunch at a place near headquarters. As soon as we sat down at our table, we heard a *slap-slap-slap* from the front of the room. Looking over, I saw a stage where a woman with the most gargantuan chest I had ever laid eyes on was rhythmically slapping her breasts together. We had blundered into a topless joint. Really, though, we were just ahead of our time. The IRS seized the place a couple of years later as part of a tax case, and it became for a time an official U.S. government topless bar.

Washington again. But in 1974, Washington came to me: I was assigned as one of the attorney general's bodyguards.

I got the job through an odd chain of circumstances. A few months earlier, newspaper heiress Patricia Hearst had been kidnapped in Berkeley by a radical group calling itself the Symbionese Liberation Army. Two months later, the group robbed a San Francisco bank—and surveillance cameras showed Hearst right in the middle of the robbery, carrying a rifle.

There was no way, of course, to tell if the gun was loaded. And there was a lot of public debate about whether she was a willing participant in the robbery or just a hostage, doing what she was told. Saxbe, President Nixon's razor-tongued attorney general, thought she was guilty, and he said so, calling her "a common criminal" during one of his speeches.

You'd have thought this would please the radicals—Saxbe was, after all, accepting their claim that Hearst had crossed over to their side—but for some reason they were incensed. They threatened to kill Saxbe, and the Justice Department decided the attorney general needed protection. Instead of asking the Treasury Department to lend some Secret Service agents, who are trained as bodyguards, Justice handed the job to the FBI.

Most of the work fell to Washington-based agents. But Saxbe, a former U.S. senator from Ohio, still had a house in Mechanicsburg, a few miles west of Columbus. When he decided to spend a couple of weeks of vacation there, headquarters wanted to add some agents to the bodyguard detail who knew the area. The initial assignment went to Emmett Scott, Hopper, and me. I was both proud and nervous that the FBI was entrusting the boss's safety to me. And I also knew that with Hopper aboard, the duty was bound to be interesting.

No one was ever surprised to learn that Hopper was a former Houston cop. With an accent that made him sound like Foghorn Leghorn, Hopper was the quintessential Texan. (The only black agent in the

Columbus office called him Hopalong Honky.) Hopper was a cop to the bone and would have taken a bullet for any agent in the office, white, black, or purple. His hobbies were tearing phonebooks in half—the day the new directories arrived at the Columbus office, there was always a line of agents at Hopper's desk, bearing sacrificial offerings—and getting up before dawn in hopes of arresting a few deserters on his own time before going to work. Once, after a bloody student demonstration at Ohio State, the morning newspaper had photos of the Columbus riot police lined up with their heavy batons. Hopper was right in the middle.

None of us was really surprised when he cut loose on Saxbe's aide. He had no patience with anyone he thought was an idiot, a designation that included entire legions of FBI supervisors. Everybody still talked about the time that Hopper, during a preraid briefing of about fifty agents, sat in the back of the room telling jokes. The diminutive supervisor who was conducting the briefing got tired of it. "Pay attention," he snapped.

"Listen," Hopper snarled back in a voice loud enough for the entire room to hear, "don't give me any shit, or I'll punch the down-button on your elevator shoes."

Somehow he always escaped from these confrontations with his life and career intact. And it happened again that day with Saxbe. Hopper bellowed at the aide so loudly that I'm certain the attorney general must have heard him. But Hopper climbed into the driver's seat of Saxbe's car, and by the time we arrived in Mechanicsburg half an hour later, they were laughing and joking like old war buddies.

Guarding Saxbe turned out to be no big deal. He played some golf, visited nearby farms to look at cattle, and went to Ohio State football games. (*There* was some tough duty, sitting in the pressbox on the fifty-yard line, eating free hot dogs.) Mostly, though, he stayed close to home, a stately old two-story farmhouse with cupolas and riverboat windows. It was located on a two-lane highway outside the little town, about 250 feet off the road at the end of a long, snaking driveway.

Mechanicsburg was a pleasant but tiny place, about half a mile from the middle of nowhere, so there was little traffic and we didn't have to spend much time watching people, wondering whether they were casual passersby or deadly terrorists. After a couple of hours the first day, I quit worrying. If terrorists really were after Saxbe, I concluded, they were far more likely to try something in Washington than out here, where any strange face would instantly be noted and reported by the townsfolk.

That was fine with me. None of us had any idea what we were doing. We didn't know anything about defensive perimeters or safe-haven fallback shelters or evasive driving techniques or any of the stuff that even the greenest Secret Service agent can probably recite backward in his sleep. In case of trouble, our plan was: Shoot the bad guy. Fortunately, we never had to. The most dangerous thing about the job was trying to avoid sitting in any of the little Styrofoam cups full of tobacco juice that Saxbe left all over the place.

We were teamed with four agents from Washington. One of them was Sheila Reagan, one of the first female agents hired in the wake of Hoover's death. I wasn't sure how women were going to fit into the White Boys' Club atmosphere at the FBI, but Sheila made me confident it was going to work.

She was an ex-marine, a big woman, husky enough that we called her Thunder Thighs (though not to her face), and yet quite feminine, too. She had an earthy streak almost as big as Hopper's. One day Saxbe asked if she wanted to go horseback riding with him. "Afraid not, general," she drawled. "I didn't bring my shitkickers with me." When Saxbe finished laughing, he went inside to get her some boots.

One day, once I was confident it wouldn't provoke a long feminist rant, I asked Sheila if she had taken much crap from male agents. "Nah, it's been okay," she said, waving her arm dismissively. "I've had some problems with my love life, though."

"What do you mean?" I asked.

"Well, shortly after I got out of the academy, I had a date," she recalled, smiling. "He was coming over to the house for dinner. He didn't know I was with the Bureau, and I wasn't sure how he'd react, so I thought I'd just keep it to myself for a while. But then I was straightening up the house and I realized my gun was out. Better hide that, I thought, it's just going to raise too many questions.

"But I couldn't think of a place to put it. I kept imagining all these bizarre scenarios where for some reason he opens a drawer and the gun falls out. It just kept getting worse and worse, and finally I put the gun in the only place where I couldn't imagine he'd have any reason to look. I put it in the washing machine."

"Not bad," I agreed.

"Yeah, except the date went really well, and I forgot all about it. The next day, I put a load of underwear in the machine and washed it. With my gun."

Saxbe was in and out of Mechanicsburg all year, and each time Sheila came with him. By her third trip, we all adored her, especially Hopper, who recognized a kindred spirit when he saw one. One day in December, when Saxbe's stay in Ohio had dragged on longer than expected, Sheila begged a day off to pick up some things from her Washington apartment. Hopper drove her to the airport. A couple of hours later, as the plane approached Washington, it hit the side of a mountain. They found Sheila's gun, the same one she laundered, lying in the rubble.


August 8 was a Thursday, miserably hot and muggy. The air was so heavy that Emmett Scott and I barely spoke as we leaned against trees in front of the farmhouse. But we turned quickly when we heard the front door open. Saxbe wasn't scheduled to go anywhere, but he might have decided on one of his impromptu cattle-buying trips.

He had an odd, pained expression on his face. "President Nixon just phoned me," he said quietly. "He's going to resign tomorrow. He says I'm the first one he's told." We all stood there silently. A few moments later, Saxbe walked back into the house. We didn't see him again that day.

I wasn't sure what to say. I don't think Saxbe did, either. His relations with Nixon had often been stormy, so much so that I could never quite figure out how he got appointed attorney general. In 1972, when Nixon ordered the Christmas bombing of Hanoi, Saxbe told reporters, "He appears to have left his senses." When the Watergate scandal started to unfold, Saxbe was even more scathing. "Nixon is like the man who plays the piano in a bordello," he cracked, "and says he doesn't know what's going on upstairs." And yet Saxbe stuck with him, right to the bitter end.

We had talked a lot about Watergate that summer. A couple of the Washington agents on Saxbe's bodyguard detail had worked on the investigation, and it rankled them that there was a public perception that the FBI had been involved in the coverup. "We were the ones who *broke* Watergate," one of the agents complained. "We did all the interviews for the Senate committee. We're doing all the interviews for the special prosecutor. And now they're even saying this guy Deep Throat who leaked all the important stuff to the *Washington Post* was getting it from FBI 302s."

And ultimately, it was fear of the FBI's investigative prowess that did Nixon in. The so-called "smoking gun" tape, the one that triggered his resignation, contained a conversation in which Nixon ordered his aides to tell the CIA to claim that investigating Watergate would compromise national security secrets. It was the only way Nixon could think of to get the FBI off the case.


After a while, I began hating the security detail. For one thing, there was no sense of accomplishment. When I made an arrest, I always felt a burst of satisfaction at knowing there was one less criminal on the streets, one less punk stealing or killing. I suppose I could have said to myself as I went home each night from Saxbe's house, "Way to go, Phil, one more day that the attorney general didn't get killed," but it didn't feel quite the same.

Another nagging problem was that, despite Hopper's brave words, we *did* start turning into houseboys. We carried the Saxbes' luggage, parked their cars, brought in their newspapers, and sometimes answered their door and telephone. Unlike real houseboys, however, we also stayed outside in nighttime snowstorms when you couldn't see ten feet away, little more than human trip wires.*

About the only (slightly) redeeming feature of the duty was that we occasionally got a glimpse of a world of sumptuous wealth that most of us could only imagine. As one of the most powerful politicians in Ohio, Saxbe had some gluttonously rich friends. When he went to their parties, we had to tag along; you never knew when some General Motors heiress might try to strangle him with her pearl necklace.

One such soirée was put on by the top executives of the Libby, Owens, Ford Glass Company in Toledo. Saxbe gave a brief speech; in return, the corporate folks presented him with a crystal spittoon that was probably worth more than my car. They also put us up at their executive retreat on the grounds of the Belmont Country Club. There was a leather manicure kit in each room as a welcome gift, and a chef was on duty twenty-four hours a day to prepare any of us a meal of our choice, any time.

Another time, we accompanied Saxbe to the home of John Galbraith, the zillionaire who owned Darby Dan farms, the Pittsburgh Pirates baseball team, and practically everything else in central Ohio. In honor of Saxbe, Galbraith invited a couple of hundred similarly bankrolled men (yes, men—all of them) to a black-tie dinner at his farm near Columbus. When I say farm, don't think of Old Macdonald; this place was about the size of the Ponderosa and included a jet landing strip, a zoo, and an auditorium.

At one point, I found myself standing beside Galbraith. Desperately fishing for something to say, I asked: "Say, Mr. Galbraith, how did you wind up with such a big farm?"

---

*Years later, I became friendly with a Secret Service agent who for a time was assigned to protect Bill and Hillary Clinton. He confirmed that Secret Service agents, too, often find themselves working as armed household help. On the other hand, he said, they got ringside seats at the First Couple's spectacular domestic squabbles, in which both parties used the words "cocksucker" and "motherfucker" with abandon.

"Well, you know how it is," he said, putting a genial hand on my shoulder. "You always want to buy the next farm over, and before you know it, you've got five thousand acres."

Jeez, why hadn't I thought of that?

My attempts at conversation with Saxbe usually came to a similar end. "Gosh, those are lovely trees," I said the first time we went out to his farmhouse. "What kind are they?"

"Oak," he replied, giving me a strange look and doubtless wondering what kind of a moron Columbus had foisted on him.

Even so, he was much easier to talk to than William Webster, who ran the Bureau from 1978 to 1987. In the mid-'80s, Webster began spending his summers at a Victorian home of his wife's family in the posh resort town of Harbor Springs, Michigan. By then, I was the senior resident agent in Saginaw, three hours south, and I once again joined the protection detail.

A cold, patrician man, Webster didn't believe in wasting a lot of effort on social pleasantries. On one occasion, he went to visit a former law partner at Harbor Point, an even more exclusive resort area nearby. Automobiles aren't allowed at Harbor Point; a horse-drawn carriage pulls up to the entrance every few minutes to pick up residents and visitors and carry them to their homes. When Webster arrived, accompanied by five agents, his former law partner was waiting at the gate. He introduced himself to each of us, shook our hands, and then turned to Webster. "Bill, how would you like to bring your agents up and show them my place?"

"Not really," Webster said, climbing into the carriage. His law partner shrugged at us, climbed in with him, and they left.

The only agent who seemed to strike up a personal relationship with Webster was Ray Jones, who was part of the permanent security detail that accompanied the director from Washington. I'm not sure why; they didn't have much in common. Webster once asked Ray what assignment he wanted when he was rotated off the security detail.

"I'm kind of tired of Washington," Ray admitted. "But I don't think I'll put in for a transfer. With the economy down the way it is, I probably wouldn't be able to sell my house."

"Oh, you shouldn't let that stop you," Webster urged him. "Just do what we did. When I became director, we just kept our home in St. Louis and bought another one in Washington."

Jeez, why didn't I think of that?

Webster's wealth didn't keep him from traveling on the FBI's aircraft. To visit Harbor Springs, Webster flew into Detroit on a commercial airliner. An FBI plane carried him from there to the little airstrip in Harbor Springs, where an FBI Cadillac diverted from surveillance duty picked him up and took him to the house. One of the Michigan agents on Webster's security detail was Gordon Nielsen, who owned a summer cottage in the nearby town of Bay View. His four-year-old son Mikey couldn't understand why Daddy was putting on a suit when everyone else was going to the beach. "Well, I have to go help the director today," Nielsen explained. "What do you do for him?" Mikey asked. "We pick him up at the airport in Detroit, fly him here, take him in a car to his house, set up his telephones, and put his bags inside," Nielsen said. Mikey contemplated this a moment, then asked: "Dad, is the director crippled?"

None of this bothered me in the least; in truth, Webster was on duty twenty-four hours a day, even on vacation. Couriers regularly visited him from Washington with top-secret messages they wouldn't leave to regular communications. But using Bureau resources for private travel, a few years later, would get Webster's successor, William Sessions, in trouble. The difference was that, while nobody loved Webster, nobody hated him. But some of the agents around Sessions detested him.

Those bodyguard details with Saxbe and Webster were the closest I ever got to the Hooverdome during my FBI career. After the May Day demonstration in 1971, it was another twenty years before I set foot in Washington.

I never met Hoover himself. Ordinarily he handed out diplomas to every class graduating from the FBI Academy, but he missed mine for some reason. The only time I laid eyes on him was during the May Day demonstration, when I saw him come out of the Justice Department building with John Mitchell, the attorney general. They got in a limousine and drove away. A year later, Hoover died in his sleep.

But I've always felt that I knew him. In my early days, the Bureau was full of agents who had worked closely with Hoover, and I spent hours listening to stories about him. Some agents loved him; some hated him. But they all agreed that, for better or for worse, he almost single-handedly invented the FBI I joined in 1969.

There were undeniably some ways in which it was for worse. His quirky ideas of how to motivate agents often made our lives pointlessly miserable. When I joined the FBI, Bucars had no air-conditioning; Hoover was certain it would turn us sluggish and lazy. He was obsessed to the point of mania about weight, firing off vicious reprimands to anyone who put on even a few pounds—although I'm sure Hoover himself could never have conformed to the charts showing "correct" weight according to height that he sent to every office. There were the stupid rules about drinking coffee, writing the letters *FBI* without periods, and a thousand more.

But how important are those things when you remember that Hoover created the FBI Academy, the greatest law enforcement school in the world? He launched the FBI lab, which in spite of criticism remains the gold standard of forensic science. He conceived the National Crime Information Center, a national computer linkup for law enforcement agencies, and then forced it through a leery Congress. Today more than thirty thousand computer terminals connect sixty thousand agencies, processing more than a million information checks a day. If you've ever had a stolen car returned or located a missing loved one, chances are it was done through NCIC.

The FBI itself might not exist if it hadn't been for Hoover. He took a small, inept, and hopelessly corrupt agency and turned it into the planet's most powerful and professional police force. Shame on Hoover for the way he treated Martin Luther King; but remember that he built the agency that solved the bombings of the World Trade Center and the federal office building in Oklahoma City in a matter of days.

I've always wondered if the spineless sycophants who clustered around Hoover in Washington didn't magnify some of his weaknesses. There's a legendary story that illustrates the point: Hoover gets a memo about a case. It comes back out of his office, with the words "watch the borders" scrawled over it. The headquarters flunkies obediently order the field offices to drop everything else and redeploy hundreds of agents to U.S. border crossings. Hoover, discovering what they've done, is astonished; he was talking about the memo's margins, which he thought were too narrow.

I have no idea if that tale is true. But here's one that is, reported to me by an agent who worked in Hoover's office the last six years of his life.

Hoover had a private bathroom right off his office. No one else was ever allowed to use it, even when the Director wasn't there.

One weekend a young clerk risked his career and possibly his immortal soul by slipping onto the royal crapper when no one was around. When he was finished, he went to the sink to wash his hands—and knocked over the expensive crystal glass on the lavatory, smashing it to slivers.

*Total panic.* Nobody gave a shit about the clerk, but how many assistant directors will be fired for failure to vigilantly stand guard over Hoover's toilet? The top brass huddles. "Can we find another glass?" asks one. "They carry them over at Woodward & Lothrop," explains Helen Gandy, Hoover's long-time secretary. "But that one had a little chip off the edge. He'll know it's been changed."

"How about asking the lab to help?" says somebody else. *Genius.* The FBI lab techs can drop all those kidnappers and serial killers they're working on to produce a counterfeit glass for Hoover's bathroom.

Trusting no one else with this delicate mission, Miss Gandy trots over to the department store, buys a glass, and takes it downstairs to the lab. A tech straps it to a vice and begins work with a tungsten chisel. Oops. The glass shatters. Miss Gandy rushes back to Woodward & Lothrop. The new glass goes back to the lab.

All afternoon the techs work at chipping Steuben glasses, going through two cases of them. A complete defeat for the war on crime: They can't do it. Every time, the glass busts. Finally, Miss Gandy calls a halt. "We're just going to have to put a new glass in the bathroom, and hope the Director doesn't notice it isn't chipped," she says mournfully. "But you know he will."

Hoover arrives, as usual, precisely at 8:30 Monday morning. All over the building people are squirming in their seats, awaiting the moment of doom. Shortly before lunch, the royal bowels rouse themselves. A few minutes later, Hoover strides out of the bathroom, enters the reception area, and plants himself in front of Miss Gandy's desk. Everyone braces. "Miss Gandy," Hoover proclaims, "I want to thank you for replacing that broken glass in my bathroom. I wondered when someone was going to get around to that."

Incidentally, after Hoover died, some of his successors liked to demonstrate their sportsmanship by using the regular men's bathroom down the hall from the director's office. This egalitarian impulse was not always appreciated by the masses. I was told that an agent was in one of the stalls when someone entered the next cubicle. What followed was so noisy and malodorous that the agent couldn't stand it. "Hey," he called, knocking on the side of the stall, "how about a courtesy flush, pal?" There was an annoyed grunt from the other side, followed by the sound of the toilet flushing. The agent finished his business, washed his hands, and left. A split second later, a very cross-looking director emerged from the bathroom.

Because he never married and spent a great deal of time with his friend Clyde Tolson, the FBI's associate director, it's become quite fashionable for the Bureau's critics to speculate that Hoover was gay. A journalist named Anthony Summers even wrote a book claiming that Hoover was not only gay but a transvestite.

I wonder what Summers and people like him would say if someone wrote a book arguing that because Janet Reno, Bill Clinton's attorney general, was well into middle age but had never been married or known to have a boyfriend, she must be gay. I suspect they would be the first to shriek "homophobia!" They'd argue that the speculation was mean and ill-willed and based on stereotypes and irrelevant—because what does her sexual orientation have to do with her qualifications as attorney general?

And, of course, they'd be right.

But there's always been a double standard among liberals. They hold the monopoly on moral righteousness. If you ever belonged to an all-white country club, you're disqualified from public life forever. If you were a member of the Communist Party, well, that was probably just youthful folly. If you supported South Vietnam, you were a fascist and a war criminal; if you backed the Khmer Rouge in Cambodia, well, who could have guessed they'd kill two million people? Sorry 'bout that. The latest manifestation of this is that it's okay to call someone a fag, as long as he was head of the FBI.

So let me go on record as saying I don't give a good goddamn if Hoover was gay or not. I don't think it's any of my business or anyone else's, and I don't think it has the slightest thing to do with how he ran the FBI.

But because the subject comes up so often, I'd like to mention a couple of things that old-time agents and headquarters staffers have said to me over the years.

I've never met a single one who believed that Hoover was gay. Of course, gay people don't have flashing neon signs in the middle of their foreheads, and homosexuals who grew up before the gay liberation movement that began in the late 1960s could undoubtedly be quite adept at concealing their sexual orientation to escape persecution. Still, when you work with someone day in and day out for years, your opinion ought to count for *something*. And in this case, the opinion is unanimous.

Certainly Hoover had plenty of enemies within the FBI, men he demoted, suspended, fired, transferred to Butte. And there were the jealous would-be directors, those who clustered below Hoover, waiting for a turn that never came. Surely if any of them had the slightest indication Hoover was gay, it would have been used against him— or by attorneys general like Bobby Kennedy and Ramsey Clark, who loathed him. By the end of Hoover's career, he was a querulous old man, and the last three presidents he served—Kennedy, Johnson, and Nixon—by all accounts longed to fire him. Homosexuality would have offered them the perfect excuse. If Hoover was really parading around New York in drag, why didn't they pull the trigger?

The final point is that one of the staffers in Hoover's office told me that he wasn't quite as uninvolved with women as some writers have made it appear. He dated several Hollywood celebrities, including Dorothy Lamour and Ginger Rogers's mother, Lela. "He also used to see several attractive Washington socialites," one of his assistants told me. "Their names were in the Rolodex, with a special code beside them that meant we were supposed to put the calls right through. And they *did* call, frequently."

Hardly any of Hoover's personal staffers, men or women, were married. How could they be? They worked ten or twelve hours a day, six or seven days a week. "His stenographer, Erma Metcalf, was married and had children," remembers one of Hoover's aides. "And we used to talk about her all the time, about how weird it was that she had a life apart from the Bureau."

But no one ever says that Miss Gandy or any of the other secretaries who went through life single were lesbians. And, of course, they weren't. Like Hoover, they were married—to the Bureau.

Though my respect for Hoover's achievements is immense, my favorite director was the last one I worked for: Louis Freeh, who took over the Bureau in 1993 after Sessions was fired. Freeh was a former federal prosecutor and judge, but as far as agents were concerned, his best qualification was that he was one of us: He spent six years in the FBI, working mostly organized crime cases in New York. Unlike Webster or Sessions, he knew firsthand what it's like to be an agent pounding the pavement.

It didn't take long for Freeh's background to show. One of the first things he did was to cut the number of supervisors at headquarters by half. Several hundred of them were immediately put on a list for reassignment to field offices where they would start working as agents again. As they sat there in limbo, waiting for vacancies to occur, street agents started calling it the "adopt a slug program."

His scrutiny of the "suits," as Bureau bosses were called, wasn't restricted to the Hooverdome itself. SACs, secure out in their little baronies, sometimes turn into the worst kind of banana republic dictators, laying down rules that can make headquarters look almost sane. As long as they don't openly defy the Hooverdome, they almost never get in trouble for it.

That was so, at least, before Freeh came along. But as he toured field offices, he paid close attention. On one of his first visits outside Washington, Freeh noticed a long queue of agents in front of a pay phone in the hallway. "Looks like you guys need some more phone lines in here," he said. "How many do you have?" Fourteen, came the answer. But seven were reserved for the exclusive use of the SAC and his supervisors, so the agents often were forced to use their own money at the pay phone when they had urgent calls to make. Guess who was looking for another job that same afternoon?

If I needed more evidence that Freeh cared for the well-being of his agents, I got it in a very personal way in 1994. For months I had been having terrible pain every time I urinated. At first the doctors couldn't find anything. But after what seemed like the dozenth round of tests, they had the answer: cancer in my bladder. I was facing a long, painful course of chemotherapy, with no guarantees that it was going to work.

I was sitting at my desk one morning soon after the diagnosis, struggling without much success to keep my head above the black waves of depression washing over me, when the phone rang. "Phil?" a voice said. "This is Louis Freeh. I hear you got some bad news from the doctors."

I thought it must be one of the guys in the office trying to kid me, but it was actually the director—calling himself, no secretary, no administrative assistant, no Washington rigmarole. He talked to me for about ten minutes, told me about the history of cancer in his family and how several of his relatives had beaten it. "You can, too," he concluded. "Hang in there."

A few days later, he followed the call with a handwritten note. And a couple of months later, when he came to Detroit to meet the staff, he sought me out to ask how I was doing. All the words in this book can't possibly express the gratitude I felt for his concern. It was as if the FBI itself was in my corner. With that kind of help, it's no surprise that so far I'm winning.

# 11

# TONY JACK

Tony Dambro eyed the man in the elegantly tailored suit sitting across the kitchen table, sipping a cup of coffee. Tall and slender, his gray hair razor-cut, he looked like somebody out of a *GQ* ad. It was hard to believe he was a big Detroit Mafia enforcer. But everybody knew that was Tony Giacalone's job. Not even his friends were off-limits, as Jimmy Hoffa may have learned the hard way. And underneath Giacalone's genteel grooming, there was a hard-edged arrogance that belied all the polish. Like the way he'd invited himself up here into Dambro's penthouse apartment, then marched through the rooms, picking things up, inspecting them. Like an inventory, almost. He even pushed his way into the bathroom where Dambro's wife, Jerri, was, putting on her makeup for the dinner party they would attend later.

That was strange, but then everything about this visit was strange. Giacalone had called from the lobby, said he'd been next door at the Saginaw Country Club playing golf. Could he come up? Well . . . sure, Dambro had said. He didn't know Giacalone, but he did have some business dealings with his nephew, a local fruit merchant named Billy Loiacano. In fact, Dambro was suing Loiacano for $10,000 over a broken contract. Could that be why Giacalone was here? Dambro discarded the thought instantly. Ten thousand dollars, though nothing to sneeze at, was not a make-or-break sum to either Loiacano or him. And to Giacalone, who everybody said controlled illegal gambling in Detroit and supposedly even had a share of the money skimmed from the Detroit mob's Las Vegas casino, it would be pocket change.

But damned if Giacalone didn't start talking about his nephew Billy. It was a long, rambling story about Billy's financial problems that Dambro couldn't follow, especially because his blood was starting to simmer. *Billy's* problems? It was Dambro who'd gotten screwed, cheated out of ten big ones he was supposed to be paid for selling Billy a liquor license and helping him set up an Italian restaurant. What, the guy doesn't have to pay his bills because his uncle's a mobster? What kind of bullshit was that? Dambro had dealt with some pretty shady characters in his construction business—you had to, it wasn't an industry run by Emily Post types—but he'd never heard of somebody just flat saying, I don't have to pay because my uncle can kick your ass. That seemed crazy, like anarchy or something.

That wasn't the way Giacalone saw it, though. The lawsuit was an insult to Billy and his whole family, he said. Reparations were necessary. *"Cento mila scudi,"* Giacalone said with an air of finality.

"What?" asked the confused Dambro. The son of Sicilian immigrants, he could swear about a thousand words a minute in Italian, but otherwise the language was a mystery to him.

*"Cento mila scudi,"* Giacalone repeated. "One hundred thousand dollars—that's what it's going to cost you to take the three contracts off your life that have been placed by my nephew."

"On *my* life!" shouted the outraged Dambro. "On *my* life! No, goddamn it, I'll put a contract on *his* life!"

In the living room, where she had overheard bits and pieces of the conversation, Jerri Dambro dropped her face into her hands. *Oh, Tony, I wish you hadn't said that*, she thought. Her husband liked that Italian tough-guy act, but that's all it was with him, an act. This Giacalone, though, didn't sound like he was acting at all. Jerri had a feeling they were in real trouble. She wondered who they could call on for help.

———

Debbie and I cried the day we left Columbus. Like so many FBI agents, I spent years trying to get home, only to discover too late that I *was* home. All our friends lived in Columbus. Our two sons, Stephen and Scott, were born there. We bought our first house there, our first Christmas tree, celebrated our first seven wedding anniversaries there. How much more of a home could it have been?

But I was burned out with bank robbers. I wanted an easier-going atmosphere and I wanted to be closer to my mother, who though remarried was still living in the Flint area.

So I put in a bid for one of Michigan's half-dozen satellite offices that report to Detroit. When I snagged an opening in Saginaw, less than an hour north of Flint, I was delighted—so delighted I didn't even visit to check it out. I had a vague memory of a bustling but charming little General Motors company town. But what we found, when we arrived in October 1977, was more like a Rust Belt poster child: high unemployment, a nearly empty downtown, and a generally seedy look of neglect. The concerts, plays, and museums that we had enjoyed so much in Columbus were like half-remembered dreams as we confronted Saginaw's stark reality.

The transition from Columbus to Saginaw was painful enough. In place of twenty-two agents, the barbecues and basketball, in Saginaw there were just five agents, and they went their own way. I was supposed to work on the office's organized-crime program, but it turned out to be nonexistent. There was a single case worth pursuing: No. 183-817, GIACALONE, ANTHONY, AKA TONY JACK, ET AL.


Until Teamster boss Jimmy Hoffa's disappearance in 1975 opened a window on it, Detroit's Mafia—born during Prohibition, when smuggling whiskey across the river from Canada changed overnight from a hobby into an industry—was little known to the rest of the world. The mobsters liked it that way. While their more famous cousins in New York and Chicago were perpetually in the headlines, with various factions trying to rub one another out in constant power struggles, the Detroit mobsters quietly went about making money.

Cooperation, not rivalry, was the watchword. The Mafia chieftains even encouraged their children to marry each other; it was much stickier to murder the boss of the territory next to yours if he was your son-in-law. Nonetheless, the Detroit Mafia could show its claws when necessary. In 1930, when crusading radio commentator Gerald Buckley threatened to identify the mob's leaders, he was gunned down in the lobby of his hotel.

Anthony Giacalone, known to his Mafia brethren as Tony Jack, grew up with the Detroit mob. His father, a Sicilian immigrant, was a Prohibition bootlegger, and Tony was arrested for the first time in 1937, at age eighteen. He beat the rap, as he would again and again over the next four decades. You name it, Tony Jack was arrested for it—felonious assault, armed robbery, mail fraud, tax evasion, loansharking, bribing cops, and every conceivable charge related to illegal gambling. But in all those years, there were only a couple of minor misdemeanor convictions. He had led a charmed life in the courts. Witnesses always seemed to disappear or change their story, evidence got lost or suppressed, and he walked away. Even convictions have been reversed on appeal.

Except for a brief stint as a bartender in the 1940s, no one back then knew Tony Jack to have a legitimate job. (For a while, he handed out business cards that said he ran an "exterminating company." Those quickly became collector's items among cops.) In the rackets, he did a little bit of everything, from bank fraud to bilking the Teamster pension fund out of $800,000. But his specialities were gambling and loansharking, which were often just two sides of the same coin. A mark would lose money in a Giacalone-sponsored card or dice game—usually rigged—and then borrow money from a Giacalone-employed loanshark standing by on the premises for just such emergencies.

The interest rates for gambling loans could be as high as 5 percent a week. Think of it: You lose a thousand bucks in a card game, and then you've got to pay fifty dollars a week just for the *interest*. Because you don't want to be in arrears with Tony Jack—that can get downright ugly—maybe you make your weekly payment to him, then borrow some of the money back to pay the rent and buy the kids some milk. Pretty soon the thousand you owe him has grown to three or five or seven thousand. Some guys wound up paying for the rest of their lives. Of course, miss a couple of payments in this world, and the rest of your life might not be all that long. In 1968, a gambler who fell too far behind on his payments was found beaten to death. His house was completely empty except for one shirt and a change of underwear.

Tony Jack was always well-known to cops—so much so that the FBI planted a microphone in the wall of his Detroit office in 1961 and recorded thousands of hours of Mafia gossip and skullduggery. Eventually his name began to creep into public, too. It started in 1961, when he was implicated in a gambling scandal involving members of the Detroit Lions football team. Two years later, he was named one of the Detroit mob's ten "big men" in congressional testimony. He grew so notorious that when he tried to take a Canadian vacation in 1966, he was picked up and deported the same day.

But his real notoriety came with the Hoffa kidnapping. Hoffa was in legal exile from the Teamsters at the time, but was threatening a comeback, which didn't sit well with the union's current management. Tony Jack called Hoffa several times, offering to mediate, and Hoffa finally agreed to meet him at a restaurant outside Detroit. He never came back from that lunch. FBI tracking dogs later picked up Hoffa's scent in the back seat and trunk of Giacalone's son's 1975 Mercury. The car was seized, and for years it sat in the basement of the FBI building in Detroit.*

Tony Jack always denied he had anything to do with Hoffa's disappearance—he was seen at the gym, getting a massage, he said—and he was never charged. But an FBI informant told us that Tony

---

*One of the Teamster bosses who disliked Hoffa the most was Anthony Provenzano. For years after Hoffa vanished, the Bureau periodically interviewed Provenzano, hoping he would tell what he knew. When I interviewed Provenzano at the federal correctional institution at Lompoc, California, Provenzano, looking perplexed, said, "Hoffa? Hoffa? Isn't that a missing persons case you boys are working?"

Jack called Teamster President Frank Fitzsimmons in 1978 and demanded $250,000 for his part in setting up Hoffa's murder. "It never ends," Giacalone told Fitzsimmons.

I don't know whether Tony Jack ever collected the money. In any event, he didn't exactly have to stand around street corners with a sign that said WILL WHACK TEAMSTER OFFICIALS FOR FOOD. In 1971, IRS investigators estimated that his *traceable* assets alone were worth $1.1 million. Concluding that he hadn't paid taxes on most of it, the IRS agents had Tony Jack indicted for income-tax evasion. He was convicted in 1976 and sentenced to ten years in prison, but his lawyers had filed all kinds of appeals, and Giacalone was still free. The way he swaggered around town, it was obvious he thought he would never serve the time. And if the past was any indication, maybe he wouldn't.

"Sure, I knew Billy Loiacano had an uncle in the Mafia when I went into business with him," Tony Dambro told me. "Who hasn't heard of Giacalone? And Billy talked about him all the time. I even met him once, for just a minute, when Billy and I had some business over in Detroit. But to me it was just sort of an oddity, like having an astronaut in the family. It was obvious—well, it *seemed* obvious—that Billy was no mobster. He just liked to impress people that he had the connections."

This was my fourth meeting with Dambro, and he was just starting to open up. When I read the case file, I assumed he would be delighted to talk to me and get the dormant investigation rolling again. Instead, he was curiously cool and reserved, answering questions yes or no, volunteering little. Then, an hour into our third meeting, he abruptly switched gears. "You wanna go to Las Vegas with me?" he asked. "Lotta fun out there, lotta blackjack tables, lotta showgirls. Let's take off this weekend—you'll be my guest."

*Is this guy going off the deep end?* I wondered. First he'll hardly talk to me; then he's my best buddy. "Tony, I can't accept gifts from somebody involved in a case I'm investigating," I replied. "Even if it wasn't against Bureau policy, it just looks terrible. And besides, I don't think I'm a Vegas kind of guy. If you want to shoot some hoops in the driveway one weekend, give me a call."

To my surprise, he visibly relaxed. The interview started to run more smoothly. As I was about to leave for the day, he explained why: a law enforcement official, who was building an addition to his house, had borrowed $6,000 in construction supplies from Dambro. When he was slow in making repayment, Dambro didn't think it was a shakedown, exactly, but it did leave him wondering how he was supposed to tell the good guys from the bad guys. The Las Vegas trip had been a little test for me, to see if I was interested in Dambro's case or his money. "You passed," he said.

Since then, our conversations had been friendlier and more expansive. I liked Dambro, a short, dapper little guy with a friendly face who looked a little bit like Dean Martin. He was an American success story, the son of Italian immigrants who came here without a pot to pee in. They went through some grim times—his father worked shoveling coal into the furnaces at a GM factory—so that their kids would have a shot at a better life, and Tony had made them proud. His construction company was one of the biggest in northern Michigan, and when he tried his hand at running restaurants, those were successful, too. In his mid-forties, he had enough money to live in this penthouse and play golf at the country club. But I didn't doubt he could still jump behind the controls of a bulldozer at one of his construction sites if it was necessary.

What I didn't understand was why he had gone into business with a member of the Giacalone family in the first place.

"Before we moved into this apartment, we lived just two or three doors away from Billy and his wife," Dambro said. "Nice couple. We met them, became friends. We used to play cards a lot at each other's house. I knew he was into gambling a little bit—if you wanted to put a bet on a football game, Billy could handle it for you—but what the hell, that didn't seem very serious. Basically, I thought he was just what he looked like, a guy who made his money buying and selling fruit."

Their business relationship began in November 1976. Loiacano wanted to open an Italian restaurant, and he offered to buy an unused liquor license Dambro was holding. Once they agreed on that transaction, Loiacano proposed a broader deal: For $10,000, Dambro would supervise construction of the building, make sure all the necessary kitchen equipment was in place, and help hire the staff—in essence, work as a consultant. They agreed, and a contract was signed.

The new restaurant, known as The Pasta House, opened a few months later. But, to Dambro's surprise, Loiacano was quibbling about the $10,000 fee. Some of the construction had been second-rate, he said. He didn't like the way the kitchen was arranged. He wasn't going to pay. They haggled and haggled, but when Loiacano wouldn't budge, Dambro filed suit. The suit named both Billy Loiacano and his wife as defendants.

A few days later, Dambro was sitting in a restaurant when Loiacano walked up from behind. "This time you went too far, you motherfucker," he murmured, leaning close. "You brought my wife into this suit. We take motherfuckers like you and cut you up in little pieces, put you in a box, and dump you in the river." He spun and walked away, leaving Dambro's jaw dangling. For Christ's sake, it was a $10,000 lawsuit. Nobody was going to be turned out into the snow and rain, no matter who won.

"It was about three weeks later that Giacalone showed up," Dambro said. "Billy invited him to play in an invitational golf tournament at the country club, so even when I heard he was around, I didn't think anything of it. And when he called me from the lobby that day, I had no earthly idea it was about the lawsuit."

After that, it was a reign of terror. If he saw the Dambros on the street, Loiacano would stop his car and dart back to open the trunk, like he was going to pull a gun. One night, when Dambro was hunched over the pool table in the country club basement, a waiter told him he had a phone call. "Are you going to stay in there playing pool, you motherfucker?" Loiacano's voice crackled from the earpiece. "We're outside, waiting to blow your head off." Dambro snuck out through the kitchen.

When the Dambros entered rooms at the country club, everything fell silent. Their houseguests from California suddenly discovered a compelling reason to return home. One evening, going out to dinner, some friends jokingly suggested Dambro start the car before they got in. When he looked at their faces, he realized it wasn't a joke after all.

The phone started to ring late at night. Sometimes the calls were from friends, sometimes from people Dambro didn't know. The message, though, was always the same: *I think you're very brave. When Loiacano and Giacalone threatened me, I just paid up.* With dawning comprehension, Dambro realized the lawsuit had nothing to do with this. It was just a trigger, an excuse. Loiacano's mobster uncle was shaking down other people in Saginaw.

But realizing that other people were scared too wasn't very comforting, was it? Dambro felt like a prisoner in his own home. Saginaw was too small, it was hard to go out without bumping into Loiacano or one of his pals. And there was always a scene. One day Loiacano walked up to him in the office of the stockbroker they shared—*right in the stockbroker's office!*—and shoved him against a wall. "Do you have any idea who I am?" he snarled. "You've got to show respect!"

It was taking a toll on Dambro's health. He suffered from a heart condition—twice he had gone into cardiac arrest, his heart just plain stopped, and if he hadn't been playing golf with doctors on both occasions, he'd be dead—as well as petit mal epilepsy. As summer passed into fall, Dambro had a haggard look. Some days, he didn't feel like getting out of bed. His own parents, their ancient memories of Sicily reignited, told him to shut up and pay.

"I guess that was about the time my attorney called the FBI," Dambro said. "He thought that would put a stop to it. But the investigation never went anywhere."

"Tell me about wearing the wire," I suggested. I knew Bureau technicians had strapped a tape recorder to his chest twice when he went to hearings on the lawsuit. The idea was for him to approach Loiacano during court recesses, say things like: "My God, Billy, why are you doing this to me?" Hopefully, the reply would be explicit enough to use in court. But the transcripts I read had been ambiguous and only mildly incriminating.

"Oh, that damn wire!" Dambro exclaimed. "You know, I never wanted to do that. A stand-up guy doesn't go around with a bunch of secret wires rigged under his shirt. It's chickenshit, you know it's chickenshit. But that agent kept after me and kept after me and finally I agreed. But they told me afterward I was sweating so much that it shorted out the recorder. Some of the stuff he said isn't on the tape at all, and some of it's so distorted you can't understand it."

He snorted. "On top of the damn thing not working, it practically killed me getting it off. He pulled the top of his shirt apart to show me the thicket of bushy black hair on his chest. "What do you think it felt like, pulling tape off of that?"

I left a few minutes later. As I walked down the stairs, I thought about the way Dambro looked in both directions before stepping out his apartment door. And I thought about an exchange I'd read in the transcripts of the bugged conversations between Dambro and Loiacano. Your uncle "scared the living shit out of me," complained Dambro. Replied Loiacano: "That's his business."


Talking to Tony Dambro wasn't my first step toward reactivating the Giacalone investigation. In reading the case file, it looked to me like the Dambro extortion was just one of a whole group of illegal acts engaged in by Loiacano and his friends focusing on gambling and related loans. Trying to get a handle on it, I went to visit a law enforcement official who, I'd been told, was a capable man.

"I may be working a gambling case soon, and I need to get the lay of the land," I told him. "Can you give me the names of a couple of bookies I can talk to informally?"

"Bookies?" the official said, like I'd asked where he kept the unicorns. "Bookies? I don't know of any bookies in Saginaw. You might be able to find some in Detroit."

I left his office wondering what was going on. I got a clue a couple of days later, when a couple of local cops called me and asked for a confidential meeting. "So, you want to know about bookies?" one of them asked as we settled into a booth in a coffee shop outside town. I wondered how he knew, but I merely nodded. "Ever heard the name Billy Loiacano?" the cop continued. This time I wasn't able to keep my face straight. "Ahh, I see the name is familiar to you," the cop said with a sardonic smile. "Well, it's a good thing you didn't mention his name when you came by the office the other day. A relative of his works there as a typist—she was sitting just a couple of desks down from you. She hears everything that goes on in there. So I guess that should tell you something about the department's commitment to fighting organized crime."

Loiacano, they told me, was doing much more than handling a few bets on football games. Besides taking in several thousand dollars a day in sports betting, he was running dice and card games around town. For big losers, Loiacano put on his lender's hat and made money available at 4 percent per week, which compounds to well over 200 percent a year. Deadbeat debtors knew in their own minds, they would not be treated kindly.

Why, I inquired, had the official led me astray? One of the cops gave an unpleasant chortle. "What do you think?" he said. "This has been going on a long time. You know, we once could have put some of this crowd away on a murder rap. There was plenty of evidence, but the case never went to trial."

The killer, the cops said, was a guy named Pete Crawford, who provided some of the muscle to help Loiacano collect his debts. In 1974, when a neighbor reported hearing shots inside an illegal after-hours club Crawford ran, police kicked in the door. Crawford was inside, wrapping a corpse's head in a plastic bag, a thick wad of bloody money stuffed in his pocket. The body, which had three bullet holes in it, turned out to be a young man named David DeLaRosa who owed gambling debts to Crawford. Though Crawford was arrested, a judge ruled there was insufficient evidence and turned him loose.

"That's it?" I asked in amazement. "Nobody protested? Nothing happened? That's the end of the story?"

"Not quite," the cop said. "A few months later, the doorbell rang at the after-hours club. Crawford's son Kim answered the door. Somebody blew his head off.

*What kind of a town is this, anyway?* I wondered as I drove back to the office.

A smarter guy, I suppose, might have been worried about taking on the Mafia—especially by himself. And that was pretty much the situation, me against them. I knew the Bureau wouldn't send me any help until I could prove it was worth the effort. The other agents had their own responsibilities.

For many years, the FBI hadn't pursued the Mafia very aggressively, either. The common wisdom explaining this is that J. Edgar Hoover claimed there was no Mafia, so how could it be investigated? The real Hoover bashers go further and say he must have been under Mafia control.

Like a lot of anti-Hoover myths, this one is exaggerated. Hoover, it is true, for years denied the existence of a national organized crime conspiracy. But that didn't mean he didn't recognize that people like Bugsy Siegel and Meyer Lansky were criminals, and the FBI went nuts trying to put them in jail. A lot of gangsters were busted on what can only be called silly technicalities because Hoover was determined to put them away even though the FBI lacked jurisdiction. During World War II, the FBI arrested several gangsters for failure to notify their draft boards of address changes. And New York mob boss Larry Gallo was jailed for exaggerating his income when applying for a federally insured mortgage.

The real problem, for decades, was that most of the things the Mafia specialized in—gambling, prostitution, loansharking, extortion—were not federal crimes. And the FBI couldn't use evidence from wiretaps or microphone surveillance—which were the best ways to trap the people at the top of criminal conspiracies—in court. Not until 1961 did Congress pass federal racketeering legislation giving the Bureau jurisdiction over mob activities, and wiretaps became admissible in court for the first time in 1968. But it wasn't until 1970, with the passage of the Racketeer Influenced and Corrupt Organization law, better known as RICO, that we had a statute that could be effectively used against the Mafia. Hoover promptly created an Organized Crime Section and unleashed the dogs. Bob Federspiel told me that when he arrived in Miami, his first office, there was an entire squad of agents whose only job was to chase mob financier Meyer Lansky.

As I prepared to go after Tony Giacalone, I wished I had an entire squad to back me up. Or even two Cub Scouts with pocketknives. My memories of those Columbus bank robbers were starting to seem positively warm and fuzzy.


The cops had given me the names of a couple of bookies who had no love for Billy Loiacano and might be willing to talk. One of them, John Bomarrito, owned a restaurant called Villa Venice, and he agreed to meet me there for a chat. He wanted to meet in a public place to avoid being seen as a snitch. This conversation would only go so far.

Bomarrito, who looked a bit like the comedian Gabe Kaplan, was a pugnacious little guy who had grown up in the streets and was pretty quick with his fists. In fact, as we talked, I realized I'd seen him beat the hell out of a Central Michigan football player in a bar back in my college days. Although the football player had about seven inches and seventy-five pounds on him, Bomarrito was harassing and taunting the guy while he tried to play pool. Finally the football player reached across the table and smacked him, and the punches were flying. The fight spilled out into the street, and the football player was beating Bomarrito's brains out, pounding him like a nail.

"Wait, wait," Bomarrito gasped. The football player backed up a step, and Bomarrito kicked him right in the balls. The big guy went down in a heap and never got back up.

"I guess you could say Billy Loiacano and I have had a falling out," Bomarrito told me. "He's been threatening me for the past six months. I've been taking more bets than he is, and in Billy's family, that's how they deal with competition—they scare you."

"Loiacano personally has come after you?" I asked.

"No, one of his goons, a guy named Bruce LaBreche. Billy uses him as an enforcer when a customer gets behind. A big guy, over six feet, and he's a typical bookie: smart as hell, and knows the streets."

One night LaBreche stalked into the Villa Venice around closing time, looking for Bomarrito. Bomarrito had been having a drink with a buddy, and they were just about to leave. "I'll deal with this guy another time," Bomarrito told his friend. "Let's just go on home." They hurried out into the frozen winter night, got into their cars, and left.

Bomarrito's friend, who knew LaBreche's reputation, watched his rear-view mirror nervously, but saw nothing during the five-block journey home. Reaching his driveway, he punched the automatic ga rage-door opener, pulled inside, and closed it again. He climbed out of the car—and screamed as Bruce LaBreche loomed in the darkness. LaBreche, approaching the car from behind in the parking lot, had slipped on the ice and gone down. His leather jacket snagged on the bumper, and he'd been dragged five blocks in the snow. As soon as he stood up in the garage, he collapsed again.

Although Bomarrito laughed as he told the stories, he ended on a note of caution. "These guys may sound like a bunch of fuckin' buffoons," he said, "and maybe they are, but you still wanna be careful. They're still mean motherfuckers."


"Is that Charlie McNally sitting over there?" I asked a waitress, gesturing at a table off to the right where several men were talking over coffee. Although I'd never met McNally, never even seen his picture, the cops had told me I wouldn't be able to miss him, and they were right: There weren't many six-foot-four men with white hair in here. I was standing in the lobby area of a restaurant called the Texan, a home-cooking type place. It was part of a chain McNally owned around the state. He was making a lot of money off them—and taking it out in cash without paying taxes, according to the IRS.

"Yes sir, that's him," the waitress confirmed. "Are you a friend of his?"

"Not exactly, but I'd like to talk to him," I said. "Could you go over there and tell him—very quietly, because I don't want to embarrass him in front of his friends—that there's an FBI agent here to see him?"

She walked over briskly, whispered in his ear, and a moment later McNally was at my side in the lobby, a guarded look in his eye.

"My name's Phil Kerby and I'm with the FBI," I said, handing him a card. "I know you're a busy man, so I'm not going to beat around the bush. I'm working a case against Billy Loiacano, and I need your help. I know you've booked some sports bets yourself, but I don't give a damn about that—I don't think you're the problem around here. I also know you have trouble with the IRS. Here's my deal: You help me with Loiacano, I'll help you on your IRS beef—the criminal part only, I can't do anything about your back taxes."

McNally pursed his lips thoughtfully. "Let me think it over for a day or two," he said finally. "Call me later in the week." We shook hands and I was on my way. He was going to cooperate, I had seen it in his eyes. The best part was, it hadn't cost anything. The IRS agents who worked down the hall from me had already decided making a criminal case against McNally was too difficult; they were just going to hit him for a ton of back taxes and penalties. But he didn't know that.


"I used to like Billy Loiacano," McNally said when we met three days later at one of his restaurants. "We used to have a kind of friendly competition—who had the bigger car, who had the nicer house, who could act more like a horse's ass with money. One day I really got him—I told him to come over to my house, which is by the country club. You know how in the movies, they're always rigging a bucket of water over a door to fall on somebody when he comes in? I rigged up a bucket—but when it fell on Billy, it showered him with hundred-dollar bills.'' He chuckled at the memory, then grew serious again.

"But the older Billy gets, the more he acts like Giacalone. Did you know I used to run the black numbers in Saginaw?" he asked. I nodded. The numbers game is a lottery, with the winning three-digit number based on stock market results. It closely resembles the legal lotteries most states run these days, but the payoffs are higher—nearly 900 to 1, compared to 500 to 1 in most state lotteries—and a numbers runner will accept bets as low as twenty-five cents. So it's a popular way to gamble in poor neighborhoods, especially black ones.

"I had a partner in that, a guy named Nick, and one day Billy invited him to come over to the Bay Valley Inn, the restaurant where he runs card games. So Nick gets there, but it turns out the meeting is not with Billy but with Tony Giacalone and his brother Vito, who's just as nasty a motherfucker as Tony. They told Nick, we're taking over the black numbers business. And when he said, wait a second, they slapped him around. No negotiation, no offer of a buyout—just, we're taking it."

"Why does Billy need to bring in his uncles for something like that?" I asked. "Why can't he do it himself?"

"Despite all his bullshit, Billy's not really part of the Mafia," McNally said scornfully. "He's not a made man. Hell, he's not even much of a businessman, much less a gangster. His parents built up that fruit company, not him."

"How is he at making loans?"

"Well, he does show some talent for that," McNally admitted. "You know, I've probably borrowed $120,000 or so from him over the past six or seven years." That didn't surprise me. McNally, I'd heard, once lost $55,000 in a single night shooting craps in one of Loiacano's games at the Bay Valley Inn. He never even spilled a drop from the drink that was perpetually balanced in his hand.

He seemed to read my mind. "It never bothered me much to lose," he explained. "I just like the action." He frowned. "But I gotta tell you, there were nights when I wondered if Billy was using loaded dice. I *never* lost like that in Vegas."

It was time to hit the street. Someone pointed out Bruce LaBreche's house near the country club to me, and I started a surveillance, parking a block or two down the street and waiting for him to come out. The results were nothing the FBI would put in a training film. My Bucar was an electric-blue Javelin, only slightly less noticeable than a flying saucer, and it never took LaBreche long to spot me.

After a few days, LaBreche gave up trying to shake me. Whenever he spotted me, he drove straight to The Pasta House, Loiacano's restaurant, and camped inside for several hours. Even before that, however, I was certain he must be using a bag man to collect bets and loanshark payments. LaBreche just didn't move around enough to be doing it all himself. So I began following men who came out of the restaurant. It wasn't much of a strategy—most of those I followed were probably just ordinary people who'd been out for lunch or an early happy hour—but one day I spotted a shaggy, hard-looking man who walked with the furtive swagger of an ex-con. *Bingo*, I thought, *this is my man*. When I ran the plate on his Chevy station wagon, it came back registered to Norman George Crawford—also known as Pete, the Loiacano muscleman who killed the DeLaRosa kid.

I followed Crawford all over town as he visited various homes and offices. At each stop, he left the car with a bag under his arm, and he never stayed inside more than a couple of minutes. He was obviously collecting and paying off bets, and probably some loanshark payments, too. And if LaBreche had warned him about surveillance, Crawford obviously hadn't paid much attention—he seemed completely unaware I was behind him.

By following Crawford for a few days, I assembled a large roster of Loiacano's clients. But I also wanted to know what was going on inside The Pasta House while I was trailing Crawford around. So I went down to Detroit to see if I could beg, borrow, or steal an undercover agent. All the Saginaw agents were too well known around town.

A trip to Detroit in those days was always a miserable experience, sort of like a Transylvanian peasant going to the castle to kiss Count Dracula's ring; the only question was how much you were going to hate it. One supervisor in Detroit had angered the agents under him so much that they stole his desk and replaced it with a child's model. This same guy, while "investigating" some damage to a Bucar in the building garage, got behind the wheel to test the brakes. Unfortunately, he tested the gas pedal instead, ripping off the whole side of the car on the garage wall.

But on this day I got lucky. After a couple of hours of kissing royal nether regions, I got the temporary services of an undercover specialist.

The notion of sending agents undercover was a relatively new one that would have been impossible under the Hoover regime. The Bureau was still feeling its way through the ethical, legal, and practical thickets tangled around the practice. Not the least of the problems was the terrible personal toll. Even agents who were good at it went bonkers in unexpected ways if they stayed undercover too long. They turned paranoid, started shoplifting, dumped their wives. Later in my career, I supervised a sting operation where the undercover agent developed a bizarre craving for bologna sandwiches. He gained sixty pounds before it was all over.

The agent Detroit sent us was a good one, but he had been undercover for nearly a year and couldn't stay there much longer. He was only able to work in Saginaw a few weeks, and he told me after a few days he wouldn't be able to burrow inside the Loiacano coterie in that time. It was too tight, too established.

"But I'll tell you this," he said. "These bars where he's running the betting are amazing places—I've never seen anything like it, and I've been helping bust these joints all over the country. Guys place bets at the bar, right out in the open—two hundred, five hundred bucks a shot. Nobody's even *trying* to hide what's going on. There was a cop sitting inside there and he didn't say a word.''

The agent had seen more than a few fistfights, too. "The bottom line on Loiacano's friends is that they're bullies. They'll pick fights over money, they'll pick fights with people who are sitting there drinking beer and minding their own business. It looks to me like they've been pushing people around so long that it doesn't even occur to them that anybody might try to stop it.''

It was true. One recent night at Holly's Landing, a rustic waterfront restaurant on the Saginaw River, Bruce LaBreche and a couple of his goons came reeling drunkenly in. As they drank more, their mood went from rowdy to something approaching berserk. They were shouting obscenities, throwing things, smashing wineglasses hanging over the bar.

Finally, with broken glass flying everywhere, a customer having an anniversary dinner with his wife walked over and told LaBreche to knock it off.

"Says who?'' he sneered.

"Says the Michigan State Police,'' the man said, flashing a detective's badge.

"Fuck you, asshole,'' LaBreche retorted, and his companions chimed in with a torrent of abuse and threats.

"That's it, you're all under arrest,'' the detective said. "Call the Saginaw police,'' he shouted to a barmaid.

As she picked up the phone, LaBreche and his pals started toward the detective. "Drop to the floor!'' he ordered them, yanking his pistol out. The sight of the gun stopped them—for a moment. Then the three men began to slowly separate, flanking the detective to both sides. He backed toward the wall. Just as it looked like LaBreche's band was ready to pounce, several uniformed cops arrived and backed them off.

"Did you file charges?'' I asked the detective when he told me the story a couple of days later.

"What's the point?'' he replied. "My wife doesn't want me to, and she's right. Who's going to protect my family?" As he spoke, I wondered if this was Saginaw, or Dodge City.

Probably the most useful by-product of the undercover agent's work was that it helped convince Detroit to send me some extra eyes. One of the Bureau's crack surveillance teams, expert at blending into the scenery—we called it the special operations group—came to Saginaw to follow Loiacano, LaBreche, and their cronies. The surveillance confirmed that Loiacano and LaBreche met every day at The Pasta House, sitting for hours at a time at the same table at the back of the dining room.

I wanted to bug it.

I'd developed a couple of snitches as the investigation inched forward. One of them would be able to give FBI technicians after-hours access to the restaurant. They could install a microphone under the table, which we could monitor in our office. A couple of weeks worth of their taped conversations, I figured, would leave a jury eager to sentence Loiacano and his pals to a long prison term, if not another solar system.

To install a microphone would require the same exhaustive legal procedure as a wiretap: a James-Michener-size affidavit explaining where the bug will go, who you'll hear on it, what you expect them to say, what makes you think it will be incriminating, and why you can't get it any other way. To back up your argument, you have to cite multiple informants who corroborate one another, and you have to cite surveillance to prove the informants really were in the place they say they were.

The finished product would read something like this: *An informant hereinafter referred to as FBI-1, known to the FBI for seven years, has furnished information in nine case, which led to seven search warrants*—you're establishing the snitch's credibility—*advised as follows: On such and such a date the informant was in The Pasta House and heard William Loiacano and Bruce LaBreche whis-*

*pering to each other at a rear table that they were going to extend loans at 5 percent interest per week, blah-blah-blah* for another thirty or forty pages. That establishes what the legal system calls "probable cause" for the microphone.

Once you've got the affidavit in order, the request for the microphone has to be okayed administratively within the Justice Department—first at the local level (in this case, the chief prosecutor on the department's Organized Crime Strike Force in Detroit) and then in Washington, by both FBI headquarters and the attorney general's office. Last and certainly not least, a federal judge must issue a court order approving it.

Working on the affidavit with me was a bright young strike force prosecutor named Dave Cook. Not only was he a keen intellect and a succinct writer, he had actually been an attorney for the federal commission that drafted most of the U.S. wiretapping laws. He was the perfect attorney to work with.

Unfortunately, though, he suffered from Crohn's disease, a gastrointestinal illness that periodically laid him low and would eventually kill him before his forty-seventh birthday. After each of Dave's bouts with the disease, we had to start from scratch. The probable cause has to be fresh. Otherwise, the judge might say: Well, it looks like Loiacano was loansharking last month. How do you know he's doing it now? Sure, he used to sit at that table with LaBreche every day, but it's been three months since you saw him. Maybe they're using another table now. So you have to check with your informants again. Maybe one is sick or out of town on vacation: delay. You have to reestablish surveillance. Maybe the team is tied up with a big case in Detroit: delay.

In August, nine months after the investigation began, Dave's health improved. To avoid the two-hour daily commute to his office, I moved into a Detroit hotel, and we worked on the affidavit for nearly one solid month. Finally we had a finished product that we were ready to present to the strike force's chief prosecutor. If he okayed it—and Dave was certain he would—it would probably take no more than a month to round up all the other necessary approvals and actually get the microphone up and working.

The morning of the meeting, I stopped at a diner to have breakfast. Comfortably slouched in a booth, I opened my *Detroit Free Press*—and promptly spit coffee all over the table. The 6th U.S. Circuit Court of Appeals had just ruled that police couldn't surreptitiously enter private property to plant bugs, even with a judge's order. That meant we couldn't put a microphone under Billy Loiacano's table unless we asked him first. Gee, maybe he'd tell us where Jimmy Hoffa was while he was at it.

The ruling would eventually be overturned by the Supreme Court, but I had no way of knowing that as I sat in the diner. All I knew was, the microphone surveillance for which I had worked so hard, which I had been counting on so heavily, was dead.


If Efrem Zimbalist, Jr., or Jimmy Stewart had been running the Giacalone investigation, they would have had a dozen backup plans ready to go when the court crossed them up on the microphone. Of all the differences between the real FBI and the silver-screen FBI, that one is the biggest: The movie agents carefully map their every move, like Eisenhower planning D-Day. In reality, we make a lot of it up as we go along. In 1978, there hadn't been a lot of effective FBI investigations directed at the Mafia, and the people who had directed the few successful cases weren't around to mentor me. It was just Phil Kerby pulling ideas out of his hip pocket, trying them out to see what worked.

Now I was down to just one: search warrants, simultaneous raids on the homes of Loiacano, LaBreche, Crawford, and the whole crew, as well as the bars and restaurants where they did business. (It would be wonderful to send agents storming into the house where Giacalone lived in the plush Detroit suburb of Grosse Pointe, but I didn't have any snitches telling me what I could find inside, and judges won't give you warrants for fishing expeditions.) Vice lords are no more capable than any other businessmen of keeping all their records in their heads, and I knew we would find betting slips, tally sheets, and paperwork on extortionate loans—hard evidence to go with the testimony of the stable of victims and snitches I'd been assembling for the past year.

Searches are always a gamble. They end the covert phase of the investigation. Not that Loiacano and his group didn't know I was after them. But they had been operating so long, they still weren't taking it seriously. The warrants would end that, as well as give them a pretty good idea of the exact dimensions of my investigation, what I knew and what I didn't. And the harsh glare of publicity would make it difficult for me to continue to quietly seek out new witnesses.

There *were* other witnesses out there, I knew it. But I also knew I was a one-man army, a one-man army that had been too long on the front lines. I was running out of steam. If that meant I had to go with a case that was 95 percent complete instead of 100, that was what had to be done.

We carried out the raids on October 22, 1978. The first one, at 4 A.M., was targeted on a little after-hours place known as the Tittabawassee Club. It was going full blast when a team of FBI agents, state police, and sheriff's deputies burst in. To say the clientele was surprised is putting it mildly. One woman, totally nude, tried to hide under a barstool. Another was caught in the middle of an act which probably would have been illegal under state law even if she were performing it for free with her husband, which she wasn't. In all, we arrested twenty people and held them incommunicado until the rest of the searches got under way two hours later.

At 6 A.M., we swept down on the homes of Loiacano, LaBreche, Crawford, and several of their friends. We hit The Pasta House, too. We found most of the records I was looking for (though some, I would discover months later, were hidden in an office at Loiacano's fruit company, which I hadn't thought to search) and there were even a few unexpected bonuses. At Loiacano's house, we seized several pairs of loaded dice. Charlie McNally's suspicion that he was being rooked began to gain credibility.

Even if we hadn't found a thing, though, the searches would have been worth it, just for the stupefied expressions on the faces of Loia-cano, LaBreche, and Crawford. The only thing I can compare it to was a few years later, when it was revealed that the Canadian embassy in Tehran had smuggled half a dozen Americans out of the country right under the noses of the Iranian thugs who had seized the U.S. embassy. One of the Iranians screamed, in outraged befuddlement: "It's illegal!"

That was pretty much the way Loiacano and his pals reacted. How dare we come into their homes and poke through the records of crimes they had been committing with impunity for the better part of a decade? At the same time, there was a visible new sense of pride on the part of the men who carried out the search. For the first time, we were playing offense, and man, it felt good!


That feeling spilled over to potential witnesses. Informants began calling the office to tell us what they knew about Giacalone and his nephew. All they had been waiting for was law enforcement to show some spine in dealing with these guys.

It was almost unbelievable, but Giacalone's reign of terror in Sa-ginaw had been worse than I thought. "He thought Jews were easy targets," one new informant volunteered. "His motto was, 'Get a Jew a day.' " Most of his extortions followed the same basic blueprint as the Dambro case: A friend or relative of Giacalone would feign injury over some minor or altogether imaginary slight. Tony Jack would show and warn the offender: "My cousin"—or nephew, boyhood friend, or business associate—"is so pissed off he's put a contract on your life. I can get it removed, but it's going to cost you fifty thousand dollars." A few brave souls bargained him down to lower amounts, but several paid in full, even if they had to borrow money from friends to do it.

Some of the people we talked to said they would never testify under any circumstances. Others would, but wanted protection in return. One of them was a big, potbellied doctor named Victor Do-minguez, who had sunk himself into a black hole of debt with an ill-fated attempt to raise show horses. He slipped deeper and deeper into debt. Then a dubious savior appeared: Pete Crawford, offering money at a mere 4 percent per week. The doctor took out a $5,000 loan.

Dominguez somehow managed to keep current on his $200 a week interest payments and retire half the loan. Impressed, Crawford offered him a new deal: The second half of the loan would be canceled. All Dominguez had to do in return was help dummy up fake insurance claims for Crawford and seven of his friends.

Dominguez was willing to take the witness stand. But he wanted to be resettled with a new identity under the federal witness protection program. When we agreed, he threw in a bonus: Alfredo Salazar, the cocaine dealer who introduced him to Crawford. Dominguez had been supplying Salazar with Mannitol—a prescription laxative that drug dealers like to use to dilute their product. Dominguez agreed to introduce Salazar to an undercover DEA agent, who promptly busted him after consummating a big cocaine deal.

Actually, Salazar was a paragon of middle-class decency next to one of our other new witnesses, a lawyer named Robert Moskal. Moskal liked to play golf more than he liked to practice law, and he started to drift into debt. The drift turned into more of a plunge. He started borrowing from Loiacano and LaBreche in 1972 at 10 percent interest a month, and eventually had paid them back $42,000 with no end in sight. Because he was such a great customer, Loiacano practiced restraint even when Moskal's payments were irregular. When the lawyer was two months behind, Loiacano didn't have his arms broken, merely observed to him: "We don't kill people anymore, but sometimes we've got to make an example." Tough love!

Getting in hock to a loanshark is stupid, but it's not despicable. It was some of the other things Moskal did to raise money that earned him a place in the Lowlife Pond Scum Hall of Fame. First he allegedly embezzled from a business partner. Then he was accused of stealing from clients, two elderly widows. Then he was accused of forging the deed to the family farm and selling it out from under his ninety-year-old invalid father. Ultimately, he was disbarred. About the only thing he hadn't been accused of—yet—was tying local virgins to the railroad tracks. I was hopeful he could manage to keep from doing that until we got him resettled as a protected witness, safely tucked away in somebody else's jurisdiction.

As we delved deeper into the case, I was staggered by the lengths to which people would go to slake their thirst to gamble. One of our new witnesses was an Irish immigrant named Mick Grant. His medical practice in St. Charles, a little town outside Saginaw, was successful. But Grant was continually betting with LaBreche and Loiacano. The reason was simple: If you wanted to lay 8-to-1 odds that the sun wouldn't come up in the morning, Grant would take the bet. He would gamble on anything, any time, any place. He flew to Europe and back to bet on a single horse race. Charlie McNally told us he went to Las Vegas once with Grant on a late-night flight. When they arrived, McNally went out for dinner, but Grant couldn't wait to get to the tables. When McNally arrived in his room forty-five minutes later, there was a message waiting from Grant: Could he borrow McNally's line of credit? He'd already lost $45,000 and exhausted his own.

Grant at least held onto his medical practice. Much sadder was the case of Gerald Yeager, whose electrical contracting company had made him a small fortune doing work for Dow Chemical. In the early 1970s, he started betting on sporting events, and pretty soon he had to borrow $5,000 at 10 percent a month from LaBreche. By 1975, his debt had ballooned to $60,000, with a monthly interest payment of $6,000. He sold his business and everything he owned and was still $11,000 short.

Yeager, a disarming little guy—he was no more than five-foot-three—with a bullfrog voice, stalled LaBreche with one story after another. But the last time he tried it was a disaster. LaBreche beat the hell out of him right in the Holiday Inn bar as several horrified patrons looked on. As he lay bleeding under the table, they took his watch and left. Pete Crawford, who had been sitting nearby during the beating, leaned over and warned Yeager: "Wise up." Yeager did:

He started carrying a shotgun with him wherever he went, and pretty soon left town altogether.

These were the witnesses we would build our case on in court. The paperwork we seized in the raids would help corroborate some of their testimony and knit it together, but the heart of the case was the witnesses themselves. They were both our strength and our weakness. Their stories of the bullying by Giacalone, Loiacano, and the rest were chilling. On the other hand, they included cheats and gamblers. I believed them, but I didn't know if a jury would. I would have loved to find more credible witnesses, but unfortunately, nuns don't often require the services of a loanshark.

The other thing that worried me was whether some of them would choke on the stand. They had every right, after all, to fear Giacalone's thugs, and to wonder about our ability to protect them. As we started taking evidence to a federal grand jury to obtain indictments, one of the witnesses we subpoenaed was a car salesman named Bob Dean. His role was minor: He had once worked for Charlie McNally and had sometimes seen Loiacano show up to collect loan payments. Soon after he testified—secretly, we thought—LaBreche and his brother Brent showed up in the showroom where Dean worked. Without any warning, LaBreche punched him in the mouth. A shower of blows followed, and soon Dean was on the floor, LaBreche on top of him, as Brent held the other salesmen back.

"What's it all about?" screamed Dean as the punches rained down on his face.

"It's about your fucking mouth!" LaBreche screamed back. We didn't know it, but one of Pete Crawford's relatives was sitting on the grand jury, relaying the identities of all the witnesses and their testimony.

The LaBreche brothers left the showroom just before police arrived. A patrol car went over to Bruce LaBreche's home. Bruce met the cops outside.

"You take care of your people, and we take care of ours," he snarled. "Now get the fuck off my lawn."

The policemen left, without making an arrest.

The grand jury handed down indictments in June 1979. Six people—Giacalone, Loiacano, Crawford, both LaBreche brothers, and Alfredo Salazar, who almost immediately cut a deal with us to testify against the others—were indicted for conspiracy to loanshark. Everybody but Giacalone was also charged with actually making extortionate credit transactions. And the LaBreche brothers got an extra count of obstruction of justice for beating up Bob Dean.

I thought we had a good, winnable case, but I wasn't blind. I knew a lot of our witnesses had credibility problems. And against Giacalone, the biggest fish, we had the least evidence. So far, the only one of his extortion victims we'd been able to persuade to testify was Dambro, who, thank God, had never had a brush with the law and was a successful businessman.* Given Giacalone's long and successful record in court, I expected his defense team would fight over every comma of the indictment.

So imagine my surprise when Brian McCormick, the veteran organized-crime prosecutor who headed our legal team, told me that Giacalone's lawyer wanted to talk about a plea bargain.

"Why does he want to do that? Is it a trick?" I asked McCormick. "He's probably beaten stronger cases than this one."

"I don't know," shrugged McCormick "You know, he just lost his last appeal on that tax conviction, and he's in prison for the first time in his whole life. Maybe he thinks the magic has worn off." Tony Jack had recently had a heart attack, too, and maybe that had something to do with it.

Giacalone was serving ten years on the tax conviction. His attorney offered to plead guilty on the loansharking charge for another ten-year sentence to be served concurrently, which would have meant no extra time. We held out for a longer sentence. Finally a deal was

---

*Because the shakedown of Dambro stemmed from a credit transaction—the $10,000 Loiacano owed him—we considered it part of the loansharking conspiracy.

struck: twelve and a half years. A few days into the new year, the plea was entered. We had won the first Mafia conviction in the history of the Saginaw office, and one of only a very few in the history of the entire Detroit division.

I had mixed feelings about the plea. On one hand, we had nailed a guy who had been avoiding almost every law enforcement agency in Michigan for more than four decades. The FBI hadn't won a lot of solid victories against the mob—the great anti-Mafia prosecutions in New York were still more than a decade off—so a guilty plea couldn't be turned down lightly.

On the other, I would have relished seeing Giacalone sitting in a courtroom, forced to play by the rules for once in his life. And after the plea-bargain negotiations began, Detroit agent Bob Neumann came up with another witness: a retired businessman who made a fortune operating several business in central Michigan. Billy Loiacano had trumped up a story that he overheard the man uttering an anti-Italian slur. Same old story: Tony Jack appears, says there's a contract on his life, it can be removed for $50,000. He paid.

In the end, I decided the guilty plea was a good deal for us. There was no guarantee we would have won at trial. And maybe my new witness could be put to use somehow later on.

The trial of Loiacano, Crawford, and the LaBreche brothers began in early February. In a lot of ways, it was a nightmare. The lead defense attorney was N. C. Deday La René, Detroit's premier defender of the mob. (A few years later, he pled guilty to various charges stemming from illicit monetary transactions with Tony Jack's brother Vito.) La Renè, a frustrated Shakespearean actor, was constantly pounding the table or loudly thumping his files in melodramatic outrage. It didn't matter to me or the prosecutors, but it rattled the witnesses and the jury.

Robert Moskal, the disbarred attorney, made a worse witness than I ever could have imagined. Sweating, his face red as a lobster, Moskal changed testimony from minute to minute, contradicted things he'd said before the grand jury, and suffered frequent memory lapses. (One of them I could understand—he said he couldn't remember why he'd been disbarred. If I'd lost my law license for bilking old ladies, I'd try to forget, too.) He topped it all off by saying Loiacano and LaBreche were still his buddies and he hoped to have lunch with them after the trial—even though he'd testified earlier that they made an implied threat on his life. After the case was over, one juror told the *Saginaw News*: "I just wish he'd been on trial and we'd have had a chance to convict him." That pretty much summed it up for me, too.

Even Dambro, our star, got carved up pretty well by the defense. Angry and combative, he blundered right into a trap the defense baited for him. He admitted he had shouted something at Giacalone about putting a contract on Loiacano's life. Banner headlines in the next day's paper: *Dambro says he threatened Loiacano's life*. To me, the difference in the threats by the two men was plain—everyone believed Giacalone had the ability to back his up, and Dambro didn't, he was just blowing off steam—but to the jurors, it just sounded like a bidding war between two Mafia dons.

The defense didn't put on much of a case, just conceded that Loiacano and his friends loaned money, but denied there was any rough stuff. During the rip-roaring inflation of the final days of the Jimmy Carter administration, Loiacano's interest rates didn't even sound that prohibitive. Cracked Loiacano during a court recess: "If they'd waited another year, we'd have been lower than the banks."

The jury stayed out three days, then came back with acquittals on all the counts of the indictments involving Moskal and one involving Dominguez. It deadlocked on everything else, voting 7–5 to convict.

I spent a day in the dumps over the outcome, but not very deeply. It was hard to get depressed when I thought of the royal fury that must be raging in Tony Jack's prison cell: *Son of a bitch, I shouldn't have pled out*. Besides, this wasn't over. We persuaded a majority of the jury, after all, on most of the charges. And at the next trial, our case would be about 500 percent stronger just through the subtraction of Moskal, who would be allowed to testify again only if I were chained inside a box and dropped to the bottom of Lake Michigan.

The defendants must have thought so, too. One by one, they offered guilty pleas to a variety of charges in return for reduced sentences. At the same time, we were hammering them with other charges that grew out of our original investigation. Loiacano pled guilty to bank fraud involving loans on nonexistent cars. Bruce LaBreche was convicted of defrauding an insurance company. Crawford, whose homes and after-hours club burned down with monotonous regularity, was convicted of insurance fraud. Soon after that, he pled guilty loansharking charges. We furnished information to Charlie Rettstadt, who worked for the state attorney general, and he developed a case leading to charges on the De-LaRosa murder, eight years after it occurred. With essentially the same evidence that hadn't been good enough to get through a preliminary hearing the first time around, he won a murder conviction this time.* By the time the last plea was entered, ten people were in prison.

Miraculously, the jail time actually seems to have rehabilitated most of them. Loiacano moved to the Tampa area and built a new fruit and vegetable empire that is, I understand, completely legitimate. Crawford opened a restaurant that caters meals to the federal halfway house in Saginaw. Bruce LaBreche has also gone straight. I see him around town; we smile and wave. He even had a Mass said for me when I came down with cancer.

One day I ran into him on the street and I asked him why we had managed to remain on friendly terms. "You always treated us like gentlemen, even when you were trying to put us away," he said. "I liked that. Making the case on us, you were just doing your job." He looked me in the eye and added: "We're all a little older and wiser, aren't we, Kerb?"

---

*It was, however, reversed on an arcane legal technicality that even the lawyers on the case had trouble understanding.

It was Bruce, also, who paid me the greatest compliment I ever heard about the Giacalone investigation—though he doesn't know I know it. But shortly after the trial, Bruce told one of my snitches: "That fucking Kerby would put his own grandmother in jail if she stepped out of line."

One who remains in the public eye is Tony Jack. He served seven years, and even if he hadn't changed a bit, you might think that at age sixty-eight he would be ready to relax. In 1996, he was indicted on sixteen counts of extortion and racketeering. He had plenty of company: the fifty-seven-page indictment covered seventeen different alleged Detroit gangsters. I'm happy to report that part of the indictment was based on work we did in the Saginaw office.

The unfortunate thing is that Tony Dambro, the first of Giacalone's victims with the courage to speak up, wasn't here to see it. The investigation and trial took an enormous toll on his health. On March 8, 1988, while he was backing out of a casino parking lot during a Las Vegas vacation, he had another heart attack. They found him, sitting in his big rented Cadillac, one of his trademark cigars still stuck in his mouth.

# 1 2

# THE AHN KIDNAPPING

**F**or maybe the tenth time that night, I glanced away from the fireplace and looked out the sliding-glass back door of the house into the night—or what I could see of it. Snow was coming down so fast and thick that it was like looking through a layer of gauze. Propping my feet up on the hearth, I wondered what it was like to be a uniformed cop on a night like this. I didn't even want to think about going out into that mess.

That, of course, was when the phone rang. "Detroit field office here," said the FBI operator. "We're patching an urgent call through to you." I sighed, but not too loudly. Since I took over as head of the resident agency in Saginaw, my paycheck weighed a little more, but along with the money, I also got most of the after-hours calls. The Detroit operators tried to screen them, but a lot of lunatics sound perfectly sane, at least at first. There was a good chance I was about to hear from yet another of the astounding number of Americans who have been forced to have sex inside flying saucers.

"Phil Kerby?" The voice on the phone was tentative, even a little fearful. It was also familiar. Dr. William Rice was the most respected surgeon in Saginaw. I'd met him a couple of times at banquets and civic club lunches, the kind of places an FBI agent goes to show the flag. But from the catch in his voice, I didn't think he was calling about a Lions Club buffet. And he wasn't the type for interstellar sex fantasies.

"What can I do for you, doctor?" I asked.

"...t's not for me," he said, the words coming slowly. "It's for a friend of mine. I think his wife has been kidnapped."

The snow, unbelievably, was even worse than it looked. John King, the agent beside me, kept up a steady stream of anxious comments as we trudged along the sidewalk. "You really think someone is watching the house?" he asked, his words oddly muffled by the snow.

"No, and the surveillance team didn't think so either," I replied as I concentrated on keeping my feet from skidding out from under me. "But the kidnapper warned he'd kill the woman if anyone called the cops. So I just don't want to take a chance pulling up here in Bucars."

It was less than an hour since Rice's phone call telling us that his medical partner's wife had been abducted. Ordinarily, I would have insisted on a meeting away from the house. But we had a bit of luck: One of the Bureau's special operations group surveillance teams was in town working a drug case. At my request, they'd done a couple of quick passes through Delevan Street in Saginaw Township, the upscale suburb where the victim lived, and reported back that nobody was watching the house. Their word was good enough for me. Being able to meet at the house meant we wouldn't have to take a chance on missing a phone call from the kidnapper.

From a strictly legal standpoint, I shouldn't have been meeting anyone, anywhere. A kidnapping doesn't become a federal offense until twenty-four hours have passed, which is when the law says it can be presumed that the victim has been transported over a state line. But one of the worst-kept secrets in law enforcement is that the FBI jumps the clock every time, plunging into kidnapping cases the moment they're reported. I've yet to encounter a judge who cares. Kidnapping is worse than a crime; it's torture, and it turns bleeding hearts into stone. The American people were hopelessly divided over Vietnam, but they were absolutely united in wanting to string the

Ayatollah Khomeini up by his beard after he seized the U.S. hostages in Iran.

I had barely touched the bell when the door popped open. The short, moonfaced man who opened it must have been standing there waiting for us ever since I hung up the phone. "Please, come in," he said. "I am so sorry you had to come out in this terrible weather. My name is Ken Ahn."

Later I learned his first name was really Kyung Sik; Ken was just a device Dr. Ahn used to avoid inflicting Korean sounds on the American tongues at St. Luke's hospital in Saginaw, where he was a vascular surgeon. I didn't know Ken, but I'd heard of him. Saginaw cops had told me stories about carting human jigsaw puzzles over to St. Luke's after bar brawls, and the immigrant doctor who miraculously put the pieces back together.

We sat down at a dining room table as an old woman in traditional Korean dress hustled two children upstairs, whispering threats each time they tried to sneak a look back at us over their shoulders. As I waited for them to get out of earshot, a framed picture on a nearby end table caught my eye. It showed a diminutive Korean woman with a delicate smile: Si Jin, Ken's wife. Debbie and the other mothers at the elementary school where my kids went knew her as Sue. She looked to be in her mid-thirties, a few years younger than her husband.

I turned to Ken. "Tell us the story from the beginning," I said. "Don't leave anything out. What might seem like an insignificant detail to you could be the key to the case."

He nodded. I could sense him willing himself to stay calm, to keep control. "I work the midnight shift in the emergency room at St. Luke's," he said in precise English, his accent making the words sound clipped. "Sometimes I stay after my shift, assisting in general surgery, and I did that today. We were very busy, and I didn't go home all day. About four o'clock, I called the house. But there was no answer. That's very unusual. If Si Jin is going out somewhere unexpected, she always leaves a message for me at the hospital. In fact, it was very unusual for me to come out of surgery and not find several messages waiting.

"I waited a few minutes, called again. Then again. A strong feeling started to come over me, a very bad feeling. I came home. My mother-in-law"—he nodded upstairs, where the old lady had gone—"said she had not seen Si Jin since the morning. I checked the answering machine. There was a message, a man's voice, saying I could find Si Jin's car in front of Frank's nursery, and to go check it right away. I went over there, and in the visor over the driver's seat, I found this letter."

He pushed a typewritten sheet across the table. Glancing at it, I recognized the ransom note I'd already heard over the telephone. Filled with misspellings and twisted grammar, it said Si Jin was being held by an "out of town" gang that wanted $10,000 for her release. The gang would be in touch by telephone later, the note said. "We are not amateurs," it added. "Do not call the police."

"What did you do when you found the note?" I asked.

"I knew I had to get ten thousand dollars," Ken said, raising his eyes slightly, as if the answer should have been obvious. "But we don't have it—we don't even have one thousand. So I called Dr. Rice to see if he could help me. He came to the house with the money, but he said we should call the FBI. He said you were experts." He paused, then locked eyes with me. "He said you would be able to get Si Jin back." His voice was neutral, but in his eyes was a plea.


If Ken had known just what kind of an "expert" was really sitting across the table from him that February night in 1982, he probably would have sold his house on the spot and started stacking ransom money on various street corners in hopes the kidnappers would trip over it. Because the fact was, I didn't know much about *managing* a kidnapping investigation.

You'd think that the FBI Academy would include a special course, or even several, on kidnappings. For one thing, it's one of the most complicated and dangerous kinds of cases that an FBI agent will ever face. Extortions usually turn on property—give me some money or I'll blow up your building. That's evil and ugly, to be sure, but it's still a *building*, and probably an insured building at that. When the threat is against a person—the wife or child of the person sitting across from you—it's infinitely more complicated and dangerous and emotional. It will rip your guts out.

Kidnapping is also the FBI's special province. It was a kidnapping that solidified the Bureau's reputation as a top-notch law enforcement agency. In 1932, Charles Lindbergh's infant son was abducted. Although Lindbergh paid $50,000 ransom, the baby was found dead. It took local police more than two years to make an arrest—and they did it without much of a case. The suspect, Bruno Richard Hauptmann, only had a single bill from the ransom money in his wallet. Try as they might, the police couldn't find the rest of the money. It was only when FBI agents searched Hauptmann's garage that another $14,000 or so was discovered in a secret compartment in the wall.

So, what do they teach about kidnappings at the academy? To spell the word with one *P* or suffer the eternal wrath of J. Edgar Hoover. The rest of it—how to make up a ransom package, the kind of electronic tracking devices available, how to integrate air and ground surveillance of a suspect or a ransom site—somehow slips through the cracks.

To be fair, I should say the Bureau did send me back to Quantico in 1980 for a week of training in hostage negotiations. A whole team of psychologists from the behavioral sciences unit spent hours and hours in painstaking explanation of the difference between sociopaths, psychotics, and schizophrenics and how they'll respond to various approaches.

Then it was time for a simulation exercise. The scenario: Puerto Rican nationalists have seized an FBI office and are holding a couple of our secretaries hostage. While the instructors watched through a two-way mirror, I sat in a room and talked on the telephone to the "terrorists," who were played by Bureau linguists. They were demanding money, as well as for one of their communiqués to be read over the radio.

At first I was a regular Dr. Joyce Brothers. "I don't give a shit if you're the *chingado* FBI, I'm going to starting beating this *puta*'s white ass if you don't get that communiqué on the radio!" one of the terrorists would scream.

"There's no need for that," I would reply in soothing tones. "We can work this out."

But after about ten minutes, one of them shouted into the phone: "Either you do what we tell you, *comemierda*, or we're going to kill this bitch right now! We're going to really fuck her up!" I could hear the sound of a woman being slapped.

"No," I roared, "we're going to fuck *you* up, you asshole!" Whoops. Phone goes dead, lights come up, the door to the observation room opens.

"Phil," said the Bureau's shrink in his sternest voice, "this is *not* the way we negotiate."

Add that episode to my only hands-on experience with a kidnapping—the disastrous Crawford case—and the picture didn't get any prettier. Nonetheless, my Bureau superiors thought I could handle it. Ordinarily a kidnapping case is run by an SAC or an ASAC, or in extreme circumstances by a supervisor. But everybody was tied up with a complicated drug wiretap in Flint. "Keep me posted," said Gene Glenn, the Detroit ASAC, when I called him to report the phone call from Ken Ahn. "Call me if you need anything or you want to talk anything over." Hidden inside that polite offer was the message: You're in charge, pal. We think you can do it. Don't disappoint us.

"Let's go over Si Jin's schedule," I said, changing the subject. "Do you have any idea where she was going today?"

"As far as I know, the only thing she was going to do was to take the car into the garage," Ken answered. "We got a call last night that said there was a problem with the brakes on Pontiacs."

"Who told you that?" I asked, instantly alert. In central Michigan, anything that goes wrong with GM cars is headline news, and I hadn't heard a word about this.

"A man at McDonald Pontiac," Ahn said. "He telephoned us to say the cars have been recalled."

I looked at King, who shook his head. "They haven't said anything about it on the TV news," he said. Reaching for the phone, I dialed the number of a friend who worked at McDonald Pontiac. He confirmed my suspicion: no recall. The call to Si Jin had been a trick to lure her someplace where she could be snatched. And, I was certain, the kidnapper had to be someone who knew her. Not only did he know what kind of car she drove, he knew her well enough to be certain she would respond immediately to the phone call. A lot of people—me included—would have said, well, yeah, I'll try to get down there sometime this week. But Si Jin agreed to go to the car dealership first thing the next morning.

"Who do you think did it?" I asked Ken. He slowly shook his head. "I have no idea," he said. "The man's voice on the answering machine—it's not familiar to me."

"Well, who are your enemies?" I asked.

"Enemies?" he replied quizzically.

"You know, people who have grudges against you," I said, a little impatiently. "Is there someone complaining that you messed up an operation? Someone suing you for malpractice? A pissed-off neighbor? Are any of the doctors at the hospital mad at you? Have your kids had trouble with anybody?"

Ken blinked in bewilderment. "Let's take them one at a time," suggested King, the agent who had accompanied me. "Let's take them one at a time, and really think them over." He gave me a sharp look. He was always plodding along. While you needed to rein me in. But he was right: I was confusing Ken, and something was going to get overlooked.

"I can't think of anyone who has complained about my work," said Ken, rubbing his chin in contemplation, "and I've never been sued for malpractice."

"Not once?" I pressed. Malpractice suits were all over the news in those days. It seemed like every sick person in America was going for an instant jackpot.

"Not once," he said gravely.

"Neighbors?"

"Everyone around here is very friendly," Ken said, shaking his head. "That's one of the reasons we live here, instead of a big city."

I felt like hell asking the next question, but there was no way around it. "Is your marriage solid?" I asked, forcing myself to meet his eyes.

"What do you mean?" he asked in confusion.

"I mean, are you seeing anyone else? Is it possible your wife is seeing anyone else?"

"Absolutely not," he said, his voice firm.

I tried a different tack. "Do you owe anybody money?"

"Of course," he acknowledged. "There is the mortgage on the house. We are still paying for the car—"

"No, no," I interrupted. Banks, no matter how far behind you get on the payments, don't generally take hostages. "I mean, persons. Have you borrowed money from any private individuals?"

"No, no," he answered.

"Well, let's look at it another way. Does anyone owe *you* money?"

"No," he replied again. "Well—maybe yes, a little. We own a duplex on Chapel Street that we rent out. The tenant, I think he is behind a month on his rent. But I'm not sure. Si Jin handles all those details."

"What's his name?" I asked. "What do you know about him?"

"His name is Richard Powell," Ken said. "I think he was living in Saginaw before he moved into our duplex. I met him once, but that's all. Si Jin takes care of everything like that."

I picked up the phone again, this time to dial Ken Ott, the township police chief. In a tiny jurisdiction like that one, the chief knows everybody who's ever jaywalked.

"Does the name Richard Powell mean anything to you?" I asked.

"Yeah, he's an asshole," Ott said, using universal copspeak for somebody who belongs in jail. "He's done time for car theft, and I think we've had some other cases on him. Why?"

"Look, Ken, we've got a kidnapping over here, but I want to keep it quiet," I explained. "The kidnapper says he's got eyes inside the police. I don't believe it, but I've got to be careful, just in case. Powell might be a suspect. Who handled his case for you guys?"

"Jim Dankert," Ott said, naming a detective sergeant King and I both knew and liked. A moment later I had him on the phone.

"Powell is a no-good son of a bitch," Dankert observed. "He's an auto thief. We've also gotten him on a couple of bad check charges, and there's another one pending now. He's big trouble waiting to happen."

"You say he worked at a Chevy dealership? What did he do there?" My skin was starting to tingle.

"Oh, the guy's a great mechanic, everybody agrees about that. Even with that car theft conviction, he never has any trouble getting a job, because he's so good. He's over at Martin Chevrolet now, but he's worked everywhere. Let's see, there was McDonald's Pontiac—"

I didn't hear the rest of the sentence. All I could think was, *we've got our man.*

Within minutes, the special operations group had Powell's duplex under surveillance—not that there was much to see. "Some lights are on, but there's no activity that we can see," one of the agents reported.

"It sounds like he's there," Ken said. "Why can't we just go arrest him now?"

"We don't have nearly enough to arrest him," I explained. "I'll bet a year's salary he's the one, but we don't have any evidence yet." The answer seemed to satisfy Ken. But actually, his question had touched on something that was already gnawing away at me. A victim who knows his or her kidnapper is almost never released alive.

That put us in the jaws of a cruel dilemma: If Powell was a lone kidnapper, we wanted to make an arrest as quickly as possible—

before he murdered Si Jin. But if he was part of a gang, we had to wait until we were sure we had fingered all the members—or the survivors might disappear forever with the hostage.

Happily for me, the doorbell rang, and I could put the thought aside. A team of communications technicians from Detroit had just arrived. "Where are you going to put the command center?" the head tech asked. I turned to Ken. "The kidnapper is going to be calling here, and we need to be around to listen and to advise you what to tell him," I said. "I'd like to stay here around the clock. It will mean bringing our radios in here and adding another telephone line."

"Of course," he said. "The sofa pulls out into a bed, so you can sleep here, too."

"Thank you, that's very kind," I said, although I doubted it would get much use. "The command center will go here," the tech told me pointing to the dining room. I went next door to see about another phone line.

We needed an extra phone in the house to use while leaving Ken's line open in case the kidnapper called. These days, that's no problem: We could just bring in a couple of cellular phones. But in the dark ages of 1982, it wasn't quite that easy.

Luckily, I knew the lawyer who lived in the house next to Ken's. Trudging over through the snow, I rang the doorbell. Although there were lights inside, no one answered for several moments. I rang again. This time the door was opened by the lawyer's twentyish son. His shirt was rumpled and only partly buttoned, his shoes and socks missing. I sensed a female presence in the background somewhere. "Can I help you?" he asked.

"Phil Kerby, FBI. Your father's not home?"

"He's on vacation," the son said, looking slightly panicked and probably wondering if there was a federal law against getting to second base. "Is there something I can do for you?"

"Yeah—I need your phone line," I said brusquely. "Our technicians are going to cut it down from your house and run it next door to the Ahn house. You won't have telephone service for the rest of the night, but by tomorrow we'll have it back on. Is that okay?"

"Sure," he said, relieved. "But what's going on?"

"All I can tell you is that if you talk about this, someone could die, and quite possibly you'll be in violation of federal statues," I said. As I turned away, his panicked look was back.

By a few minutes past ten, the techs had the second line working at the Ahn house. A trap-and-trace was already in place on Ken's phone, in case the kidnapper called. Meanwhile, Jerry Redd, the big, bearded, bearlike member of the special operations group, arrived with radios to help keep us in contact with the surveillance teams.

"What about the press?" King asked. "Are we going to have trouble with them?"

"This is so tightly held, I doubt if anything's going to leak out," I said. "And if it does, I don't think there's a reporter in Saginaw who would go with it without asking me first." King looked skeptical; like most agents, he ranked journalists slightly above rattlesnakes in nature's order. But I've always found—at least in little places like Saginaw—that if you're honest with reporters, they'll play fair with you. I was worried they would compromise us, but not too worried.

By now Ken's dining room was starting to look like a mad scientist's lab, with radios and tape recorders stacked on the table and cords and wires snaking all over the floor. A case log—a notebook in which Redd recorded every significant development and its time—lay open on a chair.

With the second telephone line hooked up, I felt more comfortable making calls. My first one was to the Michigan state police lab in Bridgeport, just a few miles south of Saginaw. Without going into detail, I told them we were working a kidnapping and might need some help in a hurry at some point during the next twenty-four hours. They agreed to put a team on standby. If this case wound up hinging on a hair or a thread or a fingerprint, we would have top-notch help in a hurry. Then I called Gene Glenn in Detroit and told him everything King and I had done; he murmured in agreement to every point and had nothing to add. He also promised to send down a dozen members of the Bureau's SWAT team the next morning.

We had a working command center, a suspect, and a surveillance team in place. Reinforcements were on the way. Now all we could do was wait.


"Can I get you anything? Would you like a beer, or some coffee?" Ken's voice was barely above a whisper. In the next room, stretched out on the sofa-bed, King was trying to sleep. It was 2 A.M. and we no longer expected to hear from the kidnapper before morning, but I couldn't sleep. Neither, apparently, could Ken. He had wandered downstairs to find me at the table, staring at the radios.

"No thanks," I said. "How are the kids?"

"It's hard to say. They know something is wrong, but they don't know what," he replied, sitting down and propping his chin on an elbow. "Or maybe they do. They were born here, and they have grown up as Americans. I don't always understand them."

"When did you come here?" I asked, genuinely interested. Saginaw was not exactly a major center of Korean culture.

"We came to the United States in 1969, first to Detroit for a year, then Cincinnati for about ten months, then here," he recalled. "I just came for the surgical training, because it's much better than in Korea. But we liked Saginaw, and we stayed."

"Did Si Jin work when you first got here?" I asked.

"Much more than I can tell you," he said, leaning forward. "She is a remarkable woman."

Si Jin had attended Seoul National University, the best college in Korea, at a time when it was almost impossible for women to get in. She got a pharmacist's degree, but when the Ahns arrived in Detroit, she discovered her credentials wouldn't be honored. So she took courses to learn to be an X-ray technician, and passed the exam with the highest scores in the school's history.

"So she worked as an X-ray technician at a veteran's hospital, and she did all the cooking and cleaning, and she did all the things that I was supposed to do as the head of the household," he recounted. "All I had to do was concentrate on what I was learning at the hospital. She did everything else, and I mean everything. Do you know, I have never been to the bank here? I have never set foot in it. Si Jin takes care of all the accounts, handles all the money, pays all the bills."

In the mid-1970s, Si Jin had to do even more. Ken's kidneys began to fail.

"She learned to run the dialysis machine. It usually takes two months of training, but Si Jin learned it in a week. Then, three nights a week when I got off work at the hospital at 10 P.M., she would put me on the machine for eight hours. I could sleep, but she couldn't. She stayed up all night, three nights a week, for a year and a half, until I could get a kidney transplant. She is a very small woman, but a very strong one."

The thought triggered a memory, and Ken laughed out loud. "When we lived in Detroit, she got her driver's license for the first time," he said. "And that same day, she drove downtown, into the very worst part of the city, just to see it. And she picked up a hitchhiker. I told her she was crazy, but she didn't understand. She is not afraid of anything."


The first call came around midmorning. It was short and to the point: "Have you got the money?"

"Yes," Ken answered, following the script we had given him, "but I want to talk to my wife to make sure she's all right."

"She's not with me," the kidnapper answered. "And she can't come to a phone. She's in a Winnebago that my partner is driving around town. I'll call back later with instructions about the money." The line went dead.

The techs quickly pinpointed the source of the call, a pay phone on the west side of town. Powell had been in the area, but the surveillance team, knowing to hang back and take no chances on being spotted, hadn't actually seen him make the call.

No matter. There was another way to confirm it. I called one of my regular snitches and asked him to call Martin Chevrolet. Later, Ken and I listened to a tape of the conversation. "How much do you charge to rebuild a blown Malibu engine?" the snitch inquired.

"That depends on the year and the number of cylinders," Powell answered in the same low, unemotional voice that we had heard asking about money half an hour earlier. As he and the snitch continued their conversation about cracked blocks and frozen pistons, the last shred of doubt disappeared from my mind.

"From now on, I don't want Powell out of our sight," I told Jerry Redd. "If there's really a partner, they'll have to be communicating somehow or other. If they do, I want to know about it. And the next time he calls us, I want visual confirmation that he's using a telephone when the call comes in."

"Our surveillance plane is already in the air, right?" I paused, thinking."

"Sure is," said Redd.

"Let's keep it in the air. Between going out to make calls from pay phones and going to ransom drops, I think Powell's going to be a busy guy this afternoon."

"You got it," he agreed, and went to work on his radios again, doubtless wondering why I had just run through a set of instructions that were second nature to him. *If you can say anything about a situation like this is lucky, then we're lucky Redd's people are here*, I thought as I prepared to call Detroit to report the latest developments. Carrying out surveillance using the eight agents I had available in Saginaw would have stretched everyone to the breaking point and created a serious risk of detection.

But Jerry had a dozen agents on his team. Breaking them into teams of four, he could shift them in and out of surveillance, minimizing the chance that Powell would notice the same face following him around all day, as well as giving the agents periodic breaks. And with air coverage as well, the chance we would lose him—due to either evasive maneuvers or just bad luck, like getting stuck at a railroad crossing—was practically nil. I didn't even have to think about any of this; Jerry just quietly went about his business, moving his agents around Saginaw like invisible chess pieces.

"Can we arrest him now?" Ken asked. "The voice was the same on the two calls. Isn't that enough?

"Ken," I answered patiently, "what if we arrest him and he says, I deny everything? We still don't know where Si Jin is. We don't know if there's really an accomplice. And if we arrest Powell and he decides to be a hardass about it, we might never find her. We don't have much leverage against him. In terms of hard evidence, about all we can prove is that he made the phone call. It's true that we can eventually get a search warrant for the house. But what if there's nothing there."

"But I'm worried about Si Jin," Ken persisted. "What if she's hurt?"

*What if it's worse than that?* I wondered, but banished the thought immediately. We had to hope Powell was telling the truth about an accomplice. If the only face Si Jin had seen was that of a man she didn't know, her chances of walking away from this in one piece increased about a million percent.

"Okay, here's what we'll do," I said. "When he calls back, you ask him something that only Si Jin would know. When he comes back with the right answer, then we'll know she's all right."

"The names of the children?" Ken suggested.

"No, if they did any research before the kidnapping, they might know," I said. "Make it something about Korea."

"The city where her mother was born?" he proposed.

"Perfect."


Around noon, the surveillance team reported that Powell was moving. He was driving his new white Camaro along a commercial strip on the west side again. "It seems like he's looking for something," one of the agents speculated.

"A pay phone," I agreed. "Ken, get ready." He moved to another room, where no radio noise would be audible when the call came.

"He's turned into a parking lot—pulled up to one of those drive-in pay phones—"

The ring sounded like a fire alarm. Ken snatched the receiver. "Hello?"

"Drive your van to the Kmart store on State Street in half an hour," Powell said, his voice now unmistakably familiar to everyone in the room. "Leave the money on the floor of the van, on the driver's side, and go inside to the store's cafeteria. Wait until you hear yourself paged over the loudspeaker. Then you can go back out to the car. Got it?

"I want to know if my wife is safe," Ken interjected. I could see the strain on his face, but his voice was calm and controlled. "I want you to ask her the name of the city where her mother was born."

"If you want to play these games," Powell replied coldly, "we might have to send you a finger or something."

The discipline of thousands of nights in the emergency room helped Ken to stifle his gasp. But his face seemed to cave in before my eyes. King and I wanted to leap through the phone and tear Powell's tongue out.

"Be at the Kmart," Powell snapped, and hung up. From Ken, I heard a wrenching sob.


I couldn't believe the words cutting through the crackling static on Redd's radio: "Subject is leaving the Kmart parking lot, heading south."

"And he never entered the van?" Redd asked.

"No, drove by, appeared to observe it, but didn't approach," the agent confirmed.

"Son of a bitch!" I exclaimed. "What's he waiting for?"

"A dry run?" King suggested. "Trying to see if there was any surveillance on the van?"

Ahn had followed Powell's directions exactly, arriving at the Kmart on time and then leaving the door unlocked to wait inside. Across the parking lot, King—a veteran Bureau sniper—observed the scene from another car. If Powell somehow tried to move against Ahn, King would put a stop to it fast.

But nothing happened. Powell cruised around the parking lot, but he never tried to retrieve the ransom money. Then he left. When Ken returned a few minutes later, he was unable to shed any light on what happened. "I waited in the cafeteria, and when I heard my name called, I went back outside," he said. "But the money was still there where I left it. Was this a joke?"

Redd's radio sputtered to life again. "He's pulling up at another pay phone," an agent announced.

"Looks like your question is about to be answered," I told Ken as he moved into the next room. The words were barely out of my mouth when the phone rang.

"That was just the dress rehearsal," Powell said. "And you did good. Now we're ready for the real thing. At 6 P.M., I want you to go to the Holiday Inn West. Leave the money in the van, just like you did before. Go into the dining room and wait at the bar. You'll get a call on the bartender's phone with instructions on where to meet your wife." Abruptly, he hung up.

I barely listened as the techs reported the number where the call originated and the surveillance agents confirmed that it was the pay phone they had been watching. All that would be important later in court, but to me it was old news. Powell was the kidnapper, or one of them, anyway. The question was, what should we do about it?

Our game plan was based on the idea that the kidnapper was rational and relatively predictable. But this "dress rehearsal" stuff was flaky, weird. What if Powell wasn't really after the money at all? What if he was some kind of loon who just got a charge out of jerking people around? This could go on for days or even weeks.

But all the arguments I had made to Ken earlier still stood. The fact was, making an arrest in a case like this was playing your last card. If it didn't work, you were busted. In this case, that meant losing Si Jin. We still didn't know where she was. We had run spot checks on Powell's house all day, but nothing was happening there. I had thought of ordering a search of the place while Powell was at work.

The Ahn Kidnapping

But what if one of the neighbors called him to tip him off as to what was happening or someone saw us at the court house?

Brushing aside a stack of crumpled Burger King sacks (it had become apparent early in the game that I had not been harboring any latent passion for Korean food), I dialed the Bureau office in Detroit to give Gene Glenn a quick sketch of what had happened.

"What's your feeling?" he asked. It was still my case all the way.

"I don't like the way it's going," I admitted. "But I think the only choice is to let it play out—make the ransom drop, and hope that Powell tips his hand."

"I think you're right," he agreed.

As I hung up, Ken was gazing at me. He could read it in my eyes: Wait. Again.


Unbelievably, Powell put us through another dry run. When Ken came to the bar telephone, Powell told him the "real" ransom drop— this would be our third attempt—would take place around 10 P.M. at the Best Western motel off Interstate 75 just outside Bay City, ten miles north. "Why are you doing this?" Ken sobbed, but Powell just hung up without replying. Back at the house, we wearily began to prepare once more to deliver the money.

By 9:30, I felt like I was conducting a covert symphony orchestra. Redd was on the radio, shuffling agents around both Powell's home and the Best Western. The SWAT team was saddled up and ready to go in any direction we chose. The state police lab was warned that the chase was drawing to a close. The ransom money was packed inside a large brown envelope tucked under Ken's arm.

"Are you ready?" I asked him. He nodded jerkily, the sign of a weary-unto-death man running on pure adrenaline. None of us had gotten more than an hour or two of sleep in the past day and a half. We were the walking dead, mistakes waiting to happen. If we could just get through the next hour without a major blunder, this thing would be over.

"Phil, I think we need to change the plan slightly," King interrupted. "I think I should go in the back of the van."

"What if Powell sees you?" I asked. "What's wrong with going in another car, like this afternoon?"

"It's night, it's snowing, it'll be a tough shot from across the parking lot if something happens," King argued. "But I can lie under some blankets in the very back of the van. In the dark, he'll never see me. And if anything goes wrong, I'll be right on top of him."

I pondered for a moment. King was not one to be modest about his shooting ability; if he said he couldn't get a shot off under these weather conditions, it must be true.

"Okay, go in the back," I told him. I started to add, don't move unless Powell tries some funny business, don't interfere with the ransom pickup. But I bit my tongue. King knew what to do. A moment later, they were out the door.

I sat at the table, sipping coffee and chewing cold french fries, for another ten or fifteen minutes. Then the radios came alive.

"The doctor's van just pulled into the hotel parking lot," said one of the surveillance agents. "He's exiting the vehicle, going inside."

"Suspect is moving," advised an agent from our airplane overhead. "Camaro headed west on the interstate."

Block by block we followed Powell's progress, until he, too, pulled into the Best Western lot. There was no sign of the fabled Winnebago. *But that doesn't mean anything*, I told myself. *If I were the kidnapper, I'd keep it as far away from me as possible, in case there's trouble at the drop site.*

"Subject approaching van . . . pausing at door . . ." I prayed King didn't suddenly decide he was the reincarnation of Melvin Purvis. "He's leaning over . . . shutting door . . . walking away . . . He's back in the Camaro."

The ransom, it seemed, had been delivered. Now what would Powell do? Contact his accomplice? Drive to the hiding place where he had stashed Si Jin?

We listened as the surveillance agents tracked him the few miles into Bay City. The Camaro turned off the highway into a residential area, then pulled up in a driveway. A minute or two later, one of the agents on the ground made a pass by the house, close enough to read off the address.

"That's Powell's daughter," said King, who had just walked into the house, Ken trailing behind him. He had spent part of the morning making phone checks on Powell's background. "She lives at that address."

"What happened at the hotel?" I asked.

"Nothing," King said. "He took the money and left."

Added Ken: "I waited a long time inside the hotel, like he said, but no message came. What do you think that means?"

"I'm not sure," I admitted. "He drove straight to Bay City, no stopping, no using the phone. Let's see what he does from there."

The answer, for the next few minutes or so, was nothing—at least that we could see. Then he left the house and drove back toward Saginaw. A few blocks from his house, he stopped at an A&P grocery to buy something.

"Have a couple of your people stay behind when he leaves," I told Redd. "Tell them to get in there and find out what he bought. And if it's possible, retrieve the money he used." The ransom had been paid in hundred dollar bills, and we had recorded their serial numbers. If he used one to buy groceries, it would be another nail in his coffin at the trial when this was all over.

Leaving the supermarket, Powell drove straight home, went inside, and shut the door. Lights went on in the back part of the house.

"He bought baloney and a loaf of bread," reported an agent at the A&P. "He used a hundred dollar bill, and we've got it."

Silently we huddled around the radios, waiting for something to happen. But as the minutes ticked by, it began to seem that there wasn't going to be anything more. It was past midnight. Surely if Powell was going to contact a confederate and order him to release Si Jin, he would have done it by now. As if to confirm it, lights started going off at the house.

"Phil, the plane's got to come down to refuel pretty soon," Redd warned me. "And I don't think it can go back up anytime soon. They've been in the air thirteen hours. Flying under these conditions is a miserable, exhausting job, and those guys have to be rested." He paused a minute, then added: "The people on the ground aren't in the best of shape, either."

The news about the airplane crystallized a decision that had already begun to take shape in my mind. Once the plane was down, what would we do if Powell came barreling out of the house and took off? Could we keep up with him? What if we lost him?

I got up from the table and moved to a chair near Ken. "I think we're about out of options here," I said softly. "I don't think there's anything left to do but go into the house. The SWAT team is good, and it's fast, and if Si Jin is inside, I think they'll be on top of Powell before he can hurt her. But you know I can't guarantee anything." My voice left a question mark for him to answer, although in truth the decision was already made.

"I believe you are right," Ken whispered.

The SWAT team was already assembled at a high school about half a mile from Powell's home. Greg Stejskal, the commander, had driven by the house several times earlier in the day, looking it over, and he already had an assault plan.

By 2:30 A.M. everything was ready. I picked up the radio microphone one more time. "He's inside the house," I told Stejskal. "The lights are out. It looks like it's over. You have permission to assault. Show the flag." Stejskal, I was certain, knew what I meant: Put the fear of God in this son of a bitch, make him wet his pants, because I want to know where that woman is and I want to know it right now. But all that came back over the radio was a laconic, "Ten-four," a simple Bureau yes.

Jerry Redd had the radio tuned to the SWAT team's frequency. We listened to them call off the distance to the house: three hundred yards, two hundred yards, one hundred. Entry made.

The Ahn Kidnapping                                                        **267**

I stared at the radio so I wouldn't have to look at Ken. The children, who had been told of the kidnapping early in the morning, were upstairs with Si Jin's mother. But Ken was here at my side, his face a strangled mixture of fear and hope. As one silent minute dragged by and then two, the tension was so heavy that I thought my lungs would stop.

The surveillance team leader's voice boomed out of the radio: "C-9 to command post." A horrible premonition made me grab for the mike to stop him, but before I could press the transmit button, he continued.

"Command post, she's dead," he said tersely.

I whirled toward Ken, who was sagging like a rag doll. "No, no, no!" I cried. "We can't be sure. That agent probably isn't even in the house. I'm going to call my people inside."

I snatched the telephone and dialed Powell's number. Jim Hiller answered.

"It's Kerby," I said, fighting to keep my voice even. "What do you have?"

"Bad news," he said quietly. "We found her body under a work bench in the garage, wrapped in plastic."

I turned to the Ahns. "I'm sorry," I whispered. Silent tears started down Ken's face. His mother-in-law, who had come downstairs, wailed and slammed her head ferociously against the wall. The children stood there, faces pale and empty. If I've ever in my life felt like dying, that was the moment.


Before I went home, Hiller gave me a brief sketch of what happened. The two burly agents who broke open the front door went hurtling down a hallway, where they collided with Powell as he came running out of the bedroom. Slamming him hard to the floor, one of the agents screamed, "Where is she?"

"Don't shoot!" Powell begged. "She's dead. She's in the garage." That was where they found Si Jin, wrapped in a plastic bag. Her hands and legs were bound with clothesline; tape covered her eyes and mouth. There was a single gunshot wound in the back of her neck.

"He's clammed up and isn't going to talk until he gets a lawyer," Hiller said. "But I don't believe anyone else was involved in this. It looks too small-time and disorganized."


I barely slept that night. But when daylight came, I couldn't get out of bed. I couldn't even answer Debbie when she asked if I was okay. All I could think of was, what will the autopsy say? When did Si Jin die? Did I kill her by waiting too long to make an arrest?

A million times I walked myself back through the case. Everything I did was right, I told myself. Everything I did was approved in Detroit. Yet that didn't hold back the dark tide of self-doubt that washed over me. All day I lay in bed, paralyzed.

Late Saturday afternoon, Debbie came into the room. "Ken Ott is on the phone, and he says it's very important," she said. Because it turned out that no state lines had been crossed in the kidnapping, Ott's police department would be handling the case. Listlessly I picked up the telephone.

"Phil, the medical examiner says Si Jin had been dead at least twenty-four hours, probably longer, when the body was found," he said. "She was dead before you got the first phone call from Powell. I just thought you'd want to know."

"I did, Ken," I said. "I really did. Thanks for calling." All day long that bastard had tortured Ken Ahn while his wife lay cold and dead on a garage floor. Tortured me, too, with a long life-and-death negotiation that was really meaningless. Nothing we could have said or done would have saved Si Jin. For some reason, I thought of Powell's late-night trip to the grocery store. Whoever said man does not live by bread alone had never met Richard Powell. With a dead woman in his garage, all he could think about was a baloney sandwich.

I got out of bed.

———

The subsequent investigation and trial tied up a few loose ends. Powell admitted that he had no partners in the kidnapping. The trip to his wife's home after he picked up the ransom was to give $1,200 to his teenage daughter, so she could buy a car.

A detailed search of the house turned up Powell's handwritten drafts of the original ransom note to Ken Ahn. They were inside four sealed garbage bags in the garage, along with clothing and other paraphernalia used in the kidnapping. Friends of Powell's said he had talked about going to Wisconsin over the weekend for a snowmobile race. Our theory was that he planned to dump Si Jin's body somewhere in the backwoods along the way, tossing it away like so much trash.

Once that was out of the way, it appeared, Powell had big plans for the future. We found a map showing the residences of two other Saginaw doctors, along with a sheet of notes describing their homes.

Powell's lawyers initially hoped to mount an insanity defense, complete with a story about his wife's picture speaking to him from the wall, talking him out of a suicide attempt. When they couldn't find a shrink who would buy it, they tried to show the kidnapping was a spur-of-the-moment thing, completely unpremeditated. Powell denied luring Si Jin out of the house with the phony call about her car's brakes. He claimed she came by the duplex to hassle him about overdue rent, and he took her hostage on an impulse. The shooting, he said, was accidental.

It took the jurors about forty-five minutes to find Powell guilty of premeditated murder, and I suspect it would have been less than that except several of them had to go to the bathroom.

Michigan law doesn't allow parole on the charges for which Powell was convicted. Nonetheless, he's working every angle trying to get out. Shortly before I retired from the FBI, he sent word to me that he used to do repairs on former Teamster leader Jimmy Hoffa's car. He got to know a lot of the people around Hoffa, Powell said, and he could tell us where Hoffa's body is—in return for a reduction of his sentence.

An FBI agent gave Powell a polygraph exam in his prison cell. It showed he was lying. Even before the results came back, though, I sent him a message: Even if you can hand us Hoffa wrapped with a bow, I won't help cut a single hour off your sentence. The FBI doesn't trade with scum like you.

Does that sound harsh? As I worked on this book, I had lunch with Ken Ahn to help me remember some of the details of the case. He stayed in Saginaw and eventually remarried, but his life has never been the same.

"My daughter is twenty-five now, my son twenty-four, but our relationship is not as good," he told me. "They never really got over what happened to their mother. Even today, my daughter has occasional nightmares." He hung his head. "It is my fault, I think. I thought the best thing was not to talk about what happened, to get past it and go on with our lives. It made the children angry."

I wanted to interrupt—to say that there's only one person at fault here, and it's not Ken Ahn—but something in his voice stopped me.

"I think I told you, many years ago, about Si Jin giving me dialysis," Ken continued. "But did I mention my brother? He had kidney problems, too. Si Jin worked for months to get him a visa to come to the United States. He got here just after I had my transplant. And then she gave *him* dialysis three times a week for eighteen months. Si Jin saved my life, she saved my brother's life, but she could not save her own.

"That was why everything seemed so unfair to me. For the first time, I was healthy, my brother was healthy. My career was good—we didn't have to work so hard as before. For the first time, our life was completely normal. And what happened?

"You know, in all those hard years, all those years of hard work in a strange country, Si Jin never showed me one tear."

And then Ken Ahn raised his face, and showed me one of his.

# 1 3

# DRUG WARS

"This is what I call a good day's work," Dave Welker said, waving at the stack of arrest reports on the desk. "Thirty arrests, six pounds of cocaine seized, five hundred pounds of marijuana, more than a hundred guns. And it's not even noon yet."

Welker, and all the rest of us, had every right to be proud. We had just pulled off the largest drug raid in Michigan history. Under Bureau direction, 350 law enforcement officers—including 90 FBI agents—had swept through the Saginaw area just after dawn, rousting drug dealers. None of them had a clue we were coming; we caught everyone we were looking for, and not a shot was fired. Operation McDope, as we called it, was a stunning success.

Welker had earned his satisfied smile. As the case agent, he had spent months overseeing two undercover officers who made $70,000 worth of drug purchases; he collected the mountain of details necessary to ask a judge for wiretaps; and he spent countless hours meeting informants, covering leads, and sitting through tedious but critical planning sessions. I intended to put him in for a bonus.

But as pleased as I was, I still felt a disquieting pang of uneasiness. In 1962, the morning's raid would have made the front page of the *New York Times* and the *Washington Post*. But today, thirty years later, I wondered if even the Detroit papers would take notice. Since 1982, when the FBI first got jurisdiction to work drug cases, I had helped put 250 Central Michigan dealers in jail. Yet out on the street, cocaine was cheaper than when I started.

During my last ten years with the FBI, when I visited clubs and civic groups, it often seemed to me there was only one question: Are we winning the war on drugs? People are usually jolted when I say no—they apparently think a cop is supposed to be a cheerleader, too—and downright disconcerted when I add that, if the war is ever won, it won't be police who do it.

But I'm not a heretic, at least within law enforcement circles. I don't know a single policeman or prosecutor who thinks the nation's drug traffic can be ended through arrests or prison sentences. While George Bush was president, he nearly tripled the federal government's anti-narcotics budget, from $4.3 billion in 1988 to $11.9 billion in 1992. You know what the result was? The supply of cocaine in the United States *increased*, from an estimated 361 tons to 376.

When it comes to drugs, the law enforcement system is just a cleanup crew, trying to keep things from getting too messy. The real solutions, if there are any, lie within society itself. Politicians have used the phrase "family values" to beat each others' heads in to the point where the words have nearly lost their meaning. But I still can't think of any other way to explain the problem of drug abuse. It *is* a by-product of deteriorating societal values, and it will continue to get worse until we figure out how to restore them.

Meanwhile, policemen will continue to do what we've always done: harass drug dealers, make them keep their heads down a bit. I firmly believe in the value of that. But sometimes, like the day we wrapped up the McDope investigation, I feel like King Canute, trying to roll back the sea.

As I mentioned before, the FBI didn't even work drug cases until 1982, when President Reagan first gave us jurisdiction. Before that, narcotics were the responsibility of the DEA and its predecessors, as well as local cops.

Why the federal government kept us out of drug cases, I'm not entirely certain. The common wisdom around the FBI is J. Edgar Hoover didn't want to fool around with dope because it would lay agents open to terrible temptations to corruption. If so, he was certainly correct. Worldwide narcotics traffic is estimated to net something like half a trillion dollars a year, and drug kingpins are happy to share some of that with cooperative police.

I learned that firsthand, soon after we began working drug cases. With two other agents, I arrested a Colombian cocaine trafficker. When we searched his car, we found $40,000 in the trunk.

"Where'd you get all that money?" I asked him.

"I don't see no money, man," he replied, looking me in the eye. It was an open invitation to walk away with the cash. I'm sure other agents who work drugs get similar offers all the time, and inevitably, some place, some day, one is going to accept.

But to me, that hardly seems a reason to give narcotraffickers a free pass. In 1984, an FBI agent in Los Angeles was caught selling classified documents to a KGB spy who had seduced him. That didn't mean we quit trying to catch spies. If we're going to stay away from any crime where large sums of money are involved, pretty soon the FBI will be the world's great jaywalking police.

When we *did* get jurisdiction, I have to admit that I knew almost nothing about dope. Drug culture came late to the small-town Midwest. I never even laid eyes on a joint until I was out of college, teaching school in Flint. A graduate student lit up a marijuana cigarette at a party at the lakeside home I shared with a couple of teachers. We told him to put it out. Later, when he did it again, we threw him in the lake.

That story may sound hopelessly square to a lot of other people who grew up in the 1960s. But I suspect almost every other agent who joined the FBI around the time I did has a similar tale. The Bureau now accepts applicants who have engaged in experimental use of marijuana and even cocaine, as long as it was fleeting and occurred in the distant past. But in Hoover's FBI, there was zero tolerance: A single puff on a joint, anytime in your whole life, and you were out.

The first time I encountered drugs during an investigation was during my first few months in Columbus, when Anson Hopper and I went out to arrest a deserter. Hopper, always one for subtlety, kicked in the guy's door and yanked him out of the bed he was sharing with his girlfriend. I walked over to the closet to get him some clothes, and I saw a shelf stacked with vials, all of them filled with powder.

"Oh, shit," I murmured. "Hey, Hop, come look at this." Leaving the deserter handcuffed in a chair, Hopper peered into the closet. "Can you tell what any of this stuff is?" I asked.

"No," he said, shaking his head, "but I kind of doubt if this guy is keeping an emergency supply of powdered milk in his closet."

We both stared at the vials for a while. "I guess we have to take this in as evidence," I finally said. "This stuff is going to have to be tested in the lab."

Hopper's face clouded. "Then we're going to have to call the local cops, get them to arrest him, and write about six hundred reports explaining why," he complained. "And maybe there's going to be some hassle about probable cause to search the closet."

He paused, and I offered a suggestion: "Let's just flush all this stuff down the toilet and forget about it. We don't even know if it's dope." My first big narcotics investigation, literally in the crapper.*

In mid-1981, gossip floated around the FBI that the Bureau would soon be permitted to take on drug cases. It piqued my interest. During the Giacalone investigation, I had stumbled across a drug operation run by a guy named Lyle Parks, part of the crowd that hung out at Billy Loiacano's restaurant. Parks was a nasty little man who was quick with his fists, "a hacksaw asshole," as one of his loyal associates described him to me. He was bringing in a load of drugs—

---

*A movie cop would have tested the drugs by tasting them, right? Whenever I see that, I have two questions. The first is, how the hell is a policeman supposed to know what heroin and cocaine taste like? This was not a subject they covered at the FBI Academy. The second is, how do you know you aren't swallowing LSD or PCP or some other hallucinogen? Or, for that matter, cyanide?

several kilos of cocaine and a few hundred pounds of marijuana—every couple of weeks.

Without any jurisdiction, I passed his name along to both the local police and the DEA. But the local cops were hamstrung: Michigan law doesn't allow police to use wiretaps, which is by far the easiest way to make cases against major dealers. The DEA—which, like the FBI, has authority for wiretaps under federal law—would probably get around to Parks eventually, but it was only a third the size of the FBI and already had too many cases of its own to deal with.

But if the gossip was correct, we could go after Parks ourselves. The idea of tying up the last loose end of the Giacalone case appealed to me. Although we had no evidence linking Loiacano or LaBreche to drug sales or even use, seeing one of their associates still strutting around Saginaw was like a pebble in my shoe. I decided to start compiling the massive affidavit we'd need to request a wiretap. On January 28, 1982, Reagan's attorney general, William French Smith, ordered the FBI to begin investigating narcotics cases. Shortly thereafter, an affidavit was submitted to a federal judge in Detroit. Within a few weeks the tap was in place, our first drug wiretap under the new jurisdiction.

The results were amazing. We were expecting to hear a lot of coded conversation: *Ruby 3 this is Ruby 5, we've got a code 7.* Instead, it was: *Hey, I need an ounce of coke. Sure, come on over.* It was so blatant that I actually wondered if Parks somehow knew about the tap and was baiting us, trying to trick us into an embarrassing raid that would yield nothing. But as the days rolled on and the open chatter continued unabated, I realized the humiliating truth: These guys had no fear of law enforcement. They were like bears in a park who go from looting garbage cans to terrorizing campers; they had gotten away with so much for so long that they thought they were immune.

Only once did we hear even a note of caution on the tapped telephone. For some reason, Parks's usual shipment of drugs did not come in from Florida, and he went to Denver to pick up a load of cocaine himself. While he was away, he left a flunkie named Bill Petersen in charge.

Apparently the prospect of working in unfamiliar territory worried Parks, because he and Petersen devised a whole vocabulary of codewords to use on the telephone. We didn't know about it until the tap picked up Parks calling his own apartment from Colorado. "I need a twelve and I'm going to be getting a seventeen," he told Petersen.

"You need a what? What did you say?" asked Petersen, who we had known for some time was dumber than a bag of rocks.

"I *said*, I need a twelve and I'm going to be getting a seventeen," repeated Parks, slowly and through gritted teeth.

"But—but—what about the cocaine?" asked the hopelessly confused Petersen.

"*Use the code, you moron!*" screamed Parks. Eventually he had to go over it word by word, right there on the telephone, while an FBI tape recorder preserved it for posterity and a jury.

Big FBI offices usually have some rooms permanently equipped to monitor wiretaps. But when we ran a tap in a smaller place like Saginaw, we rented an apartment to set up all the monitoring equipment. It isn't necessarily located anywhere near the phone you're tapping; the days are long gone when an agent had to operate the tap by pretending to be a repairman and holding a pair of alligator clips on the line. Now the phone company itself activates the tap once directed to do so by a court order.

But in the Parks case, we got lucky. There was a vacant apartment right across the parking lot from his. That meant we could keep the place under surveillance while tapping the phone, correlating calls with visits. Soon we had enough evidence of drug deals taking place in the apartment to convince a judge to let us plant a microphone in a wall inside.

That led us to an unpleasant discovery. For several weeks we had wondered about the beautiful young women parading in and out of

Parks's apartment. "Jesus Christ, Phil, I'll bet they're trading sex for cocaine," an ill-looking agent told me after monitoring the mike for a day. "They're 'coke whores.' " We had come a long way, I reflected, from the Pepsi Generation.

Parks and his pals were so open about what they were doing that we didn't have to operate the tap for long to compile a mountain of incriminating tape. In less than a month, we shut everything down and swept in with arrest warrants for about two dozen people. Most of them pled guilty rather than risk a jury's wrath after hearing the tapes. Those who didn't cop pleas were convicted in court. We didn't lose a single case out of the whole batch.

Leads generated by the Parks case enabled us to set up another wiretap in Ann Arbor. We caught a UM professor and his brother who were moving so much marijuana that they actually bought an Irish freighter to bring it in from South America. (Their eyes, it turned out, were bigger than the freighter's hold; it sank.)

*What's so difficult about this?* I wondered. Hell, at this rate we'd have the state of Michigan cleaned up by Christmas. That's when we took a little trip to the Everglades.


More than any other kind of crime, drug cases are like tumbling dominoes. When you make a case—especially as prison sentences have grown stiffer—almost inevitably the guy will roll over, offering up somebody else a notch or two higher on the totem pole in return for less jail time.

The Everglades case was the last domino from the Lyle Parks case. One of the defendants offered us a deal. He knew a kid from Saginaw we'll call Mike who had moved down to Naples, Florida, and gone into the marijuana business in a major way. He was part of a group flying thousands of pounds into an airstrip someplace in the vast Everglades swamp. With the right introduction, our new informant said, it would be easy to make an undercover buy from Mike.

Naples, way down at the southern tip of Florida, was a good

thousand miles outside my jurisdiction. So I phoned the supervisor of a drug squad in the Miami office.

"We've got a snitch who can introduce a UC"—Bureau jargon for undercover agent—"to a big-time weed dealer in Naples," I said. "Who should I talk to about it?"

"Importer of what?" the supervisor asked impassively.

"Marijuana, thousands of pounds."

The supervisor sighed. "We're not taking new marijuana cases right now," he explained. "We've got more cocaine than we can handle." He thought for a moment. "Does the case have any connection to your territory?"

"Yeah," I replied. Mike had sold a couple of loads to old friends around Saginaw.

"Then why don't you take it?" the supervisor said. "Because if you leave it for us, the guy will be selling dope from his rocking chair at the nursing home before we get to it."

Under ordinary circumstances, it wouldn't have been easy to convince my bosses in Detroit to fly a dozen agents and a Bureau surveillance plane one thousand miles to work a case in a town that the guys in the Miami office could hit with a well-thrown rock. But drugs were new and sexy, and everybody was anxious for the FBI to make a good show.

Some of the agents flew down on the surveillance plane. But I went commercial, along with our snitch and the case agent. If I believed in omens, I might have bailed on the case when we got to Miami. From there we had to fly to Naples on a tiny commuter airline that wouldn't let us carry any luggage into the cabin. Handing over the bags that contained our rifles, shotguns, and $50,000 in buy money, I felt slightly faint.

A few minutes later, you could eliminate the word "slightly." The captain boarded the plane, followed by a little girl of about seven. She went into the cockpit, sat down in the copilot's seat, and buckled herself in. I didn't want to look like a sexist or an ageist or anything, but when the captain came back into the cabin to check the door latches before takeoff, I tugged at his jacket.

"Where's the copilot?" I asked.

"Oh, he couldn't make it today," the pilot answered blandly, heading back to the cockpit.

Just a few minutes into the flight, I saw the captain whisper to the little girl, who unbuckled her seat belt and walked back into the cabin. Glancing over his shoulder, the captain caught my eye. "Could you come on up here, sir?" he asked.

I squeezed past the little girl, who immediately took my seat, and stuck my head into the cabin. "Come on, sit down here," the captain said, patting the copilot's seat.

"I don't think I know anything more about flying a plane than she did," I said, gesturing at the little girl.

"No, no," he said with a chuckle that veered toward the morbid. "I'm just having a little trouble keeping the plane's nose down, and I need to move more weight up toward the front."

Somewhat to my surprise, we landed in one piece. By that afternoon, we were setting up our surveillance. The plan was for our snitch and an undercover agent named Jerry Cox to meet with Mike and negotiate the sale of 150 pounds of marijuana. After agreeing on a price, Mike would provide a sample of twenty pounds or so. If Cox liked the looks of it, they would go out someplace in the Everglades and consummate the deal. That was one reason we needed the FBI planes—following them on the narrow, winding roads through the swamp was going to be next to impossible.

Surveillance agents were scattered all around the house where Cox was to meet Mike. I would be in a car a quarter of a mile away, monitoring the conversation through Cox's body mike.

The first part of the meeting was tense. Every time Mike seemed to be on the verge of agreement, something would snap and he'd start snarling that Cox better not be a cop. "I've got a new kid, I can't go to jail," Mike warned. "I've got five shells for anyone who tries to take me to jail." It chilled me to listen to it, and I wondered how Cox felt. Mike, I knew, was a giant, a six-foot-three bodybuilder. The words must have sounded even more threatening when you heard them come out of a body like that.

After a while, Mike calmed down. Just as we settled in for a long wait, a sheriff's deputy stopped by my car. He was part of the South Florida Drug Task Force, a multi-agency strike force organized by Vice President Bush. I'm not sure how he found out we were there—possibly neighbors had spotted some of our surveillance vehicles and called—but he'd learned of our presence. Another agent had directed him to my location.

"You guys mind telling me what your plan is?" he asked. "I'm always lookin' to steal good ideas. You gotta stay a step or two ahead of these dopers."

I gave him a quick outline. He glanced around my car. "Where are your guns?" he inquired. "You might need them before this is through."

"You've looking at them," I said, gesturing at my shotgun.

He sat there for a few moments, his chin in his hand, as if he was considering something. Then he got up. "I've gotta make a call on the radio in my car," he announced, and went out front. A few minutes later, he was back.

"I've just called for a couple of automatic rifles from my office," he said. "Somebody will be over here with them in a minute. I don't think you're familiar with the way these dopers do business in Florida. The Colombians came in here with machine guns, and now everyone uses them. If worst comes to worst in this thing, you're going to find yourself seriously outgunned."

It would have been easy to bristle at his words, to sneer and say, "Thanks, pop, but why don't you stick to the speed traps and leave the FBI to its business?" I've known some Bureau agents who, I suspect, would have done exactly that. But there was an undertone of neighborly concern in his voice that made it hard for me to take offense, even when he continued.

"It's your operation, and you have to run it the way you see fit," the deputy said. "But if you don't mind some friendly advice, I think you're heading for trouble if you go into the Everglades. No doper around here would accept those kind of terms, unless it was somebody they'd been dealing with a long time. Maybe not even then.

"Could be that fellow is onto your man. Or could be he just thinks he's a dummy who can be ripped off. Either way, I don't believe he plans for your man to come back from the 'Glades. If I was you, I'd make the bust as soon as you've got the sample, and then go on home."

My brain instantly translated the deputy's words: You guys don't know what you're doing. Get out of here before you get hurt. Following that by a beat was another thought: He was right. We *were* the new kids on the block in this game. Saginaw wasn't exactly Mayberry—we had the Mafia, for Christ's sake—but listening to Mike, I had sensed for the first time a dangerously unpredictable edge. The drug dealers we dealt with up north were essentially merchants with a mean streak. The people Cox was talking to in that house seemed about to fly off their hinges.

"Who the hell wants to go into a swamp, anyway?" I concurred. "I never liked snakes or alligators or mud. We'll make the arrest as soon as we have the sample. Deputy, if you've got time, I'd be delighted for you to join us. It sounds like we should have talked to you about this a long time ago."

Shortly after that, the negotiations stalled; Mike's people, for some reason, couldn't get the dope sample until the next day. We went back to the hotel, and I passed along the new plan: No Everglades excursions.

The next morning, with the deputies and their sleek automatic rifles, we took up our positions again. This time we didn't have to wait long. It was less than an hour before we heard Cox talking on the radio. The sample had arrived. He liked it. The deal is on. "Let's go on over there," I said. "It's time to wrap this up."

It took less than a minute for us to reach the anonymous neighborhood on the outskirts of Naples where the deal was being made. I waited until Cox was coming out of the house. He opened the trunk of his car, the prearranged bust signal to the surveillance agents. "Let's do it," said the pilot in the surveillance plane overhead.

I dashed to the back door, jerked it open, and almost trampled a little guy standing just inside. "FBI, you're under arrest," I exclaimed, shoving him toward an agent just behind me and moving inside the house, toward the front.

As I rounded a hall corner, Mike walked out of a back bedroom. There was a puzzled look on his face; he must have heard something, but wasn't sure what. I shoved him against the front door of the foyer and pushed him to the floor. "FBI, you're under arrest," I said again, moving aside to let the agent behind me snap cuffs on his wrists. As I stepped away, I marveled at his hulking size. He was even bigger than I had imagined. I wouldn't have wanted to mess with him at night in the Everglades. Or even in the day.

Mike turned his body slightly so he could look up. "Hey, man, there's some mistake here," he said plaintively. "I didn't do anything. I'm not making any trouble. Let me get up so we can talk about this." He started to lift his shoulders, but an agent shoved him back to the floor.

"Come *on*, man," Mike said, almost whining now. "Why are you treating me this way? I didn't raise a hand to anybody." He raised his shoulders once more, and again an agent pushed them down. "Ahhh, give me a fuckin' break," Mike complained. This time he pulled his knees underneath him and actually staggered to his feet.

The agent moved to confront him, but the deputy sheriff—still carrying one of the automatic rifles—swiftly moved between the two men. "Get on the floor right now," he snarled at Mike "or I'll kill you." Mike stared at him a minute, then turned toward the door. Without another word, the deputy delivered a short chopping swing across his shoulders with the rifle.

Mike crumpled into a heap on the floor. A moment later, I saw a puddle at his feet.


One of the first things I learned about narcotics is that there is no such thing as a "typical" drug user. There are black junkies who shoot a fix of heroin and nod off in doorways, and white investment bankers who snort cocaine off their office desks. There are rock and roll stars in California who fill their bodies with every illicit substance known to mankind, and New Age nut cases out in the New Mexico desert who use only ceremonial peyote. There are aging hippies who still love their joints, college students reinventing LSD, and housewives who pop pills, the Prozac Generation.

Likewise, there's not really a "typical" drug dealer, either. We once arrested a sixty-year-old grandmother who was smuggling marijuana into a prison on Michigan's Upper Peninsula. If you met on the street, you'd think she was sweet old Betty Blue Collar, on her way for a Welcome Wagon visit. More likely, she was headed for the prison with a 9mm automatic under her dress.

But I hope I can indulge myself in one tiny little stereotype without trampling anyone's ethnic or sexual sensibilities. Here it is: Outlaw motorcycle gangs sell speed. Every single one of them. Always.

Everybody's heard of the Hell's Angels, the granddaddy of all outlaw bikers. With six hundred to seven hundred members, it's still the biggest group. But there are about two hundred motorcycle gangs around the country, including the Pagans, the Outlaws, the Bandidos, the Vagos, and the Sons of Silence. All of them, at one time or another, have dealt methamphetamine in a big way. The Hell's Angels got so good at it that they were believed to control the sale of illegal speed on the West Coast.*

In the early 1980s, central Michigan had its own biker scourge, the Devil's Disciples. You know the story: big Harleys, swastika tattoos, beat your ass with a pool cue for looking at them sideways. And, of course, they dealt speed, lots of it.

We'd heard rumors about the gang's drug dealing—lots of

---

*This is, in my opinion, the fault of Lyndon Johnson. Sonny Barger, the infamous head of the Hell's Angels during the 1960s, once offered to win the war in Vietnam for Johnson. Barger said he and the top dozen Angels wanted to be parachuted into North Vietnam, where they would kick ass and take names. Johnson declined. I'm not sure the war would have turned out any differently if he'd accepted, but America would be a better place.

them—and we launched an investigation. We were already moving full-speed ahead when we got a lucky break that sent us into over-drive: A Disciple who called himself Wolf phoned us and offered to talk about his fellow gang members.

Why he did it was never too clear to me. The Michigan State Police always kept a close eye on the Disciples, looking for the slightest pretext at all to bust one of them, and maybe Wolf thought his number was up. Of course, if the other gang members had ever suspected what he was doing, his number would have *really* been up. The Disciples were the coldest, emptiest human beings I had ever encountered, and they killed for much less than this.

I once met with an imprisoned Disciple named Runner, hoping to get him to rat out a plot for a jailbreak. "What are you in here for?" I asked, trying to make a little friendly conversation to break the ice before making my pitch.

"Murder," he answered matter-of-factly.

"Who was the guy you killed?" I asked.

"*Two* guys," he corrected me.

It seemed he'd been having some differences with two members of a rival gang. When they pulled their Harleys up in front of his house one night, he came to the only logical conclusion: They were there to kill him. So he invited them in and then shooting started. One died instantly there in the house. The second jumped through a window and crawled out into the woods. Runner followed him. "There he was, lying in the bushes," he recalled.

"So what happened then?" I asked.

Runner raised his eyebrows. "Well, I capped him off."

We met Wolf in a motel room I rented for the purpose. I took another agent along in case there was some kind of trick in the works, al-though I didn't think trickery was Wolf's strong suit—it looked to me like he'd have trouble outwitting a meatloaf.

He showed up on time that evening. The minute he walked inside the motel room, we grabbed his arms and pushed him up against a wall. I gave him a quick frisk, finding a .38 revolver stuck in his belt.

"What's this for?" I demanded.

"What, are you crazy?" he asked. "I'm a fucking Devil's Disciple. You didn't know we carried guns?"

"Not when you come to visit me," I ordered him. "Not today, not ever."

"All right, man," he agreed. "But would you let go of me? I didn't know there were any rules."

We stepped back, and Wolf took a seat. For the next two hours, we went back and forth with him, implicating most of the members of the gang's Saginaw chapter in sales or use of illegal methamphetamines.

As good a source as Wolf was, I sometimes had trouble paying attention. He stunk, literally; it was like debriefing somebody inside an outhouse. I don't think he had washed his body in a week and his clothes in even longer. Fortunately, I was often distracted from the odor by the fact that he kept ramming his fingers up his nose.

As Wolf got ready to leave, I asked him one last question: Why speed? Why do motorcycle gangs always deal speed and not marijuana or LSD or peyote? He pondered the question for a minute, gazing at me gravely through dim eyes.

"It's like this, man," he finally answered. "You go to parties and shit, and you're drinking and shit. And you gotta take some crank. Because if you're the first motherfucker who falls asleep, everybody else will take your wallet and your women and all your shit. So you gotta be the last motherfucker awake." Happy to have cleared up this mystery for me, he was on his way. . . .

I was convinced that Wolf was telling the truth. But I also knew there was no way we were going to be able to put him on the witness stand in a trial without significant corroboration. By the end of his testimony, the jury would be ready to send the prosecutor to jail just for making them sit in the same building with such an asshole.

Thank God we had already decided to go undercover.

Sending agents undercover for anything longer than a day or two is always a dodgy business. You isolate them from their friends and family, then toss them in with a bunch of predatory scumbags who are waving stacks of money and drugs around. And nobody's watching; they're on their own, wandering along an ethical frontier that is mostly unmarked. If they cross it, just once, you not only lose the case but the agents, too.

Most agents aren't interested in long-term undercover work. In a lot of ways, the skills it requires are the absolute antithesis of what made them join the Bureau in the first place: an ability to lie constantly with a straight face, feeling comfortable around thieves and bullies and crackheads. Even those who want to try it aren't automatically accepted. They're sent back to headquarters for something called Operation Safeguard. It starts with psychological testing, which washes some of them out. The survivors go through classes where they (hopefully) learn to keep their feet planted firmly in reality no matter how far out their assignment gets.

Agents who work successfully undercover often stay at it, moving around from office to office as they switch roles. (Headquarters even maintains a computer data bank, listing things like hobbies, and foreign languages spoken, to help match undercover agents to operations.) But they have to return to Washington for periodic psychiatric evaluation, and undercover assignments are rarely permitted to last more than two years.

Despite all the defenses, some agents go wrong. Sometimes it's blatant. A Miami agent named Dan Mitrione, Jr., after infiltrating a cocaine ring, started skimming drugs off shipments that he knew were going to be seized. He made $850,000 before his supervisors caught on. Other times the damage is psychological. Several undercover agents have become kleptomaniacs. Others develop drinking problems. And the divorce rate for undercover agents is much higher than for the rest of the FBI.

I ran several undercover operations during my career. The most elaborate was a sting operation against a nationwide network that was stealing and counterfeiting auto parts. We rented a warehouse and set up a company that bought and sold parts. An agent named Ron Watson posed as the owner and let it be known that he wasn't a fanatic about the pedigree of the fuel pumps he bought. It didn't take long for the crooks to come calling.

As undercover operations go, this one was by no means among the riskiest the Bureau attempted. Watson was able to keep living at home with his wife. The people he was dealing with were for the most part thieves, not killers, and no one had any drugs or women that they were urging him to sample.

Still, his weight ballooned from 180 pounds to 240 in six months. The Bureau's undercover experts say that drastic weight swings are one of the clearest signs that an agent is in trouble. The case agent and I increased our meetings with him from once or twice a week to nearly every day, reminding him he was one of us, not one of them.

In the end, the talented Watson kept his head together and even got his weight back down, and the sting was a tremendous success. We recovered $15 million in stolen parts and arrested a couple of dozen people in a network that spread across seven states. Toward the end of the operation, I got a chance to see the insidious way undercover work eats away at your integrity. I went down to Dallas for a couple of days, posing as an acquaintance of Watson's, so I could be there when we lowered the boom on the thieves.

Since we didn't want to bother with a full fake identity that would include credit cards and supporting identification, I took a huge wad of cash. I was supposed to be a high roller, and I had to act the part. At the airport, I rented a Cadillac the size of a battleship. And when I checked into the swank Doubletree Inn and peeled six hundred-dollar bills off my roll for three nights, it occurred to me that I could learn to like this lifestyle. Dope may not appeal to me, but I think most people could get addicted to money after a couple of quick fixes.

Putting together an undercover scheme to penetrate the Disciples posed some different problems. Actually having an undercover agent join the gang was out of the question; he would never be accepted unless he took speed himself, not to mention having sex with the "old ladies," as Disciple camp followers were called. Feminism hadn't made much headway within the gang—each member maintained a small harem, and if a buddy lent you five dollars or a lug wrench, you sent him a girl in lieu of a thank-you note.

We decided to open a building-repair business in nearby Bay City. The two owners would be guys who rode Harleys and liked to hang around with bikers, though not such outlaws that they would attempt to join the gang. But the Disciples would be welcome to stop by their office anytime, even conduct some business deals in the backroom. In reality, the backroom was rigged to the ceiling with hidden audio and video equipment. And the "owners" were two officers on loan from the Michigan State Police.

The undercover operation against the Disciples was spectacularly effective, but it had its rough spots—mostly over offers of drugs and women. FBI agents and supervisors from the state police met clandestinely with the two undercover officers a couple of times a week, helping to keep them firmly on the right side of the law. Still, I was nervous about it, and we shut down the operation a little bit earlier than we intended. Nonetheless, we made about fifteen arrests and put the Disciples out of business in central Michigan.


State police undercover agents were available to us through a Michigan State Police unit called BAYANET, the Bay Area Narcotics Enforcement Team. About a dozen local police departments participate in BAYANET, giving it plenty of manpower. We worked closely with BAYANET, providing money, manpower, and—most importantly—legal authority for wiretaps.

Over the years, the scope and complexity of our investigations with BAYANET widened until we needed hundreds of officers to carry out the final raids, when we seized drug stashes and made arrests. Agents in the Detroit office started calling them Kerbygate or Fallfest, since we often staged them in early autumn.

We always staged the raids from a hunting club in Frankenmuth, a Bavarian-style resort town outside Saginaw. A couple of hundred

WITH HONOR AND PURPOSE

officers came from police departments all over central Michigan, along with several dozen FBI agents imported from Detroit and other offices for the location. (Some of the Detroit agents complained like hell about being assigned to this duty. Why are we going to Saginaw when there are more drugs in Detroit? they'd whine. Who's stopping you from doing this kind of investigation in Detroit? I'd answer.)

Around 5 P.M. we would have a planning meeting, breaking the group down into teams. Each team got an assignment—a search, an arrest, or both—and went over detailed photographs and charts showing the target. Anyplace where we thought there was a chance of serious trouble was assigned to a SWAT team. Trouble, though, was rare. In thirteen years of these raids, only a single shot was fired.

We were usually finished by 7 P.M. and everybody went to have one of Frankenmuth's famous dinners (family-style chicken, oddly enough, not sausage). At 5 A.M. we had another meeting to go over any last-minute changes, and by 6:15 they were streaming out of the parking lot, preparing for a simultaneous strike at 7 A.M.

I loved to stand in the parking lot as they departed, listening to the throbbing hum of a couple of hundred engines warming up, rising and falling like the breath of a giant animal. Then the parking lot began dividing, amoebalike, as the cars started to move. The blue state police cruisers were usually the first to leave, sixty or so traveling at neatly spaced intervals, like a drill team. Two or three big SWAT vans came next, followed by dozens of city and county cars, interspersed with all kinds of oddball unmarked FBI vehicles. I watched it all in awe, thinking, *how can anyone defy us?*

And yet, they did. In late 1990, we started working a case against a Mexican-American guy named Richie Castillo. A lot of law enforcement agencies had been chasing Castillo for a long time, with little to show for it. The DEA once searched his luggage at the airport in Detroit and found $24,000—but no drugs. Yet everyone knew he was making a small fortune peddling cocaine and marijuana. Although he didn't have a job, Castillo lived in a $100,000 home with a swimming pool and owned six cars, including a Ferrari, a Corvette, and a Lincoln Continental.

Dave Welker, a young agent just three years out of the FBI Academy, had become my top man on drugs. He began squeezing small-time drug dealers for everything they knew, and eventually had ten different informants reporting on Castillo. The guy was reportedly moving hundreds of pounds of marijuana from the Texas border, packed inside milk trucks. Informants said he had a car with a secret compartment to transport cocaine from Florida; he bought kilos for $21,000 apiece there and sold them in Michigan for $26,000.

The informants told us one reason Castillo had been able to stay a couple of steps ahead of law enforcement: He had an in with a cop who tipped him off whenever an operation was afoot. When we got our wiretap running, we found another reason. Castillo was incredibly careful. He never mentioned drugs or even money on the phone; all the talk was in code. Anyone who slipped got a harsh warning to shut up.

Aware the courts had ruled that no search warrant was required to sift through garbage left for pickup in front of a house, Castillo hauled his own trash to the dump. And he put all his property in his unwitting father's name, which would make it much tougher for us to seize it if we ever got anything on him.

Despite all his precautions, we eventually made a case on Castillo. The Fallfest raid on his dope houses netted $100,000 in cash, big stacks of gold jewelry and automatic weapons, and a garageful of autos and boats.

But by the time of the McDope operation the next year, the biggest narcotics investigation of my career, building the case was even tougher. The dealers were hardly talking on their phones at all. Not only did they speak in code, but they used beepers and pay telephones to evade our taps. In our game of cat and mouse with the drug dealers, the rodents were getting smarter all the time.


During my years in the FBI, there was a steady stream of new technology that helped us combat drugs. More efficient wiretapping techniques, smaller, more powerful body microphones, surveillance planes, drug-sniffing dogs: It was great stuff, and we used every bit of it.

Even better were tougher laws. By the time I retired, the stiffer sentencing guidelines on narcotics offenses were really starting to bite. In federal court one day, a judge gave a cocaine merchant named Mackie Santoya a life sentence without parole.

Santoya looked bored. He turned to his attorney. "So when's my first parole date?" he asked.

"You got a life sentence, Mackie," the attorney answered, looking at the floor.

"Yeah, I know, but when's the first parole hearing gonna be?" Mackie repeated.

"There isn't one, Mackie," the attorney said. "No parole this time."

Mackie's jaw dropped. "Oh, *man*," he complained in a voice that echoed through the courtroom. "That's *bullshit*."

But every time we come up with a new weapon, so do the traffickers. The latest gimmick that helps them beat wiretaps are these new prepaid phone cards, which make it much easier to use pay telephones. Dealers can wander the city, making calls from random phone booths. We can't tap them all. Drug delivery is getting more sophisticated all the time, too. In the last case I worked before retiring, the dealers were shipping their cocaine via Federal Express. It was wrapped inside coffee grounds (on the erroneous theory that they defeat drug-sniffing dogs), stuffed into teddy bears, and mixed in with legitimate corporate mail.

My point is that nobody's going to invent a magic bullet that will put drug dealers out of business. In fact, some dealers aren't going to be put out of business, period, no matter what we do. Nobody likes it when I say this, but marijuana has grown so ubiquitous in American society that cops rarely arrest anybody for carrying a half-burned joint. The paperwork is too much of a hassle for a case that's a misdemeanor. Instead, they sometimes take the dope and scatter it to the wind, then send the kid it belonged to on his way. The result is what is called "ditch weed," marijuana growing wild along the side of the road. Even if we domed America and sealed it forever, the marijuana supply would never run out.

As for other drugs, I've already said the answer isn't going to come from law enforcement. The United States is the largest consumer of illegal narcotics in the entire world. Obviously, something is broken inside our society, and it has to be fixed. Don't ask me what it is, or how to repair it; if I knew, I would have quit the FBI a long time ago to become president, if not pope. But I do know this: We can't arrest everybody.

Nobody likes to fight just to maintain a stalemate—ask any Vietnam veteran—and I don't believe there's a policeman alive who, at some point, hasn't felt a little discouraged about our role in the war on drugs. I certainly had my doubts. When I started working narcotics cases in 1982, cocaine cost $2,000 an ounce on the street in central Michigan. Thirteen years later, when I retired, it was $900. For all my work, there was more powder than ever out there.

But I also remember listening to a wiretap and hearing a seven-year-old kid call his cokehead mother to ask for a ride home from a playmate's house. "Ahhh, I'm not leaving the house," said the mother, obviously stoned out of her mind. "Get somebody else to bring you." And she hung up.

I thought, *if there's one kid who might have heard that who didn't because of an arrest we made, then this has all been worth it.*

And I remember, too, a town meeting in Marquette, perched atop Michigan's remote Upper Peninsula. The citizens were raising hell, demanding a tougher effort against drugs. A lot of regional law enforcement people went, including the U.S. attorney and me. A couple of Justice Department officials even flew in from Washington.

One of the guys from the Justice Department was trying to calm everybody down. "We're always grateful for public concern about law enforcement," he said. "But the fact is, you don't really need a lot of additional help up here. You don't have a significant drug problem in your community."

"You don't understand," retorted one of the people in the audience. "We *do* need more help up here, and we need it now. Because we don't want our town to become the way yours already is."

# 14

## GANGBANGERS

"**M**an, what a month," Gary Loster sighed, shaking his head as he reached for his coffee. He didn't have to explain. The day before, Saginaw had recorded its fourth street-gang murder of the month. In some cities, that's just a good night's work. But in Saginaw, where we averaged only about two dozen murders a year, it was a holocaust. Our kids were getting killed, and nobody seemed to be able to do anything about it.

Nobody felt it more keenly than Loster, Saginaw's mayor. A former suburban police chief and the chief of security at the huge General Motors plant, he was an old friend of mine. For years we had been getting together for coffee a couple of times a month, and I had watched Loster's apprehensions about the gangs grow from mere unease to something approaching anguish.

I worried, too. Originally I thought the gangs were just another facet of the drug problem—that if we got drugs under control, gang violence would diminish. Besides pressing my agents to go all-out on the drug problem, I got personally involved in some of the social programs that I hoped might heal the societal wounds that seemed to lead kids into dope. I joined the board of directors of the Girls' and Boys' Club organization, and I tramped around speaking to every civic group in the county.

But now I wondered if I had been wrong, or at least not completely right. The gangs were involved in drugs, no doubt about that, but there seemed to be more to the story. And things like the Girls' and Boys' Club, though important, were long-term solutions. They weren't going to stop all kids from being gunned down in Saginaw tomorrow night.

"What does your police department tell you?" I asked Loster, sipping from my own coffee mug.

"I don't think they really buy it," he said. "You know how it is—nobody has ever worked gangs, so nobody is *going* to work gangs, not in any serious way. There's one officer—Jim Osterman, you know him—who's been trying to develop some intelligence on it. Keeping a card file on known gang members, taking photos of graffiti to try to figure out which groups own which turf. But I think he's pretty much of a lone wolf on this." He sighed again. "The thing is, even if I could get the department to take gangs seriously, where do I find the money and manpower to go after them?"

*Money* and *manpower* made it all fall into place. "Gary, the FBI has budgeted a bunch of money to put together local task forces to attack violent crime," I said excitedly. "And that's exactly what we're talking about. Let's put together a task force on gangs."

"You mean with other law enforcement agencies?" he said doubtfully. "How are we going to get them to join?"

"You're the mayor of the biggest city around here, I'm the head of the FBI. If we throw a party, everybody will have to come."

I wish I could say that I invented the concept of the anti-gang task force that morning in August 1993. The truth is that the same thing was occurring simultaneously to a lot of agents all over the United States. And we owe it all to world communism.

Well, technically speaking, to the *end* of world communism. In 1992, with the Cold War officially ended, the Bureau shifted three hundred agents from counterintelligence work into a program targeting violent crime. Meanwhile, money was made available for field offices to establish special task forces that would coordinate law enforcement work against violent criminals. The idea was that by pooling intelligence and developing a unified strategy—instead of duplicating efforts and squabbling over jurisdiction—we could deliver a body blow to the hard-core criminal element that was making it increasingly dangerous to walk American streets.

The program gave Bureau supervisors a good deal of leeway in tailoring the task forces to local needs. Some offices went after repeat offenders. Others concentrated on fugitives.

But among the most frequent targets were the street gangs that, with little fanfare, had been turning urban America into a free-fire zone over the past few years. Everybody knew about the Crips and the Bloods, the two rival gangs that regularly shot it out in Los Angeles. Because that city is such a media hothouse, the Crips and Bloods were a regular storyline in movies and television shows.

Far less publicized was that the two gangs had expanded across America, with chapters in fifty-eight cities in thirty-five states. And in the few large urban centers without Crips and Bloods, home-grown gangs had taken up the slack. You didn't have to live in Los Angeles or New York to become an unwilling expert on drive-by shootings; they happened in Phoenix and Denver and Mobile and Wichita, too.

Street gangs are nothing new in America; they go back at least to the 1920s, and maybe even earlier. But their modern incarnation is much uglier. If you remade *West Side Story* today, Riff and Bernardo would go at it with assault rifles, not switchblades. And instead of facing off one-on-one under the freeway, they'd blow the heads off each other's mothers in drive-by shootings. Human life means nothing—literally nothing—to today's gangbangers. The Crips and Bloods routinely open fire because someone is wearing the wrong color (red belongs to the Bloods, blue the Crips) on the wrong block in South Central Los Angeles. In 1994, an eleven-year-old gang member murdered a fourteen-year-old over some trivial insult, then was killed in turn by fellow gangbangers who were afraid he might cooperate with the police.

The gangs' bloodlust is made all the worse by their size. The Crips and Bloods together are believed to have fifty thousand members. The largest of all may be the Black Gangster Disciples, headquartered in Chicago and operating throughout the Midwest. Some Chicago cops think the Disciples could have thirty thousand members. That's not a gang, it's an army. The Disciples at one point even had their own designer line of clothing (Ghetto Prisoner) and their own political action committee, 21st Century Vote, which poured thousands of dollars into Chicago elections.

The new FBI-sponsored task forces went after them with a vengeance. Two separate task forces in Connecticut zeroed in on the Almighty Latin Kings Nation gang and won a total of twenty-two indictments. In California, two chapters of the Crips were rolled up with twenty-two indictments. In Shreveport, Louisiana, the FBI office smashed a local gang known as the Bottoms Boys with forty-nine indictments. In Wichita, an antigang task force won ninety-five indictments. In Chicago, a task force won indictments of thirty-nine of the top leaders of the Black Gangster Disciples. There were other notable successes in Omaha, Portland, and Washington, D.C.

But in August 1993, when Loster and I first talked about putting together a task force, most of those success stories were still in the future. The idea of targeting the gangs was novel—and, a lot of people thought, stupid. "Why should we bother with this shit?" a cop in one of the local departments said when I first brought it up. "All they do is kill each other. It's a self-cleaning oven."

That attitude made my blood boil. For one thing, it's callous and stupid. As much as I detested the gangbangers, they were still *people*. How could you say their deaths weren't important? Who has the ability, or the right, to make that kind of calculation?

For another, it's mistaken. Gangbangers don't just kill each other; when bullets start flying in city streets, nobody is safe. One night Saginaw's TV news showed a tearful little six-year-old girl who'd been hit in the leg by a stray shot from a gang gunfight. "I don't know what I did to deserve to be in here," she wailed from her hospital bed. Self-cleaning oven, right.

But the resistance to the task force didn't just come from a few guys still living in the Stone Age. Loster had said it well: Since no one had targeted gangbangers before, no one was much interested in trying it now. Even within my own office, some agents wanted nothing to do with gangs.

"It's not exactly traditional FBI work," said one.

To which I replied: "That was what everybody said about the Mafia and drugs at first, too." The patterns of crime change, and the patterns of law enforcement have to change with them.

I did six months of quiet but relentless jawboning on behalf of the task force before Loster and I called the first meeting of law-enforcement people. I wanted to make sure the whole thing didn't collapse during the first five minutes. By the time we assembled in February 1994, I was warily confident that something could be worked out.

That first meeting looked like a real war council. We had high-ranking officials from the DEA, the Secret Service, the U.S. Marshal's office, the Bureau of Alcohol, Tobacco, and Firearms, the Michigan State Police, the Saginaw police, the Saginaw County sheriff's office, and other smaller local forces.

"Here's what I'm offering," I told them. "The FBI will provide a sixty thousand dollar budget for the task force's expenses. We'll supply a computer system, secure radios, pagers and cell phones, office space, and four vehicles. We'll also contribute two agents and a secretary. What I need from you is manpower, some cars, but most of all, your cooperation. We don't really know a damn thing about these gangs or how they operate. We're going to need a stupendous intelligence effort before we can hope to make a dent in them."

The local forces, once they knew the Saginaw police were participating, all climbed quickly on board. The federal agencies, though, were a different story. The U.S. Marshal's office turned us down, saying it just didn't have a warm body to spare. The DEA wanted to think it over. And then there was Larry Porte, the head of the Secret Service and an old friend.

"Kerby," he asked, "are any of these gangs threatening to kill the president?"

"No," I admitted.

"Are any of them counterfeiting money?"

"No."

"Are any of them engaging in bank or credit card fraud?"

"Not that I know of."

"Then there is a question whether the Secret Service has any legal jurisdiction," Porte said. "Those are the crimes we're charged with investigating." He rested his chin on his fist for a moment, a distant expression on his face. Then he grinned. "Oh, to hell with it," he said. "It's the right thing to do. Count us in."


The Saginaw Gang Crime Task Force opened its doors on April 9, 1994. "Let the word go out to parents and gang members," Loster said at a press conference in City Hall. "Today is the day to get out." One of the first questions following the press conference, as I expected, was: Isn't this just an excuse for a bunch of white cops to hassle black and Hispanic kids? Anytime a law enforcement agency tries to do anything about street gangs or dope, somebody will play the race card—even though it is precisely the minority communities who are suffering the most at the hands of gangbangers and dopers.

But in this case, we had a trump card: Loster is black. And he laid waste to the question. "I'm an African American," he said. "I'm proud to be an African American. But I support the Gang Crime Task Force. Be you black, white, or Hispanic, if you cross the Gang Crime Task Force, I'll support the Gang Crime Task Force." The subject never came up again.

Not that there weren't critics. "All it's going to cause is more killing," said Troy Rankin, a former member of the Folks, one of Saginaw's biggest gangs, who was interviewed by the *Saginaw News*. "The kids are going to be shooting."


The task force headquarters was in a downtown office building, but we didn't release the address. We wanted to create an air of mystery; we didn't want anyone to know how many officers were working for the task force, or when they came and went. We started with nine, which eventually increased to fourteen. DEA opted out, and the two agents promised by BATF somehow never seemed to be around. To resolve any questions about the FBI's jurisdiction, we opened racketeering conspiracy cases against several of the gangs. That made almost any crime committed by a gang member part of the conspiracy, even if it ordinarily wouldn't have been a federal offense.

Our first job was to find out what we were dealing with. How many gangs were there? How many members? Which parts of town did they operate in? What kind of crimes were they committing? We didn't really know much about them, and we had to learn.

Each morning the task force officers who were members of local police forces went to their departmental roll call. There they took careful notes on any gang-related activity reported by officers who were out on patrol the night before. Then they came to the task force offices for our own 8:30 roll call. The agents & officers talked over what they had heard and worked out a game plan for the day.

The details of that plan might vary from day to day, but the object was always the same: Recruit informants. Until we had people relaying information from inside the gangs, we weren't going to understand them.

Our first recruiting technique was to put the word out that we were paying for information. We offered $100 for a tip that could lead to an arrest. We quickly learned our first lesson about gangbangers: They're incredible liars. Not to us, so much—they knew we would have to verify the information before we paid—but to each other. As they gossiped among themselves, the $100 was inflated to $500. Within a couple of weeks, the task force phones were ringing as tips trickled in.

The best of those tips were the ones that identified various houses and street corners as gathering places for gangs. We'd send a police cruiser over to check them out, which usually sent the gangbangers scrambling into their cars to look for friendlier territory. That was exactly what we wanted.

Here's a little secret of police work: It seems as though there is not a single legal motor vehicle on the streets of America, not one. There are so many obscure regulations governing cars that nobody could even know them all, much less comply. Cracked windshield? Unsafe equipment, a violation. Fuzzy dice hanging from the rear-view mirror? Visual obstruction, a violation. In Michigan, even a dealer license-plate frame is technically illegal.

Technical or not, those violations are probable cause for a police officer to stop a car and question the occupants. And that's just what we did with the gang members, putting the squeeze on them in the process.

That was how Terry Williams, a task force member from the police department in the nearby town of Bridgeport, recruited one of our first valuable informants. Watching a house where gangbangers reportedly hung out, he saw a car pull away. Terry quickly called for help from uniformed officers, and quickly the car was stopped for a problem with its muffler. "The driver has some kind of a gang tattoo on his neck," one of the cops informed Terry by radio. "And he's also driving on a suspended license."

"Talk about how you're supposed to arrest him for that," Terry suggested. "I'll let him sweat for five minutes or so, then I'll come over."

Terry made sure he was wearing his task force cap and wind-breaker before he approached the car. "Hi Julio, my name's Terry Williams," he told the driver, a young Latin guy in his early twenties. He had a star tattooed on his neck, the insignia of the Latin Kings. There was another tattoo, a teardrop, under one of his eyes. That symbolized mourning for a fallen gang member. "It looks like you're in a little bit of a jam here."

"Yeah, man," Julio said, looking away. He probably wanted to tell everybody where to stick their badges, but he knew he already had enough trouble.

"Why don't you get out of the car?" Terry asked. "Come over here with me, where we can talk away from the rest of these guys." He gestured to a nearby tree.

Under its branches, he made the serious pitch. "You've got real trouble here, and you know it," he told Julio. "You don't have a license. You know I can take you to jail, I can impound your car, I can make your life miserable."

"Yeah, I know," Julio replied in a tone that was polite and even enthusiastic. He sensed there was a way out.

"You want to go home instead?" Terry asked. Julio nodded energetically. "Okay, here's the deal. I'm not making you any promises. You still get the ticket. But you don't go to jail, and I won't impound your car. And in return, you've got to meet with me and talk about your gang. I don't need you to tell me about a twenty thousand dollar dope deal. I just want to talk about how the gang is organized, who's who, develop some information."

"Yeah, yeah," Julio agreed. "I can do that."

"If this works out, I'll try to help you get your license back. You've got a job, don't you? Wouldn't it be nice to drive to work every day without looking over your shoulder?"

"Yeah, yeah," Julio repeated, shaking his head so hard it looked like it would pop off.

"Here's my card. Call me in a day or two to set up a time when we can meet." Terry paused, then locked eyes with Julio. "If you don't call, I'll get a warrant. And you know I'll find you, and you know you'll just be in a world of shit."

"No, man, no, I'm gonna call," Julio assured him, sounding slightly panicky. He didn't want this deal to fall apart. "You don't have to worry about me."

And we didn't. Julio called in two days later, and he and Terry met that afternoon in a park. He ran through a list of the Latin Kings and the highlights of their careers, almost like a baseball card giving us the names: There was one who was known for drive-by shootings and was almost always carrying a gun. Another, was the gang's chief dope merchant. He continued to tick off names, describing what kind of guns they carried and where they were usually concealed. There were also bits of fascinating trivia. We had noticed that, when gangbangers saw policemen approaching, they started yelling, "Five-oh! Five-oh!" Obviously it was slang for cops, but we always wondered where the expression came from.

"Oh, man, don't you guys ever watch *television*?" Julio said, slapping his head in amazement at the stupidity of the question. "Haven't you ever seen *Hawaii Five-O*?" Another unsolved mystery bites the dust.

As I glanced over Terry's report from the interview, I alternated between excitement and caution. This was exactly the kind of detail we were looking for. But the obvious question was, could we believe any of it?

"I think so," Terry assured me. "He knows he got the deal of the century—if we'd impounded his car, he loses his job. He's raising his fifteen-year-old brother. He's keeping his life together by a thread, and this was important to him. We're going to go to work verifying this stuff, but I'll bet you right now that at least 99 percent of it is true."

Terry was right—we started confirming bits and pieces of Julio's stories almost immediately. Meanwhile, he kept up a stream of reports. "I heard you were over visiting Chino's mom the other night," he told Terry one afternoon. Chino was a fugitive gangbanger whom we wanted to arrest on a big stack of burglary and stickup charges. We had indeed searched his mother's house, with her permission, and come up empty-handed.

"Yeah, we stopped by," Terry agreed. "Where'd you hear that?"

"Oh, man, a whole bunch of Latin Kings were watching," Julio said. "We wanted to see if you could find him."

Terry didn't know which was more surprising: the news that the Latin Kings had the task force under surveillance, or the hint that Chino had been in the house during the search. "Are you saying Chino had been hanging around there?" he asked. "You mean the mother was lying when she said she hadn't seen him?"

"I don't mean he *had been* there," Julio said, correcting his grammar. "I mean he *was* there, while you were searching. In the basement of the house, some of the bricks pull out of the wall, and there's a space back there. That's where he hides when he's visiting his mom."

"Let us know the next time he's there," Terry urged, though for the first time he wasn't sure he believed Julio. Secret rooms behind brick walls? It sounded too much like pirates and buried treasure.

But two days later, Julio called with a simple message: "Chino is there." We zipped over to the house, went straight to the basement, and started pulling loose bricks out of the wall, just where Julio said they would be. As the wall opened up, there was Chino, eyes wide. So were ours. That was the last time we doubted Julio.

Because he was so cooperative, we tried to help straighten out the mess surrounding Julio's driver's license. But it turned out to be beyond repair; he had a drunk-driving conviction. We did do him another favor, though. Terry Williams, out on uniform patrol one night, saw a car weaving from lane to lane on I-75. Flashing his light, he signaled it to pull over. When he approached the car, Terry was surprised to see Julio in the passenger seat. His girlfriend, several beers past the point of no return, was behind the wheel. "Leave the car here until morning," Terry instructed them. "I'll drive you home." From that day forward, no Latin King could burp within a hundred miles of Saginaw without Julio calling us.


Julio was by no means our only gang informant. Within a couple of months of opening the task force's doors, we had about a dozen snitches feeding us material. And we were piecing together a pretty good picture of the gangbanger landscape.

There were about thirty street gangs operating in the Saginaw area, with memberships ranging from a dozen or so to a couple of hundred. The biggest were the Folks (the oldest and best established), the Mafia Kings (who for some reason had adopted the Dallas Cowboys insignia as their own), the 4th and Kirk Gang (named for an intersection at the heart of its east side territory), the Mexican Mafia (loosely linked with the big prison-based gang in California of the same name).

A few of the groups, including the 4th and Kirk Gang and the local chapter of the Black Gangster Disciples, were black-only. But mostly they were racially mixed, open to anyone. (Women had their own gangs. The biggest was the Bitches in the Woods, who took their name from the fact that all the streets in their neighborhood ended in-wood: Glenwood, Oakwood, and so forth.) Generally speaking, members ranged in age from twelve to twenty-five. But the Folks actually operated a sort of minor league franchise, the Pee Wee Folks, for kids twelve and under. We got hold of a picture of four members: twelve-year-old boys, their fingers splayed out in the Folks' sign. One of them was holding a cocked revolver at the head of a four-year-old friend.

Secret signs were a big thing for the gangs. We learned how to read them: A hat tilted to the right identified its wearer as a member of the Folks; to the left, the People. A blue bandana tied around the ankle or poking out of a pocket was another sign for the Folks.

Many gangbangers come from broken homes, and perhaps the gangs offer them a sense of family, of belonging, that had been missing in their lives. If so, however, it's a little like joining the Addams Family, but without the laughs. Consider one of the rituals common to all the gangs: getting "beat in," which is pretty much what it sounds like. The lucky inductee stands in the middle of a circle of senior members, and they beat him within an inch of his life. He's supposed to remain stoic, which gets easier once he's unconscious.

Worse yet is getting "beat out" for breaking the gang's rules. There are long lists of rules, most of which aren't honored at all. We got hold of the Black Gangster Disciples' code of conduct, and it was nothing less than comical. "No. 4: No member should break laws. No. 5: No member should break or enter any building that is around any fellow member." Some rules, however, are taken seriously, including those against snitching and other forms of disloyalty.

Although the gangs were involved in just about every kind of criminal activity known to man, that really wasn't what they were all about. In the Mafia, for instance, the whole point is to make a lot of money and live in a nice house. For street gangs, the point is territory: This is *my* neighborhood, this is *my* block, *my* car, *my* girl, *my* shotgun. The message was for everybody—neighbors, other gangs, the police.

I talked to a nineteen-year-old member of the Mexican Mafia who we were holding on a federal firearms charge. I was curious about one of the gang's trademarks, which was walking through shopping malls four abreast, forcing everyone to scatter out of the way.

"Why do you do that?" I asked.

"We don't do it to everybody," he objected. "We respect our elders. We don't make old people move over."

"But everybody else has to get out of your way, or you'll beat their ass?"

He considered this a moment, then agreed: "Yeah, that's true."

"Why? What's the point?"

"Because we're part of the nation," he said. "We deserve respect."

"What if a bunch of us from the task force, wearing our jackets, walk up to you in the mall and tell you to knock it off?"

"We'd knock it off. But then we'd come back later, after you left, and do it again."

"And if we tell you to stop again?"

"We'll stop again. But we'll come back again, too. We've got to show everybody that we don't take orders from anybody, not even the FBI. *Especially* not the FBI."

Now it was my turn to think for a moment. Finally I asked: "What if we caught you doing it a third time and took you out in the parking lot and beat the living shit out of you?" (Note to any ACLU attorneys who managed to choke down the first thirteen chapters and are still with us: No, no, we don't do that. But I was curious what his answer would be.)

His reply was chillingly simple. "We'd come back with guns."


As we learned more about the gangs, our campaign to squash them gathered steam. One of the first things we did was to solicit donations of paint and cleanup materials from local merchants. Then, whenever new gang graffiti was spotted, Loster sent out city workers immediately to get rid of it. This wasn't just a campaign to keep Saginaw pretty. We wanted to keep the gangs from staking out turf.

More concretely, we wanted to put some gangbangers in jail. We were able to start right away, because a large number of the gang members caught up in our traffic stops turned out to be carrying illegal weapons. We filed federal charges against them whenever possible, because parole is much more difficult to obtain in the federal system.

We landed our first really telling blow against the gangs just a few weeks after the task force started operations. The Mafia Clan gang had been conducting a show of strength in a west Saginaw neighborhood near the river, parading around like it owned the place. To show them otherwise, task force officers were rousting the gangbangers, busting them on legitimate but minor offenses. A lot of the Mafia Clan guys had the same complaint: "How come you harass us and you leave Jamal White alone?" But, when we tried to question them further, they clammed up.

Jamal White's name was familiar to some of the officers. He was believed to have supplied the guns that were involved in a gang shootout at a party in Bay City that left three people dead earlier in the year.

"I think I've got a snitch who might talk about this," said Brian Berg, a task force officer from the Saginaw Township police. He arranged an interview, and I tagged along, hoping to learn more about the inner workings of the gangs.

The snitch, a young member of the Mafia Clan, did indeed know Jamal White. "That motherfucker sits over there in his house on Stone Street, watching out the window," the snitch said. "And if he sees somebody from another gang coming down the street, he shoots him."

"Shoots him?" Berg echoed in disbelief.

"Yeah, shoots him," the snitch repeated. "Jamal don't tolerate no disrespect."

On one hand, the snitch's story seemed fantastic. Didn't the neighbors complain? Didn't the police notice anything? On the other hand, we couldn't see any reason for him to make it up. We asked the Saginaw police to check their records. Sure enough, two shootings had been reported in the same block of Stone Street a few months apart. Both the victims were young men. Neither was killed, but one was hit in the chest, one in the hand. And both cases were unsolved.

We went back to the snitch for more information. "Jamal's the one everybody goes to when they need a gun," he said. "He sells them out of his house. He don't go out very often, but when he does, he's always packin'. He don't go nowhere without a gun, never. He's the warlord of the Folks."

We checked around some more and discovered an old warrant against White for a misdemeanor assault charge. After some discussion with prosecutors, they agreed it could be upgraded to a felony. Then Berg and Bill Lauman staked out White's house. It took a week, but finally he left the house. Our men pounced. In jail, White freely admitted one of the shootings. After his arrest, his neighbors said they'd never called the police about White because they were afraid of him.

It was an enormously satisfying arrest for the gang task force. We stopped a one-man crime wave that had terrorized an entire neighborhood. And without the task force canvassing informants and checking records, it would never have happened.

A couple of months later, we made another big-time score. This one involved a Mafia King gangbanger named Osbaldo Urivez.

Urivez and a couple of other Mafia Kings pulled into the parking lot of a convenience store around three o'clock one morning. Urivez was standing up in the car, his chest and head sticking through the open sun roof, giving the Mafia King sign. A kid in the parking lot very ostentatiously flashed back the gang sign for contempt. Urivez promptly whipped out a gun and shot him in the face, then disappeared into the night.

This was exactly the kind of pointlessly cold-blooded killing that had made Loster and me so anxious to do something about the gangs in the first place, and we were determined to track Urivez down. Agent Bob Lucas put a full-court press on all our informants, and a few weeks later he was arrested by a couple of Bureau agents in Kansas. I felt like having a victory party. Everybody—cops and gang-bangers alike—recognized that, without the task force, Urivez would not have been caught so soon.

The gangbangers offered their own singular tribute to the task force one evening a few weeks later. We had scheduled a street operation that night—we had a list of gang members to be targeted for guns and dope—and task force officers met at McDonald's for a quick dinner and last-minute planning. When they were finished, they headed for the south side.

Lucas of the FBI, Jim Osterman of the Saginaw police, and Terry Williams were driving along in a white Chevy Caprice, a vehicle so obvious it might as well be marked. Suddenly there was a loud *ca-chung!* outside the front passenger door.

"What was that?" Lucas asked. "Did we hit something?"

"I think we've been shot at," Williams replied. They pulled around a corner and stopped. There was what looked like a .32-caliber bullet hole in the lower part of the door.

"Lucky for you we're dealing with a bunch of incompetent ass-holes," Osterman told Williams. "Three feet higher, and you're dead."

By then, the arrests were coming fast and furious. In its first six months, the task force made more than seventy felony busts and so many for misdemeanors that we stopped counting. Violent crime was down 10 percent and murders 20 percent. The pace kept up over the long haul; by the task force's second birthday in 1996, it was credited with more than three hundred felony arrests. More than 80 percent of them included the seizure of guns.

Gary Loster was as proud of the task force as I was. Not that we agreed on everything. He once proposed bringing in Edward James

Olmos, director and star of *American Me*, a terrifyingly accurate film about the Mexican Mafia, to speak to gang members.*

"Don't do that," I urged him. "Bring in a movie star to talk to the kids who *don't* join gangs. Otherwise it's like you're saying, act like a scumbag and we'll do something special for you." I've always been against having movie stars and athletes who've kicked drugs talk to kids, too. It seems to me the message they unintentionally convey is, use dope, you can always come back and be a star.

He listened to me. And I listened to him, a year or so into the task force, when he came back from a trip to Los Angeles.

"We don't have a gang problem," he announced.

"*What* did you say?" I asked sharply.

"We don't have a gang problem," he repeated. "In Los Angeles, I met some guys who were fifth- and sixth-generation gang members. They pointed out somebody on the street and they said, 'That guy owns eighty blocks.' "

"What do you mean by that," I asked.

" 'That means he owns the right to sell drugs on eighty blocks in East L.A.,' they said. That's like the Mafia. And that's where we're going if we let down for one minute."

---

*The Mexican Mafia indirectly endorsed the movie by doing in several people who helped make it.

# 1 5

# OKBOMB

April 19, 1995

The secretary rushed through the door and, without a word, flipped on my office television set. Before I could even ask what was going on, I was transfixed by the scene on the screen: a towering column of dust swirling above a hulking pile of rubble.

"What is it?" I asked in a voice tinged with awe.

"A federal office building in Oklahoma city," the secretary answered. "CNN says it just blew up a few minutes ago."

Within minutes my office was crowded with agents and typists, eyes glued to the television as dazed, bloodied survivors staggered out of the wreckage.

"Was it a bomb?" someone asked.

"They don't know yet," someone else answered. "It might have been a natural gas explosion."

Gazing at the remains of what had been the Alfred P. Murrah Federal Office Building, I wondered how much natural gas would have to explode to do such damage. The entire facade of the building was torn away, the floors inside collapsed on one another.

"If it *was* a bomb, who do you think did it?" a secretary asked.

"Who knows?" said an agent. "But it sure looks like the marine barracks in Beirut did after one of those radical Muslim groups bombed it."

And later in the day, when Oklahoma City police confirmed that the explosion had been caused by a bomb, most of our speculation centered on Middle Eastern terrorists.

But one of the interviews I'd heard on CNN stuck in my mind. A terrorism expert noted almost in passing that today was the second anniversary of the dreadful day in Waco, Texas, when the FBI tried to end a seven-week standoff by breaking into the Branch Davidian religious sect's compound. A fire broke out, and more than eighty Branch Davidians died in the flames.

When I realized the bombing fell on the same date as the Waco fire, a chill ran down my spine. The leaflets I frequently saw from the Michigan Militia and other right-wing groups up in the northern part of the state had begun to focus on the death of the Branch Davidians as evidence that the federal government was running amok and had to be stopped.

*I'll bet this turns out to be some kind of home-grown, right-wing thing*, I thought to myself, *and has nothing to do with foreign terrorism at all.*

But I didn't share my thoughts with anyone. The FBI was running the investigation in Oklahoma City—it was code-named OKBOMB and got a MAJOR CASE designation, only the 117th time in FBI history that label had been used—but there was nothing at all connecting it to Michigan, hundreds of miles away. The Oklahoma City office, I was certain, had generated hundreds of leads, but not a single one had come our way. Oklahoma City remained for our office, just as for most of the rest of America, a place to watch on television and remember in our prayers. By Thursday evening, a day and a half after the bombing, search parties had pulled fifty-two bodies out of the wreckage. They weren't even halfway through the building.

But while I slept that night, FBI agents all over the country kept beating the pavement, following a trail of clues out of the still-smoking hulk of the Murrah Building. It started with the identification, in Oklahoma City, of the vehicle that had held the bomb: a Ryder rental truck. From one twisted, blackened axle, agents were able to retrieve the vehicle identification number, which led them to a rental depot in Junction City, Kansas, a couple hundred miles north of Oklahoma City.

They quickly established that the truck had been rented under a false name. But, working from descriptions provided by the depot's workers, the agents put together a sketch of two suspects. Then they went door to door, asking if anyone remembered them. At the Dreamland Motel, the owner knew one: The man had rented a room from her on April 12, one week, cash in advance. He registered as Timothy McVeigh.

On Friday morning, as agents all over the country looked for McVeigh, an FBI computer found him: Arrest records showed he was sitting in a jail in Perry, Oklahoma, barely sixty miles from the scene of the blast. A traffic cop had pulled him over a little more than an hour after the bombing for driving without a license plate, then arrested him for carrying a concealed pistol. The thin, flinty-faced McVeigh was just fifteen minutes from making bail and disappearing onto the Oklahoma prairies.

When he was arrested, McVeigh listed his home as Decker, Michigan, a tiny pinpoint of a town about an hour east of Saginaw. Although he hadn't really lived there in more than a year, we quickly learned that McVeigh had stayed in Decker for several months at the home of a couple of local farmers who were involved with the Michigan Militia. One of them, an old army buddy of McVeigh's named Terry Nichols, would soon be under arrest himself on charges stemming from the bombing. By noon Friday, I was up to my eyebrows in OKBOMB.

The investigation, after moving at warp speed for the first ninety-six hours, settled into a routine. Not that we slacked off—the Bureau set up ten computer-linked command centers around the country, manned by more than one thousand federal agents (BATF and Secret Service joined in) to focus exclusively on OKBOMB. But most of the giant leaps forward came during the first few days. After that, blitzkrieg turned into trench warfare as we methodically built a complete picture of what happened.

With Frank Laudan, who ran the FBI office in Mt. Clemens, Michigan, I took over the command center in Sandusky, a town near Decker. (Since it was his territory, Frank was first among equals.) It was easily the biggest assignment of my career: Frank and I supervised seventy-five agents, more than some SACs. Every day I got up at 5 A.M. to make the hour drive to Sandusky, where, with Frank, I checked the overnight teletype traffic and put the finishing touches on the day's plans. At 8 A.M. we did a roll-call style briefing, handing the various agent teams their assignments. At 5 P.M. there was another briefing, where each team reported its results for the day. After that, Frank and I began mapping out the next day, and most of the agents went back to work, too. For the first couple of weeks, almost no one arrived home before 10 P.M.

Our team knocked out an amazing five hundred interviews a week. To me, though, the numbers weren't the most astonishing thing. It was the way people talked during the interviews: sometimes whispering, even in their own living rooms. There were days when I felt like we were running an investigation in Nazi Germany. How ironic, that an organization like the Michigan Militia that said it was promoting freedom made people feel afraid to speak out loud inside their own homes.

OKBOMB generated such a blizzard of paper that the Bureau told us to use a new computer program called Rapid Start to keep track of it all.

Here's how it worked: Let's say we get a tip that Joe Smith on Elm Lane knows something about the bombing. Obviously, Smith needs to be interviewed. I write down the assignment on a triple-copy form. One copy goes to the agent who will do the interview, one copy stays with me, and one copy is sent to the Rapid Start computer. Immediately the computer will tell us if someone has already talked to Joe Smith, and, if so, what he said. If not, I can check in the computer later to see if the interview has been completed and what the results were. And periodically the computer will belch out a list of assignments that haven't been completed, so we can check with the agents and find out what's wrong.

The theory sounds great. There was one big flaw in the execution:

For some reason, the Decker command post couldn't get a Rapid Start computer terminal. Instead, a courier arrived once a day to pick up the forms and carry them the two-hour drive south to Detroit to be keypunched into the computer. The couriers were not necessarily among the Bureau's most dedicated agents; they tended to stick their heads in the door just long enough to ask, "Anything for the computer?" If the janitor happened to be standing there and answer "no," that was good enough for them. As a result, the computer data base always lagged behind the investigation, and we started calling the program Fairly Rapid Start.

Laudan—whose astounding litany of complaints about the command center, the Bureau, and the world in general quickly won him the nickname Frank the Crank—decided he was going to put an end to this. One morning he lay in wait for the courier, determined to carve him a new orifice. The courier was supposed to arrive at 11 A.M. He didn't show at eleven, or twelve, or one. Shortly after two, Frank popped across the street to buy a Coke. He came back less than three minutes later, only to discover the courier had come and gone. Frosting the cake, nobody could find the forms—Frank had been holding them on his desk in anticipation of the great showdown—and the courier left empty-handed. For a few minutes there, I thought Laudan's new nickname was going to be Frank the Stroke Victim.

As OKBOMB created a tight prosecutorial mosaic from tens of thousands of bits of esoteric information, I was proud of the FBI. No other law-enforcement agency in the world, I am sure, could have solved the case so quickly. But there were bitter moments, too, especially whenever we found something linking McVeigh to the Michigan Militia. Years ago in Ohio, there were no shackles on me as I went after Afro Set. And, I'm certain, we saved a lot of lives when we broke it up. Two decades later, the rules had changed, and I couldn't pursue my instincts about the festering right-wing sore in northern Michigan. America's civil liberties were protected. Too bad the lives of those one hundred sixty-eight innocent people in Oklahoma City weren't.

I spent a lot of time wondering about that, how it could be that some congressmen could fear the FBI more than they did terrorists sworn to overthrow the government. It was a sad thought to have on my mind as my career neared its end. And I knew that was true; these daily drives east to Decker, through the rolling farmland, the fields of green spring wheat dotted with red barns, were going to be among my last tasks for the Bureau. I found myself thinking about old cases and old faces. And one morning, I reflected back on a dope case we worked in Saginaw a few years back. The case, I realized, spoke volumes about the FBI—my FBI.

The target was a guy named Barry Cashin, a star outfielder on a nationally known fast-pitch softball team sponsored by a local Cadillac dealer. Cashin was something of a local celebrity, and even our agents were skeptical when an informant told us that he was dealing marijuana in thirty-gallon bags. But through surveillance and a careful sifting of his trash we were convinced the informant was right. Cashin wasn't the smartest dealer in the world—once he showed up to a buy with a sack full of cash, only to discover he'd picked up his groceries by mistake—but he must have been doing something right. When we got a search warrant for his home, we found $300,000 in a small tin box behind his freezer in the basement.

About six months after Cashin was arrested, we got a call from an inmate at the county jail where he was being held awaiting trial. "Cashin doesn't have any sense of humor about this," said the inmate. "He's asking if I know anybody who could break some arms and legs of witnesses for fifteen hundred dollars. And he'll throw in some extra money if one of your agents winds up at the bottom of the river." The money, the snitch said, would be delivered by Cashin's brother Brian.

We wired the snitch and got Barry Cashin on tape, talking about beating up witnesses and their families and repeating that he wanted the agent who arrested him to wind up "at the bottom of the river." At the same time, we sent an undercover state cop to meet brother Brian, posing as the hit man. Brian handed over $1,000. The next day, we had an arrest warrant for Brian.

We decided to use the SWAT team for the bust. For one thing, we knew Brian was a hunter who probably had guns in the house. And of course we knew he didn't exactly have strong feelings about the sanctity of FBI agents' lives, either.

It was after dark by the time we were ready to move. Half a dozen SWAT agents formed a loose perimeter around the house; an equal number prepared to go in the back door. Everybody was wearing a jacket marked *FBI*; the last thing you want to do on one of these raids is to mistake one of your own men for a bad guy.

"FBI!" shouted the team leader. "You're under arrest! Come out with your hands up!" For two tense minutes, the agents waited, but there wasn't a sound or a sign of movement from inside the house. Finally they burst inside.

Brian Cashin was just inside the house, standing in the kitchen, and made no move to resist as a couple of the agents slapped hand-cuffs on his wrists. "I want to talk to my lawyer," was all he said. The rest of the agents moved through the house, searching for evidence or other people.

As they moved toward the rear of the house, a boy of about ten darted down a hallway and into a bedroom, slamming the door behind him. A couple of agents, hurrying after him, heard the crash of breaking glass. Yanking the door open, they found the room empty— but a window was shattered, the jagged shards of remaining glass jutting out like teeth. Rushing over, they peered out. The boy's body was sprawled on the ground outside, two other agents already huddled over it.

"Believe it or not, he looks okay," one of the agents called out. "He's just got a few scratches. But we need to get him to a hospital to make sure."

The boy rode to the hospital in a county sheriff's patrol car, and long before it arrived it was obvious to the deputy that the kid was okay. He was chattering away, asking questions about the siren and the flasher. The deputy decided to ask a question of his own: Why did you jump out the window?

"My uncle deals drugs," the boy replied. "And my dad always

said that if someone came to the house they might try to kill us. So when I heard men inside the house, I thought I'd better run away. But then I saw those letters that said *FBI*, and I knew everything was going to be okay.''

OKBOMB was my biggest assignment in the FBI, and also my last. At the end of the year, I retired. I was overwhelmed when, at my farewell luncheon, I got a framed photograph of Louis Freeh. Across the bottom was inscribed: "Dear Phil—My best wishes and appreciation for your dedicated service to the FBI and the nation." He signed it "Louie."

They also mounted my badge and credentials on a beautiful plaque as a going-away gift. I asked for my gun—the same old Smith & Wesson Model 10 revolver they gave me at the academy, back when Lyndon Johnson was president and the Beatles were still together. That model has long since been retired, but the Bureau wouldn't let me have it. Rules, you know. But I've had my revenge. In the pages of this book, you won't find the letters FBI separated by periods, not a single time.

But as I look back on my twenty-six years in the Bureau, the silly stuff is fading away. Mostly what I feel is pride. Although I received sixteen incentive awards containing substantial cash bonuses for work on people like Tony Jack and Monk Huffman, I didn't work for money. I worked for the safety of my fellow citizens. I had them in my heart—the heart of the FBI. Thank God I didn't have to pay the price she did, but like Martha Dixon Martinez, I tried to work every investigation with honor and purpose.